D0742476

STUDIES IN HISTORY, ECONOMICS AND PUBLIC LAW

Edited by the
FACULTY OF POLITICAL SCIENCE
OF COLUMBIA UNIVERSITY

NUMBER 251

THE PAN-GERMAN LEAGUE, 1890-1914

BY

MILDRED S. WERTHEIMER

PROFESSOR DR. ERNST HASSE

THE PAN-GERMAN LEAGUE

1890–1914

BY

MILDRED S. WERTHEIMER

1971

OCTAGON BOOKS
New York

Reprinted 1971
by special arrangement with Columbia University Press

OCTAGON BOOKS
A Division of Farrar, Straus & Giroux, Inc.
19 Union Square West
New York, N. Y. 10003

Library of Congress Catalog Card Number: 79-159257

ISBN-0-374-98352-6

Printed in U.S.A. by
NOBLE OFFSET PRINTERS, INC.
NEW YORK 3, N. Y.

DB 119
W4

Woe unto us .... if we cannot see, written in blood, in the dying civilization of Europe, the dreadful result of exaggerated nationalism as set forth in the patriotic histories of some of the most eloquent historians of the nineteenth century. May we not hope that this will be but a passing phase of historical writing, since its awful sequel is so plainly exhibited before us, and may we not expect that the historians of the twentieth century may seek rather to explain the nations of the world to each other in their contributions to the progress of civilization and to bear in mind the magnificent sentiment of Goethe: "Above the Nations is Humanity." H. MORSE STEPHENS.

CONTENTS

PAGE

CHAPTER IV

THE FINANCES OF THE PAN-GERMAN LEAGUE

CHAPTER V

THE AIMS AND IDEALS OF THE PAN-GERMAN LEAGUE

CHAPTER VI

METHODS OF ACTION OF THE PAN-GERMAN LEAGUE

PAGE

CHAPTER VII

THE PAN-GERMAN LEAGUE AND THE REICHSTAG

CHAPTER VIII

THE MAJOR ACTIVITIES OF THE PAN-GERMAN LEAGUE, 1894–1914

CHAPTER IX

THE PAN-GERMAN LEAGUE IN GERMANY

CHAPTER X

Non-German Opinion of the Pan-German League ; Conclusion

APPENDICES

PREFACE

THE Great War focused the attention of the world on a phenomenon called propaganda. We have heard of Allied propaganda, of German propaganda, and most of all perhaps, of Pan-German propaganda. Germany, the German government, the German people have been accused of conspiring to spread their *Kultur* over the entire globe through a vague movement called " Pan-Germanism ", which is generally considered to have been one of the major causes of the War.

This study will attempt to describe the German patriotic society—the *Alldeutscher Verband,* or Pan-German League as it is usually translated—which gave its name to the movement. Its origin, aims, membership, financial status and history up to the outbreak of the War will be considered in an endeavor to determine—in so far as it is possible to evaluate such an intangible thing—the significance of " Pan-Germanism " in the history of the two decades before 1914.

The study is based for the most part entirely upon primary sources: the publications of the Pan-German League itself, the Reichstag debates, official collections of documents, periodicals, newspapers and memoirs. For assistance in locating and procuring the material the writer wishes to acknowledge her indebtedness to the officials of the Columbia University Library, the *Auskunftsbüro der deutschen Bibliotheken* (Berlin, Germany) and the Mayence *Stadtbibliothek,* (Mayence, Germany), as well as to Dr. Herman Escher of the *Centralbibliothek* (Zürich, Switzerland), for suggestions and advice. The librarian of the Mayence library has been especially kind in verifying references and assembling bibliographical data. The author wishes also to express her appreciation to Miss Isadore G. Mudge of the Columbia University Library for her interest and assistance in preparing the bibliography and the list of German chauvinist publications which appears in the appendix.

Professor Sidney B. Fay of Smith College has read parts of the manuscript and offered much constructive and helpful criticism which the writer wishes most gratefully to acknowledge. She also desires to thank Miss Katharine Snodgrass of Leland Stanford University for her assistance in the preparation of the diagrams in Chapter III.

The study was inspired by work with Professor Carlton J. H. Hayes in German history, and the writer welcomes this opportunity to express her indebtedness and deep appreciation of his constant and unflagging interest, encouragement and advice, without which the work would never have been possible.

CHAPTER I

INTRODUCTION

IN the sentiment of nationality there is nothing new. It was one of the main keys of Luther's Reformation. What is new is the transformation of the sentiment into a political idea. Old history and fresh politics worked a union that has grown into an urgent and dominating force. Oppression, intolerable economic disorder, governmental failure, senseless wars, senseless ambitions, and the misery that was their baleful fruit, quickened the instinct of Nationality. First it inflamed visionaries, then it grew potent with the multitudes, who thought the foreigner the author of their wretchedness. Thus Nationality went through all the stages. From instinct it became idea; from idea abstract principle; then fervid prepossession; ending where it is today in dogma, whether accepted or evaded.

VISCOUNT MORLEY [1]

The roots of modern German nationalism lie in the French Revolution. The rotten foundations of the Prussian state had been exposed to view by the humiliating defeat inflicted by Napoleon in the campaign which opened at Jena and closed at Tilsit. And the defeat was laid in part to the revolutionary spirit of *Fraternité* which inspired the armies of France. In the brief period between the peace of Tilsit and the War of Liberation Prussia was rejuvenated physically and spiritually. Stein and Hardenberg freed the serfs, abolished feudalism and created a free peasantry; Scharnhorst and Gneisenau reorganized the army and introduced compulsory military service, and Wilhelm von Humboldt

[1] *Politics and History* (New York, 1914), pp. 128 *et seq.*

founded the University of Berlin and established a common school system. The work of regeneration and reorganization was aided by the fact that the Holy Roman Empire had collapsed in 1806 and that there had been a diminution in the number of small states that comprised the Germanies. The Prussian leaders recognized that the strength of France lay in the individual and national self-consciousness that had been born of the Revolution. It was this spirit they worked to inspire in the Prussian people.[1]

The work of the philosophers and poets further fired the clear flame of the new nationalism. The poetry of the young Romanticists, especially Fichte, Arndt and Körner, and Schiller's *Wilhelm Tell*; the theories expounded by Kant and Hegel—all together had a large share in the development of the new spirit of patriotic nationalism that finally won the battle of Leipzig in 1813 and liberated Prussia. Indeed Kant's philosophy was of great prophetic significance, for he helped to formulate a sense of national mission and destiny and to give the Germans the consciousness of fulfilling an ideal mission in whatever they accomplished by way of material conquest.[2] Fichte, in his *Reden an die deutsche Nation,* set forth an exalted conception of the character and mission of the Germans [3] and put forward the idea of a geographically isolated and economically self-sufficing community as the ideal nation (*geschlossener Handelsstaat*). Hegel glorified the state and raised it to the altars. " The State is God on Earth! " he said,[4] and by stressing

[1] Gooch, G. P., *Nationalism* (London and New York, 1920) ; Stocks, J. L., *Patriotism and the Super-State* (London and New York, 1920).

[2] Dewey, John, *German Philosophy and Politics* (New York, 1915), pp. 28 *et seq.*

[3] Dunning, W. A., *A History of Political Theories from Rousseau to Spencer* (New York, 1920), pp. 137 *et seq.*

[4] Hegel, *Grundlinien der Philosophie des Rechts*, vols. viii-ix, sec. 258, p. 313.

political self-consciousness as a criterion of a people (*Volk*), he too gave great stimulus to the doctrine of nationalism. Furthermore, Hegel pictured mankind as progressing through all the ages, steadily but unconsciously, toward the Germanic perfection of the nineteenth century.[1]

But the German people were still primarily citizens of their separate kingdoms, duchies and principalities. The fires of nationalism were not hot enough in 1848 to weld these petty states into a sovereign empire. Austria's loss of prestige in 1866, as a leader of the Germanies and Prussia's consequent gain which Bismarck aided and manipulated with such skill until in 1871 the Empire was formed exclusive of Austria, was the triumph of the so-called " Little German " or *Kleindeutsch* idea. In contradistinction is the " Great German " or *Grossdeutsch* idea which includes Austria among the Germanies. The Pan-German League, into the history of which we are about to inquire, was *Grossdeutsch* in its ideals and felt itself called upon, among other things, to continue the old struggle between the two ideas.

In the growth of German unity one is struck by the important part played by historians. By preparing the nation for unification by means of their precepts and lessons, they became leaders of German nationalist thought. Gustav Schmoller has said that without the cooperation of the historians, the Empire would never have been set upon its feet.[2]

First there is the *Monumenta Germaniae Historica* which was the product of the spirit of the War of Liberation, and was started by that great German statesman, Baron vom Stein, in an attempt to arouse popular interest in German history. The Congress of Vienna and the period of reac-

[1] Dunning, *op. cit.*, pp. 154 *et seq.*

[2] Guilland, Anton, *Modern Germany and her Historians* (London, 1915), pp. 9 *et seq.*

tion following it aroused Stein to the need of such a work, and although he failed to secure governmental support for it, he raised the necessary funds from the resources of himself and his friends. This collection of the sources, ably begun by G. H. Pertz and carried forward by George Waitz, has made possible much of the work of succeeding generations of historians.[1]

Histories lauding the Hohenzollerns, the glories of the German mediaeval period, German prowess in the crusades, and the deeds of the Teutonic Knights contributed to the nationalist fervor. The work of Duncker and Droysen did much to convince the German people of the " mission " of the Hohenzollerns and of Prussia. The founding of the University of Berlin gave great impetus to the development of glorious national history, past, present and future, supported by the Hegelian theory of the State.[2] Leopold von Ranke in part shared Hegel's notion which became that of most Prussian historians—that civilization is spread only by war. But his interest was mainly in the triumph of civilization, which he believed to be above the rivalry of races, peoples and religions. Von Treitschke's *Deutsche Geschichte im neunzehnten Jahrhundert* ranks as one of the literary masterpieces of modern historiography. He too was imbued with the idea of Prussian leadership and his work is full of enthusiasm for the national cause; yet adequate attention is given to the cultural forces in national development. In von Sybel, the third of the leaders of the Prussian school, we have a complete advocate of German unity through Prussian leadership. His *Begründung des deutschen Reiches* is clear and masterful but entirely unreliable in spots, especially when dealing with Bismarck's foreign policy.[3]

[1] *Encyclopedia Americana* (1920 edition), vol. xiv, pp. 234 *et seq.* H. E. Barnes, " Nationality and Historiography."

[2] Guilland, *op. cit.*, pp. 94 *et seq.*

[3] *Encyclopedia Americana* (1920 edition), vol. xiv, *loc. cit.*, p. 235.

The work of Mommsen was in part responsible for a new so-called science, " *Völkerpsychologie* ", by which professors of history and geography, ethnographists and schoolmasters sought to explain the superiority of the German race over all others.[1] Mommsen was an ardent German patriot, and his whole *Römische Geschichte* becomes, in a sense, an apology for the German race. To him as to von Ranke the object of history is civilization; but in order to triumph, civilization demands the suppression of races less capable of, or less advanced in culture by nations of a higher standing. War thus becomes the great machine which elaborates progress; and in the German universities Mommsen represents best, perhaps, the religion of force and the realistic spirit which were rife in Prussia after 1850.[2]

" *Völkerpsychologie* " was further supported by the publication in 1854 of the work of a French writer. This was the *Essai sur l'inégalité des races humaines* by Count Joseph Arthur de Gobineau (1816-1882). The work did much to strengthen the cause of nationalism in Germany. To Gobineau the racial question overshadowed all other problems of history. It held the key to them; and according to him, the inequality of the races from whose fusion a people is formed explains the whole course of its destiny.[3] He asserted the inherent superiority of the " Aryan " race and held that racial degeneration was the inevitable result of its mixture with inferior races. " I can say positively ", declared Gobineau, " that a people will never die, if it remains eternally composed of the same national elements." [4]

[1] Guilland, *op. cit.*, pp. 151 *et seq.*

[2] *Ibid.*, pp. 128 *et seq.*

[3] Gobineau, *Essai sur l'inégalité des races humaines*, 2 vols., Paris, 1884. *Cf. The Inequality of the Human Races* (translated by Adrian Collins), New York, 1915, p. xiv (from the author's introduction).

[4] *Ibid.*, p. 33. (English translation).

He believed in race and aristocracy as the first condition of civilization and disbelieved in the influence of environment. Further, he distrusted the efficacy of religion and morality.

As a philosopher, Gobineau might have exercised an influence merely pessimistic and wholly vicious; but as a pseudo-scientist, in his doctrine of Aryan supremacy, he paved the way for the Teutonic effusions of Houston Stewart Chamberlain in Germany and Charles Kingsley in England, for the Gallic frenzy of Maurice Barrès in France and the Saxon songs of praise of Kipling and Homer Lea in England and the United States.[1]   In Germany, his doctrines, interpreted by Chamberlain, Ludwig Schemann and the so-called Gobineau school, were made the vehicle of much patriotic prattle, and were found capable of broad and elastic interpretations.   Schemann, himself a member of the Pan-German League, founded in 1893 the *Gobineau Vereinigung* of which the League itself was a corporate member.   The purpose of this society was to spread the works and ideas of Gobineau and to erect on his grave a tombstone that would be worthy of him.[2]   In 1906 a collection of Gobineau relics, everything connected with his work and life, was placed in the university library at Strasburg.   It is Schemann who is largely responsible for Gobineau's popularization.   His biography of the count is a monumental work in two volumes, glorifying " his hero ", as Schemann always calls Gobineau, and laying great stress on the latter's *penchant* for the Germans over the other Germanic peoples.   It is a book calculated to stir patriotic pride in the most callous breast. Though the first volume was not published until 1913 and the second did not appear until 1916, they were the fruits of many years of work, and for a long time Schemann had

[1] *Encyclopedia Americana* (1920 edition), vol. xiv, *loc. cit.*, pp. 234 *et seq.*

[2] Schemann, L., *Gobineau, eine Biographie* (Strasburg, 1916), vol. ii, pp. 590 *et seq.*

been the foremost authority on Gobineau and had written and lectured untiringly.

Houston Stewart Chamberlain's *Grundlagen des neunzehnten Jahrhunderts,* which appeared in 1899, is a remarkable example of what might be termed the higher guesswork, and the author jumps through all sorts of controversial anthropological data to his own conclusions. Chamberlain's *Leitmotiv* is the assertion of the superiority of the Teuton family over all the other races of the world. He says: " The awakening of the Teutonic peoples to the consciousness of their all-important vocation and culture forms the turning-point (in the history of Europe) ; the year 1200 can be designated the central moment of this awakening." [1] The book was widely read and discussed in Germany; it became a " best seller ", and was particularly popular with the Kaiser. Appealing as it did to the innate egotism of a people, its popularity is easily explicable.

It is impossible to estimate accurately the extent of the influence of such works as Gobineau's and Chamberlain's, but doubtless they were of considerable importance in refreshing and nourishing German national egotism, patriotism and nationalism. Professor John Dewey says that

the philosopher sees movements which might have passed away with change of circumstance as casually as they arose, acquire persistence and dignity because thought has taken cognizance of them and given them intellectual names. The witness of history is that to think in general and abstract terms is dangerous; it elevates ideas beyond situations in which they were born and charges them with we know not what menace for the future.[2]

[1] Chamberlain, H. S., *The Foundations of the Nineteenth Century* (English translation by John Lees, London and New York, 1911), author's introduction, p. xv.

[2] Dewey, John, *German Philosophy and Politics* (New York, 1915), p. 12.

Philosophy and theory alone could never have accomplished the unification of the German Empire in 1871, but they formed a firm intellectual support for Bismarck's more practical efforts. The wars of unification were a tremendous stimulus to German nationalism, and whether this intellectual support was dynamic or a matter of rationalization in retrospect, it received credit and honor.

In 1871 Germany had achieved unity. Her prosperity, prestige and power henceforth increased by leaps and bounds, and as her economic development gained strength, there grew up a desire for expansion, for the acquisition of a colonial empire. Prevailing opinion has long maintained that Bismarck was reluctantly dragged into the struggle for colonies in the year 1883 by the efforts of the merchant class. Recent research in the subject indicates that as usual Bismarck said one thing and did another, and that in reality he was actively if cautiously in sympathy with the acquisition of German colonies as far back as 1876.[1] Be that as it may, early in the decade of the '80's the interests concerned fanned the fires of latent nationalism into a blaze of patriotic feeling which forced the Reichstag to indorse a state-directed colonial policy.

To interested business men the primary consideration was a practical one—markets and raw materials, and government aid and protection in their acquisition. The development of a strong national consciousness was a secondary consideration, a means to an end. It was thought to be highly idealistic and beautiful; but consciously or unconsciously it was felt also to be capable of serving practical ends by awakening the people to an understanding of their inherent greatness and by making them sensitive to the

[1] *Cf.* Townsend, Mary E., *Origins of Modern German Colonialism* (New York, 1921), also Fuller, Joseph Vincent, *Bismarck's Diplomacy at its Zenith* (Cambridge, 1922), *passim.*

slightest, even to an imaginary, reproach to their national honor. Since Germany had become a nation, she must expand as a natural outlet for her enthusiasm, her feeling of patriotism, her nationalism, and her manufactures. She must express herself accordingly, and her consciousness of self must take the form of creating a colonial empire. This intensified nationalism was both the cause and the effect of a spirit of imperialism; for it worked toward colonial expansion as the latter in turn did toward further nationalism.

It was the feeling of the need for an intense nationalism at home, in order to further the expansion of the Empire abroad, that led directly to the formation of the Pan-German League. In this we find an organized effort to keep frenzied nationalism at fever heat. It was a truly idealistic, though entirely misguided, movement to awaken public opinion to the past, present and potential greatness of the German Empire. The history of the Pan-German League is particularly worthy of notice, because its name — Pan-German — has come to connote one of the most potent " perils " ever invented to strike terror into the hearts of unsuspecting peoples. The aim here is to show what the Pan-German League was, what it did, and to what extent it was influential on German thought and action.

CHAPTER II

THE ORIGINS OF THE PAN-GERMAN LEAGUE

THE Pan-German League may be regarded as a direct outgrowth of the desire in Germany for colonial expansion. The colonial party that had been agitating so untiringly for German colonies overseas had succeeded in making *Kolonialpolitik* a national and political issue,[1] and secured at last the support of Bismarck, who forced the Reichstag to accept a state-directed colonial policy in the form of a Steamship Subsidy Act (March 23, 1885).[2] In order to secure the passage of this bill, Bismarck was called upon to awaken public opinion to its support, against the prevalent opposition in the Reichstag. Great Britain had recently negotiated treaties with France and Portugal dealing with territories in Africa, and it was fairly easy for him to make her African policy appear selfish. By skillfully drawing attention to this fact, and thus making Great Britain the scapegoat, Bismarck caused an outburst of patriotic and national enthusiasm strong enough to force the passage of the bill. Aided by the colonial societies which protested violently against British policies in Africa, patriotic excitement spread throughout Germany and public opinion arose against England. " To the popular mind, England appeared to wish to monopolize the control of all affairs in Africa." The *Kolonialverein* (Colonial Society) rushed

[1] Townsend, *op. cit.,* p. 112; *cf.* also Fuller, J. C., *op. cit., passim.*
[2] Townsend, *op. cit.,* pp. 163 *et seq.*

22

publicly to Bismarck's aid, as did the *Central Verein für Handelsgeographie* (Central Society for Commercial Geography) ; and the more staunchly the Reichstag blocked the bill, the more people joined the colonial societies. Finally, after the members of the opposition had been branded as cowards and pro-British and lacking in sentiment for the national honor, they surrendered and assured the chancellor that when it was a question of defending the honor and prestige of the Empire, the Reichstag would never be found wanting. The "fire of chauvinistic patriotism, so carefully prepared, lighted and kept alive by Bismarck" had reduced the opposition to silence or consent, and had completely destroyed the last obstacle to the adoption of a national colonial policy.

Dr. Karl Peters, the man who had been responsible for the acquisition of a large share of Germany's African colonies, returning about this time from fresh African explorations and conquests, determined to capitalize to as great an extent as possible the enthusiasm which had been stirred up by the struggle in the Reichstag over the Steamship Subsidy Bill. He issued a call for a " General German Congress for the promotion of the interests of Germany overseas" (*Allgemeiner deutscher Kongress zur Förderung überseeischer Interessen Deutschlands*), for the autumn of 1886. This call was issued in cooperation with the *Westdeutscher Missionsverband* (West German Mission Society) and the *Central Verein für Handelsgeographie.* It was published in the *Kolonialpolitische Korrespondenz,* and other German societies, interested in colonial matters were invited.[1] The *Central Verein für Handelsgeographie,* which was the more important of the two societies cooperating with Peters, had been founded in 1863 by the traveler and explorer, Otto Kersten, and in the early '70's developed into

---

[1] Bonhard, *Geschichte des alldeutschen Verbandes* (Leipzig, 1920), p. 1.

one of the most important means of fostering German commercial interests overseas, since it represented the only hitherto organized agency for promoting the aims of economic colonial policy at home.[1]   The society recognized as its aims: 1. to establish and build up real intercourse between Germans living in foreign countries and those in the fatherland; 2. to secure and to disseminate information about the natural and commercial conditions in those countries where Germans had settled; 3. to direct emigration toward those countries which were known to be favorable to German colonization, and in which German national consciousness (*Volksbewusstsein*) might be kept alive; and 4. the society hoped to aid in the founding of German colonies through the establishment of commercial and naval stations.[2]

Peters' General German Congress met in Berlin, September 13-16, 1886, and busied itself with the following questions, all of which are closely related to the tenets of the *Central Verein* stated above: 1. extension of the colonial movement to practical results; 2. the exploitation and expansion of the oversea regions already won for Germany; 3. the German emigration question; 4. German missions overseas; 5. the augmentation of German exports; 6. the retention of the German language and of German customs overseas; and 7. the strengthening of the bonds between Germans in foreign parts and those at home.[3]

By the cooperation of several societies working toward these common ends, a " General German Society for the Furthering of German National Oversea Interests "[4] was

---

[1] Townsend, *op. cit.*, pp. 51 *et seq.*

[2] Jannasch, " Central Verein für Geographie," Schmoller's *Jahrbuch*, 1883, p. 177.

[3] Bonhard, *op. cit.*, p. 2.

[4] *Allgemeiner deutscher Verband zur Förderung überseeischer deutschnationaler Interessen.*

formed. But the men taking part in the movement were
entirely occupied with their own work in the colonial movement both inside and outside the Empire; each society had
its own point of view as to how the common goal could
best be reached, and its own special aims for which it worked
in preference to more or less outside appeals. The result
was that they began to quarrel among themselves; Peters
went off to Africa and, there being nothing left to hold it
together, the Society dissolved.[1]

This abortive attempt to capitalize the intense feeling
which had been worked up over a specific issue, and to
turn it to the more general matters of colonial policy and
strengthened nationalism, has a very direct bearing upon
the foundation of the Pan-German League. The next attempt to found a society which should arouse the patriotism
of the German people came in 1890 as the direct result of a
specific " grievance ". The founders again called upon
Dr. Peters, again freshly returned from African triumphs,
to lead them. He and a few of the hardier souls who had
survived the struggles of 1886 joined forces with some
gentlemen to whom the full honor for starting the movement of 1890 belongs; and the *Allgemeiner deutscher Verband* (General German League) was founded, the direct
predecessor of the *Alldeutscher Verband* (Pan-German
League). As will be shown later, the executive committee
of the former society merely changed the name in 1894 to
Alldeutscher Verband so that, to all intents and purposes,
the story of the foundation of the *Allgemeiner deutscher
Verband* is the story of the foundation of the Pan-German
League.

The specific grievance which occasioned the founding of
the *Allgemeiner deutscher Verband* was the Anglo-German

[1] Grell, Hugo, *Der alldeutche Verband, seine Geschichte, seine Bestrebungen und Erfolge* (*Flugschriften*, no. 8), (Munich, 1898), p. 3.

treaty of July 1, 1890, by which Germany engaged to recognize a British protectorate over the islands of Zanzibar and Pemba and over the dominions of the Sultan of Witu.[1] In return, Great Britain ceded the island of Heligoland to Germany.[2]

This period, it must be remembered, was the beginning of a new era in German affairs, the *neuer Kurs* (" new course "), as it is often designated. The old pilot had been dropped and General von Caprivi had taken his place as chancellor of the German Empire; the young Kaiser, well-disposed toward his English grandmother, seemed to have been working for more cordial cooperation with Great Britain ever since his accession to the throne. The Anglo-German treaty, signed in the year that the German reinsurance treaty with Russia was allowed to lapse, appeared to make a critical departure in foreign policy.[3]

With augmented vigor, the *neuer Kurs* was combated by those who were opposed to the Kaiser's policies, especially by the " Bismarck Fronde "[4] that was developing. In general the struggle was carried on in accordance with the wishes of the old recluse at Friedrichsruh. Bitter and spiteful after his retirement from office, Bismarck felt no compunction in opposing everything accomplished or attempted by the new government. No longer bound by the responsibilities of office, he gave free rein to his pen. Because the great figure of the old Prince appeared again and again in back of the almost daily press battles, the " Fronde " won strong aid from the ranks of followers who had remained

[1] Hertslet, *The Map of Africa by Treaty* (London, 1909), vol. iii, pp. 899 *et seq.*

[2] Herstlet, *The Map of Europe by Treaty* (London, 1891), vol. iv, pp. 3286 *et seq.*

[3] Dawson, W. H., *The German Empire* (New York, 1919), vol. ii, p. 392.

[4] The group of people rallying to Bismarck's standard.

true, and to whom the honoring of Bismarck meant a worth-while form of opposition to the new Kaiser's ways. Bismarck himself, influenced more by personal emotion now that he was no longer directly concerned with the government than when bound by the exigencies of party politics, championed causes and criticized policies entirely inconsistent with his past opinions and acts. In his bitterness and his hatred of everything done by the Caprivi government and the young Kaiser, he was probably little concerned with the real wisdom of the policies which he so harshly condemned.

But these considerations were not taken into account by the developing " Bismarck Fronde ". The professors and students of the *Hochschulen,* the teachers of the *Gymnasien* and even the *Volkschulen* stood in the foreground of this opposition, though the Agrarians formed the picked troops of the " Fronde ".[1]

On February 14, 1893, the Agrarians formed their own organization—*Der Bund der Landwirte* (Agrarian League), as an offensive and defensive alliance against the commercial policies of Caprivi. It was essentially representative of the large landed proprietors, while some of the professors and students who were most violently anti-Caprivi joined the Pan-German League. Their battle-cry was raised against the grasping Anglo-Saxons.

Bismarck expressed his views on the Zanzibar treaty in the recently published third volume of his memoirs. He wrote :[2]

That the Heligoland Treaty was a very great disappointment to us, is now the judgment of people other than those whose

[1] Hammann, Otto, *Der misverstandene Bismarck* (Berlin, 1921), pp. 25 *et seq.*

[2] Bismarck, *Gedanken und Erinnerungen,* vol. iii (Stuttgart and Berlin, 1919), pp. 147 *et seq.*

major interests are in oversea possessons. In the official justification of this affair the compensation, which is invisible to the naked eye, must be sought in the realm of things imponderable, in the fostering of our relations with England. Reference has been made in the affair to the fact that I, while I was in office, had set a high value upon these relations. That is undoubtedly correct; but I never believed in the possibility of a lasting guaranty of these relations and never intended to sacrifice a German possession in order to gain a good-will whose duration would have had no prospect of surviving an English ministry. . . . However the renunciation of equal privileges in the commercial city of Zanzibar was a lasting sacrifice for which Heligoland offered no equivalent. Free trade with that single great market on the East African coast was the bridge that joined our commerce with the mainland, which today we can neither dispense with nor replace. . . . . The tendency of Caprivi to make me responsible for doubtful political measures which he undoubtedly advocated at the command of a superior, was not exactly a proof of political honesty; any more than was the attempt to ascribe to me the treaty concerning Zanzibar. On February 5, 1891, he said in the Reichstag (Shorthand Reports, p. 1331) : " I will consider the reproach which has repeatedly been made against us, namely that Prince Bismarck would scarcely have been responsible for this cession. The present government has been compared to the previous one, and the comparison was to our disadvantage. Indeed, should I not have been a man entirely lacking in sense of duty, and the more so considering what an important man my predecessor had been if, when I took over this office and all that that implies, I had not formed my own opinion on what was going forward, what the policy of the government was in the affair, and what it had at stake? That was of course a perfectly obvious duty and you may believe that I have applied myself to this duty most zealously."

How he had informed himself I do not know. If it was by reading the reports of the transactions, he could not have interpreted those reports to mean that I had advised the Zanzibar treaty. The proposition that England is of greater importance to us than Africa, which I have occasionally advanced in connection with over-hasty and exaggerated colonial projects, may be just as pertinent under certain circumstances as the statement that Germany is of greater importance than East Africa to England; but this was not the case at the time that the Heligoland treaty was concluded. It had not occurred to the English to expect us to renounce Zanzibar; on the contrary, people in England were becoming accustomed to the idea that German trade and influence there was increasing and would finally secure the upper hand. The English in Zanzibar itself were convinced at the first news of the treaty that it was a mistake, for they could not comprehend why we should have made such a concession.

There was considerable irritation, then, over the treaty and excitement grew when Bismarck appeared on the side of those who opposed it.[1] The *Hamburger Nachrichten* praised the intention of the treaty to care for relations with England, but gave assurance also that Bismarck had not concluded the treaty as it was signed.[2] " In the event of war," the old chancellor said, " it would be better for us that Heligoland should be in the hands of a neutral Power. It is difficult and expensive to fortify."[3]

[1] In 1884, in letters to the German Ambassador to Great Britain (Count Münster), Bismarck had expressed himself concerning the great value of Heligoland to Germany. But he seemed even more concerned with the maintenance of friendly Anglo-German relations. *Cf. Die grosse Politik der europäischen Kabinette 1871-1914* (edited by Lepsius, Mendelssohn-Bartholdy and Thimme) (Berlin, 1922), vol. iv, pp. 51 *et seq.*, p. 56, pp. 61 *et seq.* In 1889, Bismarck's son, Count Herbert von Bismarck wrote his father advising acceptance of Joseph Chamberlain's offer to exchange Heligoland for German Southwest Africa. The old chancellor did not commit himself and advised delay; before the matter was settled, he was no longer in office. *Cf. ibid.*, pp. 408 *et seq.*

[2] Hammann, Otto, *Der neue Kurs* (Berlin, 1918), pp. 19 *et seq.*

[3] Busch, Moritz, *Bismarck, Some Secret Pages of His History* (New

In colonial-political circles, the treaty was of course judged most unfavorably. Even the African explorer, Stanley, said that a new pair of trousers had been given away for an old trouser button; Karl Peters raged that two kingdoms, Witu and Uganda, had been exchanged for a bath-tub.[1]

The bad feeling, moreover, that had been stirred up against Great Britain in the campaign to pass the Steamship Subsidy Act had not entirely disappeared. Some individuals, at least, remembered that Great Britain's colonial policy— especially in Africa—had been shown to be very selfish, and the new Anglo-German treaty was to their minds proof positive of that fact. The German Empire was being scorned; its sacred honor had been tarnished; its sovereignty might even be impaired; for German citizens seemed to have no rights overseas but those allowed them by the omnipresent British.

On June 24, 1890, there was printed in the *Kölnische*

York and London, 1898), vol. ii, p. 547. Bismarck said further: " I would never have made this treaty. Zanzibar was already half German when he gave it to the English. German commerce greatly exceeded the English commerce there, and in from five to ten years the most important town and harbor would have been entirely German. As to the value of Heligoland; to my mind it is a weakness and a drain rather than a support for Germany in any future war with France. For formerly the numerical supremacy and strength of the French navy made no difference to us simply because there was no harbor in the North Sea or the Baltic Sea where the French navy could coal. They always had to return to Cherbourg for coal. As long as Heligoland was in the hands of a neutral power, England, it was closed to the French as a coaling station. But in the future, the French fleet needs only to silence the few forts on Heligo- land which nothing can fortify against the power of modern artillery, and it has a coaling station in the North Sea for further ravages on our coast." Penzler, *Fürst Bismarck nach seiner Entlassung* (Leipzig, 1897), vol. iv, p. 206.

[1] Bornhak, Conrad, *Deutsche Geschichte unter Kaiser Wilhelm II* (Leipzig, 1921), p. 73.

Zeitung [1] and the *Frankfurter Zeitung* and circulated through the south and west of the Empire,[2] an appeal entitled *Deutschland wach auf!* (Germany awake!). In frantic phrases this outcry attempted to arouse the German people to the grasping policy of Great Britain, who was seeking to cheat Germany out of her rightful possessions overseas:

The diplomacy of the English works swiftly and secretly. What they created burst in the face of the astonished world on June 18 like a bomb—the German-English African Treaty. With one stroke of the pen—the hope of a great German colonial empire was ruined. . . . Shall this treaty really be? No, no, and again no. The German people must arise as one and declare that this treaty is unacceptable! . . . . Men of all parties who, in this situation, think of themselves only as Germans wish to take the matter into their hands. The Reichstag will, we hope, go to the government with an overpowering majority and say: The treaty with England harms our interests and wounds our honor; this time it *dares* not become a reality! We are ready at the call of our Kaiser to step into the ranks and allow ourselves dumbly and obediently to be led against

[1] Printed as an advertisement in the morning edition of June 28, 1890 of the *Kölnische Zeitung*, signed by Adolf Fick, M. D., in the name of a group of Germans in Zürich. Fick was the son of a professor of anatomy; he himself was a practising oculist. He was born in 1852 at Marburg, served as a volunteer in the Franco-Prussian War and participated in the triumphal German entry into Paris. After demobilization, Fick studied medicine at the universities of Würzburg, Marburg, Freiburg and Zürich, and in 1884 married the daughter of Dr. John Wislicenus, professor of chemistry in Leipzig, who will appear again in these pages. The children of Marie Wislicenus and Adolph Fick, six in number, bore the Teutonic names of Hildegarde, Roderich, Brunnhilde, Ingeborg, Roland and Waltrut. Dr. Fick practised medicine in Cape Colony in 1886, and in 1887 took up his Zürich practice. Many medical books came from his pen; and he lectured on a wide range of subjects including colonial expansion, poetry and prohibition. *Wer Ist's* 1914, p. 417.

[2] Bonhard, *op. cit.*, p. 2.

the enemy's shots, but we may also demand in exchange that the reward come to us which is worth the sacrifice, and this reward is: that we shall be a conquering people which takes its portion of the world itself, and does not seek to receive it by the grace and benevolence of another people.

Deutschland wach auf!

JUNE 24, 1890.[1]

The summons was followed three weeks later by a second document, a letter, which was sent to interested people. It said in part:

We have in Germany a body of nationally-minded citizens to whom it seems inconceivable that our government should give up lands, rich with promise for the future, without pressing cause. This section of German citizens remains silent because on the one hand the opinion is widely held—though not held by us—that the Anglo-German treaty is an unalterable fact; on the other hand there stands that portion of the Germans who, through the twenty-year period of Bismarck's leadership, have considerably lost their own initiative. They are united in following the government without coming to any judgment of their own on the method or aims of the government. . . . Whether or not our government recognizes the value of a burning, national public opinion, it seems to us to be our duty to the fatherland to set forth our views again at a fitting moment, just as we did a short time ago in our " Wach auf!".

Such an expression can have real results only if a large number of Germans living in the Empire work together in this same direction. There seems to be an actual prospect of it. In the numerous letters that came to us as the result of the " Deutschland wach auf " the thought was expressed that all the people feeling as we did should join together in a sort of National League, the purpose of which should be to give expression to what we wanted and expected of a national gov-

[1] *Ibid.*, pp. 233 *et seq.*

ernment in situations similar to the situation created by the Anglo-German treaty. . . . The first preparation must consist in this: to see a large number of people who agree with us. We ask you to inform Albert Müller, book-seller in Zürich, whether you are inclined to participate in an association of like-minded people, such as has been sketched above. As soon as a sufficient number of acceptances have come in, we shall send the entire correspondence together with a small sum of money already in our hands, to a comrade living in Germany to carry the plan further.

ZÜRICH, JULY 15, 1890.   FELIX, FICK, LUBARSCH, MÜLLER.[1]

This communication seems to have had the desired effect; for on August 1, 1890, another letter was sent out by Dr. A. Hugenberg of Hanover, saying that he had undertaken the temporary business management of the affair. The path of action along which their endeavors should lead them was made clear. The letter states: [2]

There are also still larger territories—one need only think of Central Sudan, the natural hinterland of Kamerun, the fate of which has not as yet been settled by any treaty. He who seizes these territories quickest and holds fast the most tenaciously will possess them.

Finally, does not *everything,* and especially the slowness with which the German government moves to assert itself in colonial affairs, point to the fact that our fatherland, be it from one side or the other, will not be spared a new war if it wishes only to maintain the position which it won in 1870? . . . . The official memoir which has just appeared concerning the motives of the Anglo-German treaty, leaves no doubt but that a certain indifference to colonial expansion exists in official places. In a tone of contempt it has been said that " the period of hissing the flag and shooting at the treaty must now be ended ! "

[1] Bonhard, *op. cit.*, pp. 238 *et seq.*

[2] *Ibid.*, pp. 240 *et seq.*

. . . . Similar reverses can be prevented in the future only if foreign countries deal with a sensitive German nationalism. . . . . The question is how this ideal is to be realized. . . . No one would be a more fitting person to lead the movement than Dr. Karl Peters, . . . he who acquired East Africa. It is intended that as soon as he returns to Germany he shall be asked to place himself at the head of the association to be founded. Competition with the *Kolonialgesellschaft* (Colonial Society) will not be undertaken, but the association shall rest on deeper foundations, supplementing those to which the aims and composition of the *Kolonialgesellschaft* do not reach, in particular with respect to propagandist activities. If Dr. Peters declares himself ready to lead this movement, its success will presumably be assured. . . . The primary consideration is naturally the willingness of a sufficiently large number of gentlemen to sign their names to the petition to Dr. Peters. . . . . But always the most important thing is, not the number of names but the complete agreement with the specific aims of those people won to the cause; for we must be able to assure Dr. Peters that among those who are asking for his cooperation are to be found only trustwofthy supporters of the movement.

HANOVER, AUGUST 1, 1890.   A. HUGENBERG,
                                                    Dr. rer. polit.

The petition which was presented to Karl Peters on his return from Africa asked him to place himself at the head of an association to stimulate intense nationalism.[1] It ran :

. . . . It is our wish and our intent to prevent such possibilities in time, . . . by creating an independent association, with its roots firmly established in the citizenry (*Bürgerschaft*), a center for all the national aspirations of our people; an association whose first aim shall be to work for a united, fundamental patriotic view of life for all citizens, in the sense of creating a National Morale.

[1] Bonhard, *op. cit.*, p. 243.

In detail, the aims of this association shall be:

1. The bringing together of nationally-minded citizens, without consideration of party, in the thought that the accomplished unification of the German race is only the foundation of a larger national development; that is, the development of the German people into a cultural and political world power, as the English people already are and the Russians doubtless will become.

2. The beginning of an energetic colonial policy for the acquisition of wider colonial possessions and the organization of our emigration.

3. The widening of interest in the oversea commercial and civilizing tasks of Germany in the widest fashion.

4. By the firm presentation of the views expressed here against indifference and indolence, against a superficial cosmopolitanism and against the very widely over-rated world position of Germany to-day and the value of one-sided continental politics, may such desires as ours finally be felt on the side of the parties of the government.

This petition to Dr. Peters was circulated among the same people to whom the letters quoted above had been sent. Dr. Peters was informally approached as to his willingness to head the projected organization. Although he strongly condemned the Zanzibar treaty, he seems to have demurred [1] at first, because he wanted governmental backing when he returned to East Africa, and therefore did not wish to antagonize the government unnecessarily.

On September 28, 1890, a meeting of people interested in the movement started by Dr. Fick was held in Frankfurt-am-Main under the presidency of his father-in-law Professor Dr. John Wislicenus.[2] The gathering was a very

[1] Bonhard, *op. cit.*, p. 3, footnote.

[2] Professor Wislicenus was a man of great sincerity and kindliness. Born in 1835 of a family whose free religious beliefs were of long standing, he had shared in the many vicissitudes resultant upon his pastor-father's participation in the revolutionary movement of 1848. After many

small one, attended by only seven people; but they decided that the appeals which had been made must be upheld and that the movment must not perish. September 28, 1890 accordingly is designated by Class and Bonhard as the birthday of the Pan-German League. As the result of this meeting, Hugenberg and Wislicenus issued another call to action,[1] in which it was declared that " *das Deutschtum*,[2] wedged in between nationally self-sufficient peoples and itself

hardships the family had fled to America where the young Wislicenus, with his chemical knowledge, was their main support. In 1856 they returned to Zürich "in free Switzerland" to live, the young man going to Halle in 1857 as a chemical assistant. Aside from chemistry, music was one of his main interests, but above all he was interested in the "Struggle for Freedom". He lectured on reformed religion and on political subjects, and when offered a position by the government on condition that he give up his political views, he emigrated to Zürich. He lived there until 1872, becoming professor of chemistry at the Polytechnic, but was called to the University of Würzburg and then to Leipzig where he remained until his death (1902).

While living in Zürich, Wislicenus was chosen president of the Germans there who were celebrating the victory of the Franco-Prussian War and the foundation of the Empire. Unluckily the celebration was rudely disturbed by some wounded French officers and prisoners of war in Zürich, but Wislicenus calmed the meeting with a few well-chosen patriotic words, and when a young English student attempted to set the meeting-hall on fire and a stairway actually burst into flames, Dr. Wislicenus, finding that there was no water at hand, was equal to the occasion and catching up a keg of beer put out the fire. (*Alldeutsche Blätter*, 1902, pp. 453 *et seq.*)

Wislicenus seems to have been a man with a real social conscience and a tireless worker, very much interested in the welfare of his countrymen. Often besought by the Leipzig National Liberals to stand for the Reichstag, he would never accept candidacy; but he did hold a small political post in the city of Leipzig where at the same time he could carry on his academic work undisturbed. Interested in colonial problems, and related to Dr. Fick, his presence at the Frankfurt meeting of intense patriots is easily explained.

[1] *Ibid.*, p. 455.

[2] The expression *das Deutschtum* means the German nation; used without the article, *Deutschtum* has the wider connotation "Germanism" and is used in the same sense as "Anglo-Saxonism" or "Americanism."

having only very lately achieved a national unity of its component parts, must fight for its development against greater odds than almost any other great people."

Finally, after the struggle over the Zanzibar treaty had become less acute, Peters changed his position and agreed to join forces with the Fick-Wislicenus-Hugenberg group that had been issuing these appeals and letters. The African explorer stipulated for the inclusion of the remains of his *Allgemeiner deutscher Verband* of 1886, and on January 25, 1891, at the personal invitation of Peters, a number of Reichstag deputies and other people [1] met in Berlin with Wislicenus and Hugenberg, who represented the 1890 movement. The purpose of the meeting was to call to life again the old *Allgemeiner deutscher Verband* with a wider and more timely platform and aims, and the result was that the ground was prepared for a sort of constituent assembly, which met in Berlin, April 9, 1891, and formally resurrected and revamped the old organization of 1886.

The expressed purposes of the new organization were: [2] to arouse patriotic self-consciousness at home and to oppose vigorously any development of the German people along unpatriotic lines; to support and aid German endeavors in all lands where members of the German people must struggle to retain their individuality, and the union of all Germans on the earth for the furthering of these aims; to promote an energetic German policy of might in Europe and oversea; above all to carry forward the German colonial movement to tangible results.

The words of the Great Elector, " *Gedenke dass du ein Deutscher bist* ",[3] were taken as the motto of the League.

[1] According to Bonhard.

[2] Bonhard, *op. cit.*, p. 4.

[3] This was changed later to " *Bedenke dass du ein Deutscher bist* "— Remember that you are a German.

Karl Peters assumed the leadership as president,[1] and the organization was launched.

The period between 1891 and 1894 was a very difficult one for the *Allgemeiner deutscher Verband*. History repeated itself, and Peters soon went back to East Africa, this time as a government commissioner. He resigned the presidency of the League in order to contaminate neither the Foreign Office nor the *Allgemeiner deutscher Verband* by serving both simultaneously; a banker, Karl von der Heydt, assumed the presidency, and a man named von Eyken took over the business management.[2]

However, the work of von der Heydt and von Eyken was for several reasons not successful. In the first place, the League's annual dues were set at the very low figure of one mark, in order to open the membership to as many people as possible; but as a result, sufficient funds to finance the organization were not forthcoming, and the work stood still —and even retreated. In the second place, a regular issue of reports concerning the League's work was badly needed to hold it together. Even the intermittent *Mitteilungen des allgemeinen deutschen Verbandes,* which were issued only seven times between 1891 and 1893, did not reach all the members because there was an extra charge for it. Lack of money cut off publicity in the daily press as well. Thirdly, the members of the League outside Berlin lacked competent leadership. Only a few branches were formed, and all the work and responsibility rested on the central office, which had to waste time and energy on details. Nor could branches be formed at this time in Saxony or Bavaria because of the peculiar legislation of these States in regard to associations.[3] In the fourth place, anti-Semitism broke

[1] Class, *Zwanzig Jahre alldeutscher Arbeit und Kämpfe,* (Leipzig, 1910), p. viii.

[2] Bonhard, *op. cit.,* pp. 5 *et seq.*; *cf.* also Grell, *op. cit.,* p. 4.

[3] Theodor Scheffer in *Die Zeit* (Vienna), Sept. 22, 1900, no. 312, p. 178.

out in the influential Berlin branch, and this weakened the League's prestige in the public eye,[1] for before this time the organization had not been avowedly anti-Semitic.[2]   In the fifth place, the members of the executive committee disagreed among themselves; and finally, to cap the climax, the president and the business manager and some others in the League, toward the end of 1892, tried to start a movement for the foundation of a new political party—a " national party ".   A circular letter was sent around through the ranks of the Free Conservative and National Liberal parties, openly advocating the splitting of these parties, to which many members of the *Allgemeiner deutscher Verband* belonged, so as to allow for the formation of a new party.   The result was, that not only was dissension stirred up but the energy of the leaders, which might have gone into work for the *Verband,* was dissipated in work for the projected party.   The League had been founded as an organization standing above parties; and that had been and continued to be its prerequisite for existence.   Thus the fact that its leaders were starting to mix in politics threatened the very roots of its being.   Bad matters were made worse by the failure of a *Kalender aller Deutschen,* (Calendar of all Germans) compiled by Karl Pröll,[3] which resulted in a deficit of 6,000 marks.[4]   In a short time the membership shrank from 21,000 to 5,000; the organization was in debt and seemed about to expire.

In the summer of 1893 a crisis was reached, and a meeting of protest was held in Frankfurt-am-Main.   This meet-

[1] Bonhard, *op. cit.,* pp. 6 *et seq.*

[2] Schultheiss, Dr. Franz Guntram, *Deutschnationales Vereinswesen* (*Kampf um das Deutschtum,* no. 2), (Munich, 1897), p. 77.

[3] Pröll was a very active member of the *Allgemeiner deutscher Schulverein* (*Alldeutsche Blätter,* 1901, p. 505).

[4] Grell, *op. cit.,* p. 4.

ing, engineered by west Germans, was called entirely against
the wishes of the central organization of the *Allgemeiner
deutscher Verband,* and stated as its avowed purpose the
" dissolution or reorganization of the League." [1]   However, Dr. Wislicenus again presided, as he had at the first
assemblage of the League, and his attitude was that of a
staunch supporter of the existing order.   The upshot was
that another meeting was arranged, to be held in Berlin,
July 5, 1893.   President von der Heydt resigned, after
covering 4,000 of the 6,000 marks deficit on the *Kalender
aller Deutschen* out of his own pocket.   Dr. Karl Peters
paid the remaining 2,000 marks with a gift for that amount
donated to him by a friend.   Most of the earlier executive
committee of the *Allgemeiner deutscher Verband* followed
von der Heydt's example and resigned.[2]   At the advice of
Dr. Wislicenus,[3] Professor Dr. Ernst Hasse of Leipzig, a
friend and colleague of Dr. Wislicenus, was elected president.   Dr. Hasse placed himself entirely at the service of the
League and, aided by his friend Dr. Adolf Lehr, who took
over the office of business manager,[4] he rescued it at the
eleventh hour and gave it a new lease on life.

Hasse's acceptance of the leadership of the *Allgemeiner
deutscher Verband* had been tentative; he had made his permanent tenure of the office conditional upon the acceptance
of certain proposals which, in his opinion, would put the
League on a firm financial basis and infuse fresh life into
its activities.[5]   He advocated a more active exchange of
views between the leading members of the League, outside
of Berlin, by means of correspondence between the ex-

[1] *Alldeutsche Blätter,* 1902, pp. 455 *et seq.*
[2] Schultheiss, *op. cit.,* pp. 77 *et seq.*
[3] *Alldeutsche Blätter,* 1902, pp. 455 *et seq.*
[4] Class, *op. cit.,* p. viii.
[5] Bonhard, *op. cit.,* pp. 7 *et seq.*

ecutive committee, the local branches and individual members. Since it had been suggested that the Germans oversea could be drawn together more easily if the cooperation of the German consuls were assured, he believed that this was possible only in so far as the complete independence of the League could be assured in making use of such service. The previous failures had been very largely due to lack of financial support. Hasse, therefore, made his acceptance conditional upon financial assurance that the remaining debts of the League would be entirely paid within three years at the most, and that the money to do it should be raised by voluntary contributions.[1] He further advised the wide foundation of branches. This was particularly near to his heart for he lived in Leipzig, while the central organization of the League was in Berlin. The difficulty was overcome, however, by the choice of Dr. Adolf Lehr as business manager, with headquarters in Berlin; and these two men, feeling great mutual confidence, cooperated in holding the League together. Finally, Hasse felt that a journal, serving the exclusive wants of the League was a *sine qua non* of its success.

It took considerable activity on the part of the League to comply with these suggestions and conditions. The executive committee held two meetings, on November 5 and December 10, 1893, respectively, and issued an appeal for funds to found the weekly journal; enough money was secured by voluntary contributions to begin the publication of the *Alldeutsche Blätter.*[2] On January 1, 1894, under the editorship of Dr. Lehr, the first issue made its appearance, announcing that the League now felt that its foundations were

[1] This was really accomplished in spite of the fact that the amount was not inconsiderable. Bonhard, *op. cit.*, p. 8.

[2] Grell, *op. cit.*, p. 5, and *Alldeutsche Blätter*, 1894, p. 1.

more securely laid and that it could face the future full of hope and confidence.

At a meeting of the executive committee held on April 1, 1894, it was decided to change the name of the *Allgemeiner deutscher Verband* to *Alldeutscher Verband.*[1] Negotiations had been in process for some time for the amalgamation of a society called the *Allgemeiner deutscher Verein,* which had for its aim the support of *Deutschtum* along educational lines, with the *Allgemeiner deutscher Verband.* The *Verein* had sprung to life shortly after the League, but had not succeeded in developing to any extent.[2] Its president, the president of the Reichstag, von Levetzow,[3] determined therefore to attempt amalgamation with the League, and the arrangement was effected on April 12, 1894.

With the change in the name of the League to *Alldeutscher Verband,*[4] the organization wes really launched and the stage set for saving *das Deutschtum.*

The name "*Alldeutsch*" (Pan-German), now so universally known, had been suggested to Dr. Hasse by an old gentleman named August Diederichs as a title for a fund which he was donating to the League to aid them in their work.[5] Of it he said:

As regards the name for my national foundation (*Nationalstiftung*) I suggested the word, previously neither heard nor seen, "*Alldeutsch*". . . . At the time when Professor Dr. Ernst

---

[1] *Alldeutsche Blätter*, 1894, p. 109.

[2] Bonhard, *op. cit.*, pp. 8 *et seq.*

[3] *Stenographische Berichte des Reichstags, IX Legislaturperiode, 2te Session* (1893/94), *33 Sitzung* (January 23, 1894), p. 809. Von Levetzow was not on either the executive committee or the business managing committee of the Pan-German League. *Cf.* Bonhard, *op. cit.*, appendix 11 and 12 for list of members.

[4] The actual change of name did not take place until July 1, 1894.

[5] See *supra*, p. 77 *et seq.*

Hasse took the leadership of the *Allgemeiner deutscher Verband,* I sent him the first draft of the aims of my "national foundation", which was at that time still in an embryonic stage. Dr. Hasse joyfully acclaimed it in his reply to me as an everlasting monument (*Denkmal*). A few weeks later he rechristened his League, and the League's official journal as well, with the cognomen "*Alldeutsch*". Thus it would appear that the credit for the word *Alldeutsch* should belong to me, while to Dr. Hasse belongs the honor of having spread it broadcast.[1]

The two men who really set the Pan-German League on its feet were Dr. Adolf Lehr and Dr. Ernst Hasse. Lehr, who died in November 1901, had the less influential personality of the two; but as business manager and editor of the *Alldeutsche Blätter,* and as a member of the executive council of the League, he did his share for the advancement of *Deutschtum.* Born in 1839, of a middle-class family in Wiesbaden,[2] he studied engineering and chemistry, and then, for ten years, held various positions in foundries and factories in the Ruhr and in Aschaffenburg. Later he became connected with an accident insurance company in Leipzig; but in 1887 a new corporation law in Saxony caused the dissolution of the company and Lehr was without a position. He took a doctor's degree at the University of Leipzig in 1888, studying statistics with Dr. Hasse. Finally, in 1894, Lehr assumed the business management of the Pan-German League and devoted his entire attention to it. He was

[1] *Satzungen der Diederichsstiftung des alldeutschen Verbandes,* pp. 20 *et seq.*

The term *Alldeutsch* has been indiscriminately applied by the outside world to all imperialists and chauvinists in Germany where, on the other hand, super-patriots are often derisively dubbed *die Alldeutschen,* without regard to membership in the Pan-German League itself. It has become a convenient slogan, comparable perhaps to "100% American."

[2] *Alldeutsche Blätter,* 1901, p. 498.

elected to the Reichstag in 1898, taking his seat as a National Liberal. On the whole, he seems to have been a more or less ineffectual person, though absolutely sincere in his devotion to the cause of super-patriotism and super-nationalism.

The captain of the Pan-German ship was Dr. Ernst Hasse. Born of a long line of middle-class and professional forbears, Hasse's father was a pastor and his maternal grandfather, an officer.[1] Ernst Hasse was born in 1846,[2] and worked on a farm in his early youth.[3] In 1866 he began the study of theology at the University of Leipzig, though his interests were turning towards law and political science; but his studies were soon interrupted by military service, and when the Franco-Prussian War broke out in 1870, he was a reserve officer and working hard for his state jurist's examination. He went to war at once and served gloriously, according to the account, finding time to write accounts of the campaigns for the *Leipziger Tageblatt*; after the war he returned to Leipzig at the head of his regiment. In 1875 Hasse became statistician for the city of Leipzig, and carried out some reforms in taxation and poor relief. Incidentally, he wrote a history of the Leipzig Fairs and won a prize for it. Then, in 1885, he became a *Privatdocent* at the University of Leipzig and in 1886, *ausserordentlicher Professor,* teaching statistics until 1888, when he instituted a course on colonial politics, the first regular university course on the subject in Germany.[4]

Hasse's colonial-political activities had begun as early as 1878, when, with such men as Hübbe-Schleiden, Robert Jannesch and Friedrich Fabri, he endeavored to launch a

[1] *Nachrichten über die Familie Hasse* (Leipzig, 1903), *passim.*
[2] *Wer Ist's,* 1906.
[3] *Hasse als Politiker* (Leipzig, 1898), pp. 1 *et seq.*
[4] *Ibid.,* pp. 9 *et seq.*

colonial movement which, at that time, was contrary to the customary currents of public thought. The Leipzig *Verein für Handels-Geographie* was an outgrowth of this movement, and Hasse was its president from 1879 to 1896. He was on the executive committee of the *Deutsche Kolonialgesellschaft*, (German Colonial Society), and published many articles in the first number of *Export*[1] and the *Deutsche Kolonialzeitung*.[2] His interest in the colonial movement centered in the colonization of South America and, for a time after Karl Peters' expedition had turned public attention from South America to Africa, Hasse withdrew somewhat from the movement. But the Zanzibar treaty aroused him to the need of freeing Germany from British influence and interference, and in 1893 he was persuaded to take the presidency of the Pan-German League. In 1898 Dr. Hasse was elected to the Reichstag by the National Liberal Party in Leipzig, winning over his Social Democratic opponent by a bare 2,000 plurality in an election in which approximately 30,500 votes were cast in the district.[2] He held his seat until 1903, when his Social Democratic rival finally defeated him.[3]

Hasse was a man of great sincerity of purpose and singleness of aim.[4] He was a man of conservative ideals, believing that the foundations of the German Empire must be kept inviolate; a strong German army and navy and universal military service he considered a great support to

[1] The organ of the *Central Verein für Handels-Geographie*. Townsend, *op. cit.*, p. 52.

[2] The organ of the *Kolonialverein*. Townsend, *op. cit.*, p. 144.

[3] *Hasse als Politiker*, p. 41.

[4] *Alldeutsche Blätter*, 1903, p. 234. Professor Hans Delbrück has told me that Hasse was a sincere man, though a fanatic and a person of limited intelligence; Dr. Paul Rohrbach, that Dr. Hasse received no honorarum during his entire service as president of the Pan-German League.

German nationalism and an aid towards the consummation
of a truly national German state.   He felt that Germany
was possessed of such an abundance of native man-power
that it did not need the immigration of foreigners.   Especially, he felt that the immigration of Slavic and Semitic
peoples into Germany should be discouraged, for since these
peoples demanded naturalization and the enjoyment of equal
rights with native-born Germans, they were striking at
the roots of the German and Christian character of the
state.   Not only was immigration a source of grave danger
to the German and Christian character of the state, but international political views of any sort were a menace.
Hasse said : [1]

*I fight internationalism in every form, the red as well as the
black and the yellow, the Social Democratic as well as the Jesuit
and the power of international finance.*[2]   It is this internationalism which, opposed as it is to religion and monarchy, is peculiar
to the Social Democracy ; their stirring up of the masses without offering them a better constructive program ; their exclusive demand for rights without recognition of correspond-
ing duties ; in a word, their unpatriotic and immoral politics is
what separates me from the Social Democrats.   On the other
hand, *I recognize the justice of the efforts of the working classes
to better their commercial and social condition* [3] and to introduce a better division of incomes and property, and, for my
part, I am as always ready to support strongly these efforts
in the future.

Naïvely and fanatically intolerant in his views, this university professor was sincere to the core in his belief that
das Deutschtum must be saved and made all-powerful.   In
our own days of war-stirred passions and intolerant nation-

[1] *Hasse als Politiker*, p. 41.

[2] Italics Hasse's.

[3] Italics Hasse's.

alism, it ought not to be too difficult to understand his point of view. He saw Germany's star rising suddenly upon the great commercial horizon and striking consternation into the hearts of the powers already engaged in dividing up the globe. Believing firmly (and perhaps rightly) that each nation was as selfish and intolerant as he himself desired Germany to be, he looked around and saw the Powers staking out private preserves and putting up "No Trespassing" signs and Germany left outside the fence. He had a clear conception of Germany's future status should she lose a great commercial war.[1] He therefore felt that she must arm to the teeth, but that besides arming, she must secure herself by winning new commercial and political power. He urged the formation of a central European customs union, even as Friedrich List and Nebenius and others before him had urged; but in all sincerity Hasse affirmed that Germany would never seek to obtain sole control of the world but merely to be *equal* to other powers. "My ideal, the object of my love and my anxiety, is my German people", said he.

Obviously intensely sincere in his ideals, Dr. Hasse worked tirelessly for the Pan-German League. The aims and ideals of the League were synonymous with his own; he was the mainstay and guiding spirit of the organization until his death in 1908.

Before proceeding further, it would seem advisable to summarize briefly what has gone before: First of all it must be borne in mind that Bismarck, aided by the colonial party, had stirred up sufficient patriotic anti-British feeling in Germany to force the Reichstag to support a state-directed colonial policy. Then Karl Peters endeavored to start a society that should capitalize this patriotic enthu-

---

[1] *Hasse als Politiker*, pp. 18 *et seq.*

siasm to further German oversea expansion. This society was unsuccessful, but the virus of patriotic Anglophobia was merely dormant until another outstanding " grievance " against Great Britain, the Zanzibar treaty of 1890, aroused it to new life. A small group of individuals, bound together by common hatred of Great Britain in general, and of the Zanzibar treaty in particular, decided that the time was ripe to form a society for the stimulation of patriotism. They were further encouraged by the fact that Bismarck opposed the treaty, and a common antagonism to the new government made them feel even more keenly the necessity for such an organization. Peters was approached with a proposal to lead them, and after some preliminary skirmishing, an amalgamation was affected between those who had remained faithful to the colonial promoter during and since the struggles of 1886, and the newer anti-Zanzibarites. Thus Anglophobia and partisanship for Bismarck formed a common meeting-ground and, united under the banners of super-patriotism, the *Allgemeiner deutscher Verband* marched forth to do battle for *das Deutschtum*. This *Verband* in turn, was reorganized in 1893 by Dr. Hasse as the *Alldeutscher Verband* and became under his leadership a vigorous society.

CHAPTER III

The Constitution and Membership of the Pan-German League

THE structure and methods of action of the Pan-German League were defined and ordered by a written constitution that was a marvel of detail. This document, adopted in its final form in 1903 [1] (with another minor change in 1905), was in force in 1914 and will be found in full (in translation) in the appendix.

According to the constitution, membership in the League was open to every German in sympathy with the ends for which the organization stood, regardless of his citizenship. The annual dues [2] were set at a minimum of two marks, with an initiation fee of one mark and an extra fee for subscription to the *Alldeutsche Blätter*. It was further provided that members acting contrary to the ideals of the League might be forced to resign, and that such as were more than a year in arrears could not vote until their full indebtedness was discharged.

The constitutional provison concerning local organization was as follows:

The League is formed of local branches of at least ten members; several local branches may band together in a district organization. In communities where there are no local branches, the executive committee of the League may name

---

[1] *Alldeutsche Blätter*, 1903, p. 190.

[2] For more detailed account of the finances of the Pan-German League see chapter iv.

agents (to represent it). The local branches and district organizations elect their own officers and make their own constitutions.[1] The business of the local branches and district organizations is to provide for the local needs of *das Deutschtum,* and in particular to see to it that there is discussion of questions of the day significant in the light of the League's aims.

The local branches and agents were authorized to make recommendations to the executive council of the League, which had to consider them if they were received ten days before its meeting; in this way there was a semblance of democratic control of the policies of the League by its members. The local branches held regular meetings of a more or less social character [2] at which they sometimes had special speakers who were either designated by the central office or procured by the local leaders.

The executive direction of the League was of course the most important part of its organization. According to the constitution,[3] the League was " to be directed by the executive council,[4] the business managing committee,[5] the executive committee,[6] and the League convention." [7] The executive council consisted of: (1) the honorary members of the League, (2) the members of the executive committee, (3) the members of the business managing com-

---

[1] Subject to the approval of the executive committee of the League, however.

[2] The *Alldeutsche Blätter* carried a weekly column devoted to news of the local branches. Their meetings are described in a more or less general fashion; and the applause is always " hearty " and the meeting always " well attended ".

[3] *Handbuch,* 1914, pp. 9 *et seq.*

[4] *Vorstand.*

[5] *Geschaftsführender Ausschuss.*

[6] *Hauptleitung.*

[7] *Verbandstag.*

mittee, (4) the presidents of all the district organizations, (5) the presidents of all the local branches, (6) the local agents. (7) members at large elected by the council itself, bringing the permanent membership of the council up to one hundred, (8) representatives of local branches having a membership of more than one hundred.[1]

The executive council, besides deciding the policy of the League in all fundamental questions, had power to change the constitution (by two-thirds vote) and to dissolve local branches and district organizations whose activities were deemed to be counter to the aims of the League. It elected annually twenty of its own members to form the business managing committee of the League for the following fiscal year, and every three years it elected (also from its own membership) an executive committee of not less than three nor more than six members, two of whom were president and vice-president of the League. Furthermore, the council was empowered to receive reports of work on hand from the business managing committee and to apportion the work to be done between the latter and the executive committee. The constitution required the council to meet twice a year in ordinary session, but it could be convened in extraordinary session for a specific purpose, on four weeks' notice, at the request of the business managing committee or of ten local branches or of twenty members of the council.

The business managing committee of twenty members, elected annually by the council, was headed by the president, who represented the League legally and whose business it was to arrange meetings of this committee and the executive committee and council. He arranged for the League conventions as well, directing their procedure and carrying out their decisions. The business managing committee directed

[1] Local branches having more than 100 members had the right to elect one representative on the executive council for each 100 members.

the affairs of the League, overseeing all its activities. It
was empowered to choose and to dismiss the editor of the
Alldeutsche Blätter and the business manager or managers.
Moreover this committee handled reports and expressions of
opinion and requests from the local and district organizations, and to it the constitution delegated the task of prod-
ding these bodies to the discussion of important problems
and the formulation of expressions of opinion concerning
them.

The executive committee of from three to six members,
elected by the council, for a three-year term, was designed
to " support the president in the management of the League
and prepare work for the committees, for the council and
for the League's convention, and to decide on the agenda." [1]
The president and vice-president were *ex-officio* members of
the executive committee. Furthermore, this committee
was empowered to choose and dismiss the local agents [2] of
the League and to receive all reports, opinions and proposals
from local and district branches.

One more part of the constitutional frame-work of the
League must be dealt with—the convention (*Verbandstag*).
Constitutionally it was provided that such a meeting must
be held every three years; [3] as a matter of fact, conventions
were held every year but two (1895 and 1901) from 1894
to 1913 inclusive, [4] and in the years 1905 and 1908, respectively, there were two. [5]   These annual meetings were held

---

[1] *Handbuch,* 1914, p. 10.

[2] *Vertrauensmänner.*

[3] *Handbuch,* 1914, p. 12.

[4] *Ibid.,* pp. 44 *et seq.*

[5] In 1905, a second convention was held in Leipzig, December 16 and 17.
The navy, the Russian revolution and Austria-Hungary were discussed.
Alldeutsche Blätter, 1905, pp. 433 *et seq.* An extraordinary convention
was held Nov. 21 and 22, 1908, in Leipzig and concerned itself with the
Daily Telegraph incident. *Alldeutsche Blätter,* 1908, pp. 407 *et seq.*

in different cities in Germany, and dealt with widely vary-
ing subjects.

These component parts—the local and district organizations, the executive direction and the League convention
comprised the constitutional skeleton through which the
League did its work. The methods of action which it employed to carry·on the work will be described in a later
chapter. Our attention must now be turned to consideration
of the membership of the League.

From 1894 until 1905 the membership statistics of the
Pan-German League were published regularly in annual reports in the *Alldeutsche Blätter.*[1] After 1905, the membership was almost stationary, any change having been on the
downward side,[2] and the League's leaders seem not to have
been anxious to advertise their exact status to the world.

The accompanying tables will give some idea of the
League's development and growth. Table I shows as far as
possible the annual membership statistics of the League:
Table II shows the organization of the members into local
branches and under agents, and Tables III and IV show the
number of local branches and agents.

The growth of the League was slow during the early
years (1894-96), its first noteworthy advance synchroniz-
ing with the agitation for a larger navy. It seemed to many
people that a convenient way to work for the passage of the
Navy Bill was to join a super-patriotic organization such as
the Pan-German League. Following closely upon the navy
agitation came the Boer War in South Africa, and the
League, always in the extreme van of Anglophobes, took up
the cudgels for its half-brothers, the Boers, the low Ger-

---

[1] Except for 1901 when a larger report was made and printed separately, and for 1902 when no report seems to have been made.

[2] See Table I.

TABLE I

MEMBERSHIP OF PAN-GERMAN LEAGUE

Year	Number of Members[1]	Source of Information
1890–1892	21,000	Wenck, *Alldeutsche Taktik*, pp. 28 *et seq.*
1893..............	5,000	*Alldeutsche Blätter*, 1894, p. 1.
1894..............:.	5,742	" " 1895, p. 78.
1895..............	7,715	" " 1896, pp. 101 *et seq.*
1896 (April 1)	8,601	" " 1896, pp. 101 *et seq.*
1896 (end of year)..	9,443	" " 1897, p. 89.
1897 (April 1)	10,217	" " 1898, p. 90.
1897 (Dec. 1)	12,974	" " 1898, p. 90.
1897 (end of year)..	13,240	" " 1898, p. 105.
1898 April 10).....	15,401	" " 1898, p. 90.
1898 (end of year)..	17,364	" " 1899, p. 161.
1899..............	20,488	" " 1900, p. 182.
1900 (April 1)	21,361	" " 1900, p. 182.
1900 (end of year)..	21,735	" " 1901, p. 350.
1901..............	21,924	*Der alldeutsche Verband im Jahre 1901,* pp. 16 *et seq.*
1902..............	......	No figures—membership receded—*Alldeutsche Blätter*, 1904, p. 192.
1903..............	19,068	*Alldeutsche Blätter*, 1905, pp. 160 *et seq.*
1904	19,111	" " 1905, pp. 160 *et seq.*
1905	18,618	" " 1906, p. 208.
1906..............	18,445	" " 1906, p. 208.
1912..............	17,000 (app.)	Wenck, *Alldeutsche Taktik*, p. 29.

[1] This does not include the "corporate" members of the League. See *infra*, p. 56 for further information on this subject.

TABLE II

ORGANIZATION OF MEMBERSHIP OF PAN-GERMAN LEAGUE

Year	Members in local branches	Members under local agents	Unorganized	Total number members	Source
1894..	3,374	1,729	639	5,742	*Alldeutsche Blätter*, 1896, pp. 101 *et seq.*
1895..	5,455	2,629	517	8,601	" " 1896, pp. 101 *et seq.*
1896..	5,338	2,937	568	8,843	" " 1897, p. 89.
1897..	7,990	4,482	768	13,240	" " 1898, p. 105.
1898..	13,481	3,023	860	17,364	" " 1899, p. 161.
1899..	16,883	2,595	1,010	20,488	" " 1900, p. 182.
1900..	18,313	2,310	1,112	21,735	" " 1901, p. 350.

TABLE III

LOCAL BRANCHES OF THE PAN-GERMAN LEAGUE

Year	In Germany	Outside Germany	Total	Source
1894	....	....	33	*Alldeutsche Blätter*, 1895, p. 78.
1895	29	17	46	" " 1896, pp. 101 *et seq.*
1896	43	23	66	" " 1897, p. 89.
1897	70	28	98	" " 1898, p. 105.
1898	102	27	120	" " 1899, p. 161.
1899	149	27	176	" " 1900, p. 182.
1900	173	28	201	" " 1901, p. 350.
1901	....	....	215	" " 1901, p. 259.
1906	190	15	205	*Handbuch*, 1906, pp. 8 *et seq.*
1908	184	13	197	" 1908, pp. 8 *et seq.*
1913	239	11	250	" 1914, pp. 8 *et seq.*

TABLE IV

NUMBER OF AGENTS OF PAN-GERMAN LEAGUE

Year	Number	Source
1894	180	*Alldeutsche Blätter*, 1895, p. 78.
1895	157	" " 1896, pp. 101 *et seq.*
1897	151	" " 1898, p. 105.
1898	132	" " 1899, p. 161.
1899	92	" " 1900, p. 182.
1900	76	" " 1901, p. 350.

mans of South Africa.   Many intense England-haters joined
the ranks of the Pan-German Leaguers and sought thereby
to turn the German government against the British.[1]   It
may be seen from Table I that the high-water mark in membership was reached in 1901.   Peace was signed in South
Africa in the spring of 1902 (May), and the membership
of the League shows a decrease of 2,856 by 1903.   Nor
do the international complications of the succeeding decade
seem to have had much effect on the League's membership
statistics.

[1] *Alldeutsche Blätter*, 1899, p. 166.

Corporate bodies affiliated with the Pan-German League were counted as single members, so that the total membership of the League was in fact somewhat greater than the figures in the above table indicate. In 1898 about three thousand additional members were to be accounted for in this way,[1] and in 1906, 101 clubs with a total membership (in round numbers) of 130,000 were corporate members.[2] However, the *Alldeutsche Blätter* is not explicit as to what clubs, etc., belonged to the League and these do not seem to have added much to its importance or potency.[3] The number of subscribers to the *Alldeutsche Blätter*[4] as compared even with the number of individual (as opposed to corporate) members of the League, makes this clear.

The gradual decrease that began in 1902 continued down through 1906, the last year for which official figures are available. According to Bonhard,[5] this was due to two causes—the lack of a sufficiently energetic program and the opposition of the government, which had become more and more severe. "For," said he, "a large membership such as the other national societies have could only be acquired through a program which did not criticize the government. Moreover, it was not detrimental to the inner life of the League that it was not burdened with 'also rans' who contributed nothing to its work."[6]

It is generally considered that the election of 1907 in

[1] *Alldeutsche Blätter,* 1898, p. 255.

[2] *Ibid.,* 1906, p. 208.

[3] Dr. Paul Rohrbach told the author in conversation, that many yacht-clubs, singing societies, rowing-clubs, etc., belonged corporately to the Pan-German League, but since they were not interested *per se* in politics, they contributed little.

[4] See table, *infra,* p. 121.

[5] Bonhard, *Geschichte des alldeutschen Verbandes,* p. 23.

[6] Bonhard, *op. cit.,* p. 132.

Germany determined finally the direction of affairs along the path of *Realpolitik* (practical politics). In that election, the Center party and the Social Democrats who had joined hands to defeat the government's policy of war against the Hereros in German Southwest Africa, were defeated by a combination of all the other parties. Fought on the issue of national patriotism, the election temporarily discredited both the Center and the Social Democratic parties, though the Centrists were returned in slightly greater strength while the Social Democrats lost nearly one-half of their eighty-one seats to the Conservative and Liberal groups. After 1907, the Centrists did not again oppose army, navy, or colonial bills.[1]

However, in 1912 we find that the members of the Pan-German League numbered about 17,000—less by some 5000 than in 1901. Evidently the general tendency of Germany towards intense nationalism did not serve to increase the numerical strength of the League. Too extreme in its demands to lead in time of peace, it did not exert any considerable influence until after 1914.

The founding of the Navy League[2] and of the National Security League[3] naturally did not add to the Pan-German League's membership. Founded in April, 1898, under the presidency of Count William of Wied and the "protection" of Prince Henry of Prussia, the Navy League reached the height of its power and the high-water mark of its membership between 1904 and 1908. At that time it boasted a membership of over a million, and a subscription list to *Die Flotte*, its official publication, of 375,000. During this period the Navy League was a not inconsiderable political factor in Germany, and after the elections of 1907 a complete reorganization of its administration

[1] Dawson, W. H., *The German Empire*, vol. ii, p. 333.

[2] *Flottenverein.*

[3] *Wehrverein.*

placed it under the leadership of Grand Admiral von Köster who guided it according to the wishes of the Imperial Naval Office.[1]   The business manager of the Navy League from 1904 to 1908 was General Keim, an enthusiastic member of the Pan-German League, who repeatedly addressed the members of the latter organization on questions dealing with the navy and the security of the state.

In January, 1912, the National Security League was founded wih General Keim as president.   Every German over eighteen years of age and every German club was eligible for membership.   Its aims were " the strengthening of the national (*vaterländisch*) self-consciousness and the maintenance of a manly spirit in the German people.   In particular it entered the lists to make the German means of defense as great and strong as possible, so that the Empire might be unconditionally protected and its powerful position in the world maintained."   The widely-felt dissatisfaction with German policy in Morocco in 1911 aided the National Security League tremendously,[2] and by the autumn of 1912 this new organization of super-patriots had enrolled over 40,000 individual and 100,000 corporate members.[3]   In comparison with these two Leagues—Navy and National Security—the Pan-German League seems small.

Without doubt, [says the *Alldeutsche Blätter*,] [4] the League finds grave difficulty in its work.   Because of the indifference of the large mass of the German people to national affairs, the national associations (*Verbände*) are forced more or less to cover the same fields.   It is naturally much easier to arouse interest and understanding in a specialized field such as the colonies or the navy than to cover an entire national

[1] Meyers, *Konversations Lexikon* (Supplement 1909-1910) vol. 22, p. 308.

[2] Meyers, *Konversations Lexicon* (Supplement, 1911-12), vol. 24, p. 986.

[3] *Alldeutsche Blätter*, 1912, p. 375.

[4] *Ibid.*, 1905, p. 161.

world outlook as the Pan-German League endeavors to do. In every national task that the League undertakes for itself, it feels, of course, that it serves to aid the work of those more specialized national associations; it feels that in fostering in its members a general national *Weltanschauung*, (outlook) it is preparing the ground for each and every special national movement, so that its work may be compared with that of the general practitioner while the other associations may be likened to specialists.[1]

The relations of the League with the other nationalistic associations[2] were quite friendly and according to its own statement led to useful cooperation, particularly in the case of the General German School Association[3] and in that of the German Navy League. When the Navy League was attacked as " a danger to the community ", the Pan-German League came openly to its support. In the case of the Association for the promotion of Germanism in the Eastern Marches,[4] many members were also members of the Pan-German League.[5] Hansemann, Kennemann and von Tiedemann, the three founders of the Eastern Marches' Association, had been recipients of a manifesto of Dr. Hasse's concerning the Polish question. Their association was known by the Poles as the *H. K. T. Verein* from the initials of the names of its founders. It was formed for the defense of Germanism in the Polish provinces and " became a potent agency for fomenting ill-feeling between the two nationalities." [6]   In 1909 it had a membership of 52,000 and 431 local branches and capital amounting to 694,000 marks.[7]

[1] *Ibid.*, 1906, p. 208.

[2] For complete list of the societies, etc., regarded as " national " by the Pan-German League, see appendix no. 2.

[3] *Allgemeiner deutscher Schulverein.*

[4] *Verein zur Förderung des Deutschtums in den Ostmarken.*

[5] *Alldeutsche Blätter*, 1895, p. 78.

[6] Dawson, *The German Empire*, vol. ii, p. 278.

[7] Meyers, *Konversations Lexicon*, (Supplement 1909-10), vol. 22, p. 192.

Bonhard says that doubtless Hasse's manifesto influenced Hansemann, Kennemann and von Tiedemann and indirectly aided them to found their association.[1] Whether this was the case or not can only be a matter of conjecture. At any rate, the Pan-German League and the Eastern Marches' Association were at one as regards the Polish problem.[2] Never slow to take credit to itself, the Pan-German League maintained that it had launched the original idea of enlarging the navy and dealing with the Polish problem, since the Eastern Marches' Association and the Navy League were founded after the Pan-German League had broached these matters.[3]

The aims of the General German Language Association [4] bore a close resemblance to some of the Pan-German League's ideals and the relations of the two societies were most cordial. The declared purpose of the Language Association was the purification of the German language by the removal of unnecessary foreign words and the restoration and preservation of the true spirit and individuality of the German tongue.[5] The General German School Association,[6] an outgrowth of an Austrian society of the same name, was another of the Pan-German League's sister societies in the fight for *das Deutschtum*; the German branch, founded in 1881, antedates the League. The platforms of the Austrian and German societies were the same: To aid in the erection and maintenance of German schools in the parts of Austria-Hungary where German schools were not built at public expense. The German society worked

---

[1] Bonhard, *op. cit.*, pp. 10-11.

[2] For the League's stand on the Polish question see *infra*, pp. 163, 168.

[3] Bonhard, *op. cit.*, p. 106.

[4] *Allgemeiner deutscher Sprachverein.*

[5] Meyers, *Konversations Lexikon* (1906 edition), vol. iv, pp. 738 *et seq.*

[6] *Allgemeiner deutscher Schulverein.*

outside of the German Empire, and in 1902 numbered 33,594 members in 282 local bodies with a net capital of 126,498 marks.[1]

The general relationship between the Language Association, the School Association and the Pan-German League is well shown in an article in the *Alldeutsche Blätter*[2] reporting the celebration of the eighty-fifth birthday of August Diederichs, one of the League's staunchest supporters. This old gentleman, the originator of the term *Alldeutsch*, had been for many years the master of a boys' school in Geneva, Switzerland, and was the author of several books on phonetics. An entirely sincere person, he believed heart and soul in *Deutschtum* and desired to make it as strong and pure as possible. As means to his ends, he supported (financially) the *los von Rom* movement, not primarily for religious motives, but because to him the relation of the papacy to Germany was a question of *national power,* and likewise he had helped to finance the three associations we have just described.[3] Therefore, many people belonging to the language and school associations and to the Pan-German League, gathered on his eighty-fifth birthday to do him honor. Speeches were made extolling the venerable patriot and describing the work of the societies. Among other remarks made on the occasion, it was explained that the Language Association had an uphill task, for all over Germany French menus were used, German women followed the French fashions, children counted their tennis scores in English! Many toasts were drunk and Herr Diederichs must have felt well repaid for his investment.

Another kindred association of the Pan-German League

---

[1] Meyers, *Konversations Lexikon* (1906 edition), vol. iv, p. 738.

[2] *Alldeutsche Blätter*, 1904, p. 177.

[3] See *infra*, p. 77 *re* the Diederichs' Fund. The Pan-German League received 20,000 marks, the other two 15,000 marks. *Satzungen der Diederichsstiftung des alldeutschen Verbandes,* pp. 10 *et seq.*

was the Society for Germanism Abroad.[1] This society, which worked for the preservation and aid of *das Deutschtum* in foreign lands, expended on its work in the one year, 1910, the sum of 197,727 marks,[2] chiefly in Austria-Hungary. Since all these associations covered much the same ground,[3] they naturally cooperated more or less with one another and their membership lists must have shown a good deal of similarity. In 1906 the Pan-German League had official representatives at the convention of the Navy League and at the celebration of the twenty-fifth anniversary of the School Association,[4] while at the 1912 annual convention of the Pan-German League, representatives of the following associations were present:[5] Navy League, Society for Germanism Abroad, National Security League, Society of German Students,[6] Evangelical Society for German Settlers,[7] German National Society for the Aid of Commerce, Rüdesheimer League of German *Burschenschaften,*[8] Society of Germans in Bohemia,[9] Society of the Southern Marches,[10] German National Society of Krems on the Danube.[11]

The close connection between the German colonial movement and the foundation of the Pan-German League has been brought out in an earlier chapter. After the first years, however, the League does not seem to have maintained

[1] *Verein für das Deutschtum im Auslande.*

[2] Meyers, *Konversations Lexikon,* Supplement 1911-12, vol. 24, p. 228.

[3] Herr Geiser, the business manager of the Pan-German League, left in 1908 to work for the Society for Germanism Abroad. (*Alldeutsche Blätter,* 1908, p. 394).

[4] *Alldeutsche Blätter,* 1907, p. 172.

[5] *Ibid.,* 1912, p. 333.

[6] *Verein deutscher Studenten.*

[7] *Evangelischer Hauptverein für deutsche Ansiedler.*

[8] *Rüdesheimer Verband deutscher Burschenschaften.*

[9] *Bund der Deutschen in Böhmen.*

[10] *Verein Südmark.*

[11] *Deutscher National-Verein, Krems, a. d. Donau.*

especially intimate relations with the colonial societies, though colonial questions always occupied a position of major importance in League affairs.

But in the earlier period, A. Lucas, a director of the German East African Society,[1] was treasurer of the Pan-German League from 1893 until the end of 1902, and on the original executive council of the *Allgemeiner deutscher Verband* are found the names of Dr. Fabri[2] and Dr. Hübbe-Schleiden,[3] two of the foremost propagandists for a vigorous German colonial policy. Fabri, for twenty-seven years inspector of the Rhine mission, had become a prolific writer urging the cause of German imperialism, and had founded (1880) the West German[4] Society for Colonization and Export.[5] He represented the economic aspect of the question of German colonialism. To Dr. Hübbe-Schleiden, on the other hand, has been ascribed the doubtful distinction of being the first to elevate the acquisition of colonies to the plane of a distinctively national policy and of having " cleverly linked up colonialism with the contemporary transformation in the outlook of the Empire from a liberal, *laissez faire* cosmopolitanism and internationalism to a conservative, individualized and narrow nationalism." Hübbe-Schleiden was a friend of Dr. Hasse's, and the political philosophy of the two men was much the same. Though his only official connection with the Pan-German League was through the executive committee of the old *Allgemeiner deutscher Verband*, Hübbe-Schleiden's views on nationalism are of interest here because they are representative of certain aspects of the German colonial movement, in that they por-

---

[1] *Deutsche-ostafrikanische Gesellschaft. Handbuch,* 1906, pp. 42 *et seq.*

[2] Dr. Fabri died in 1891.

[3] *Handbuch,* 1906, pp. 32 *et seq.*

[4] *Westdeutscher Verein für Kolonisation und Export.*

[5] Townsend, *Origins of Modern German Colonialism,* pp. 85-88. See *Allgemeine deutsche Biographie,* vol. xlviii, pp. 473-475.

tray a tendency towards intolerance of other peoples. It is a tendency of which the Pan-German League itself is the exemplar *par excellence*.

Always feeling himself a member of the younger and more progressive generation which must fight against the conservatism of the old, Hübbe-Schleiden strikes this note on the very fly-leaf of his *Deutsche Kolonisation* [1] by a quotation from Schiller's *Wilhelm Tell*—" *Es lebt ein andersdenkendes Geschlecht*".[2] " For ", says he,[3] " to the older generation the term ' nationality' had merely an ethnographic meaning, while for the younger it has a political. . . . Wherever Germans in foreign lands have been respected they have earned this respect by their personality, not by their nationality; they are not honored as Germans but as pleasant and diligent men."

He expresses very strong feeling against the Anglo-Saxon peoples and " *Los von England* "[4] and " *Los von Nord-Amerika* " are his slogans. Like Hasse, Hübbe-Schleiden is resolute against internationalism in any form; he compares it to Nirvana, and says that for any non-Anglo-Saxon race it is today only a betrayal to the English. Agreeing as he did so exactly with Dr. Hasse, it is no surprise to find such a man connected with the Pan-German League.

As regards the matter of the relationship between the Pan-German League and patriotic societies of the same sort, it may be said in general that the League tended more and more to feel itself superior to all other organizations, because it was enabled by its elastic constitution to deal with any and all problems; while the other societies, founded for more specific purposes, were bound to follow special aims.

[1] Hamburg, 1881.

[2] There lives a different thinking generation.

[3] Hübbe-Schleiden, *Deutsche Kolonisation* (Hamburg, 1881), pp. 14 *et seq.*

[4] "Away (free) from England"; "away (free) from North America!"

In particular, the Pan-German League seemed to have fewer dealings with the colonial societies as time went on, and more with other associations. This may have been due to the position and professions of the members of the League, and to this question attention must now be given.

Statistics concerning who and what all the members of the Pan-German League were and how they earned their livings, are available for only one year—1901. However, since that was the year when (before the war) the membership was largest, it may be taken as fairly typical. The following table (V) gives the data: [1]

TABLE V

PROFESSIONS OF MEMBERS OF PAN-GERMAN LEAGUE, 1901

Source: *Der alldeutsche Verband im Jahre 1901*

Profession	Within Germany	Outside Germany	Total
Academic	5339	560	5899
Business men	4905	383	5288
Liberal professions[2]	3760	262	4022
Industrial and hand-workers	2673	186	2859
Farmers	416	28	444
Miscellaneous	1091	193	1284

Total membership accounted for 19,796.

Total membership (1901) of Pan-German League 21,924. (excluding corporate members).

Since lists of the officers of the local branches, etc., with their professions, are available, it has been possible to check the analysis for 1901. The following tables show the professions of the men who were leaders of the League—the officers of the local branches, the agents, the district leaders and the executive council — and since the results of this tabulation coincide for the most part with the official table for 1901, the professions of the leaders may be taken as typical of the occupations of the rank and file.

[1] This table is a translation of a table taken from *Der alldeutsche Verband im Jahre 1901*. The other tables have been prepared by the author from lists given in the sources named. This accounts for the slight difference in nomenclature.

[2] Artists, officials and teachers according to the original table.

TABLE VI

PROFESSIONS OF OFFICERS OF THE LOCAL BRANCHES

	1894[1]		1896[2]		1898[3]		1906[4]		1908[10,11]		1914[10,12]	
	Number	App. %	Number	App. %	Number	App. %	Number	App. %	Number	App. %	Number	App. %
Teaching Profession	7	15%	28	25%	41	24%	161	36%	104	27%	148	24%
Business Men	21	44%	33	29%	53	31%	83	19%	97	24%	179	31%
Officials	8	17%	23	20%	26	16%	53	12%	61	15%	71	12%
Physicians	5	10%	9	8%	13	8%	43	10%	36	9%	44	8%
Technical Men	..	..	6	5%	13	8%	30	7%	27	7%	48	9%
Lawyers	2	4%	7	6%	8	5%	23	5%	25	6%	30	5%
The Church	1	2%	3	2%	4	2%	12	3%	9	2%	14	3%
Writers and Editors	1	2%	2	2%	3	2%	11	2%	10	3%	9	2%
Landowners	3	6%	2	2%	2[5]	1%	2	<1%	1	<1%	2	<1%
Nobility	..	..	..	..	1[7]	1%	2	<1%	1	<1%	2	<1%
Military Men	..	..	1[7]	1%	1	<1%	4[6]	<1%	3[13]	1%	4[14]	1%
Reichstag Members	..	..	..	..	1	<1%	{ 3[7] / 1 }	<1%	{ 5[15] / 1 }	1%	{ 6[6] / 1 }	1%
Miscellaneous	..	..	..	..	..	<1%	22[8]	5%	15[17]	4%	17[18]	3%
Number of above having degree of *Geheimrat*	..		1		2		2		2		4	
Number of above having degree of Ph. D.	3		23		40		85		91		69	

PROFFESIONS OF OFFICERS OF LOCAL BRANCHES GRAPHICALLY REPRESENTED

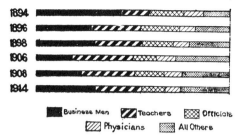

[1] *Alldeutsche Blätter*, 1894, p. 16.

[2] *Alldeutsche Blätter*, 1897, pp. 93 *et seq.*

[3] *Alldeutsche Blätter*, 1898, pp. 117 *et seq.*

[4] *Handbuch*, 1906, pp. 8 *et seq.*

[5] Baron and count.

[6] Three barons and one count.

[7] Retired major.

[8] Clerks, librarians, foresters, persons of private means.

[9] An honorary title.

[10] The figures for 1908 and 1914 include both officers of local branches and local agents.

[11] *Handbuch*, 1908, pp. 8 *et seq.*

[12] *Handbuch*, 1914, pp. 18 *et seq.*

[13] Count and two barons.

[14] Count and three barons.

[15] Two retired majors, one active lieutenant colonel, two retired lieutenant colonels.

[16] Two retired majors, one captain, one lieutenant colonel, one retired major general and a retired naval captain.

[17] Persons with private means, accountants, librarans, head forester, a royal lottery collector, a painter, a clerk and a cabinet maker.

[18] Clerks, librarians, statisticians, foresters, an accountant, master carpenter, orchestra leader and chimney sweep.

TABLE VII

PROFESSION OF AGENTS OF THE PAN-GERMAN LEAGUE

Profession	1896 [2]		1898 [1]	
	Number	Approximate %	Number	Approximate %
Business Men............	62	45%	39	32%
Teachers................	21	15%	21	16%
Officials................	17	13%	21	16%
Physicians	15	11%	15	12%
Technical Men...........	7	5%	9	7%
Lawyers	5	4%	3	3%
Editors	2	1%	2	2%
Landowners.............	2	1%	1	1%
Church.................	2	1%	4	3%
Military Men............	2[4]	1%	2[4]	2%
Miscellaneous...........	4[5]	3%	7[6]	6%
Number of the above having degree of Ph. D.	27	....	25	....
Number having title of *Geheimrat*.........	2	....	1	....

100 Per Cent

1896
1898

Business Men   Teachers   Officials   Physicians   All Others

[1] For the years 1908 and 1914, the figures concerning local agents are combined with those of the officers of the local branches.

[2] *Alldeutsche Blätter*, 1897, pp. 95 *et seq.*

[3] *Ibid.*, 1898, pp. 119 *et seq.*

[4] Lieutenant colonel (retired) and captain (retired).

[5] Gardeners, a head forester and concert master.

[6] Gardeners, procurator, manager, person of private means and director of an institute of correction.

TABLE VIII

PROFESSIONS OF LEADERS OF THE DISTRICT ORGANIZATIONS OF THE
PAN-GERMAN LEAGUE

Profession	1906 [1]		1914 [2]	
	Number	Approximate %	Number	Approximate %
Business Men	5	25%	4	18%
Teachers................	4	20%	7	31%
Officials	5	25%	4	19%
Physicians	2	10%	1	5%
Lawyers	2	10%	1	5%
Nobility................	1 [3]	5%	2 [4]	10%
Editors	..	....	1	5%
Chemist	..	....	1	5%
Men with private means ..	1	5%	1	5%
Number of above having degree of Ph. D........	3	....	8	....

[1] *Handbuch,* 1906, p. 6.

[2] *Handbuch,* 1914, pp. 16 *et seq.*

[3] Count.

[4] Count and baron.

TABLE IX

PROFESSIONS OF MEMBERS OF THE EXECUTIVE COUNCIL OF THE
PAN-GERMAN LEAGUE

Profession	1906 [2]		1914 [3]	
	Number	Approximate %	Number	Approximate %
Teachers.................	22	26%	23	25%
Business Men............	14	17%	21	23%
Officials	12	14%	13	14%
Physicians.	7	9%	8	9%
Reichstag Members	5	6%	1	1%
Editors	5	6%	5	5%
Technical Men	5	6%	7	8%
Military Men............	3[4]	4%	4[6]	4%
Lawyers	2	2%	3	3%
Landowners	2	2%	..	....
Nobility.................	2[7]	2%	4[3]	4%
Church	2	2%	4	4%
Miscellaneous	3[5]	4%	..	....
Number of above having degree of Ph. D........	26	....	32	....
Number of above having title of *Geheimrat*	5	....	7	....

100 Per Cent

1906
1914

■ Business Men   ▨ Teachers   ▨ Officials
▨ Physicians   ▨ All Others

[1] The executive council consisted of the honorary members of the League, the members of the executive committee, the business managing committee, the presidents of the district organizations and of the local branches, the local agents, members of the League elected to the council and representatives of local branches having a membership of more than 100 (see *supra,* p. 51).

[2] *Handbuch,* 1906, pp. 5 *et seq.*

[3] *Handbuch,* 1914, pp. 14 *et seq.*

[4] Lieutenant colonel, retired first lieutenant and retired captain.

[5] A farmer, member of the *Landtag* and the president of the German National League for the Aid of Commerce.

[6] Retired captain, major and lieutenant colonel and a major general in active service.

[7] Two counts.

[8] Three barons and one " excellency."

The most striking fact about these tables is that the first four professions most largely represented in each are the same—business men, teachers, officials, and medical men. The teaching profession for the most part contends with the business men for first place and wins in some cases. The race seems to have been fairly even, though the fact that there are a great many more men in business than in teaching, makes the relative position of the latter profession considerably higher.   A closer analysis of these leading professions is essential to an understanding of what strata of society composed the membership of the Pan-German League.

Let us first consider the teachers.   These may be divided roughly into two classes, the university professors and the teachers in *Realschulen, Gymnasien,* etc.   The following table (X) shows the percentage which these two classes of teachers bore to each other among the League's leaders. It is a closer study of the subdivision " teaching profession " in the previous occupational tables.

TABLE X

Year	Among Local Branch Officers		Among League Agents		Among District Organization Officers		In the Executive Council	
	Pro-fessors	Teach-ers	Pro-fessors	Teach-ers	Pro-fessors	Teach-ers	Pro-fessors	Teac-ers
1894	57%[1]	43%[1]	....	....	...	....	....	....
1896	57%[2]	43%[2]	38%[7]	62%[7]	....	....	....	....
1898	49%[3]	51%[3]	33%[8]	67%[8]	....	....	....	....
1906	22%[4]	78%[4]	....	....	50%[9]	50%[9]	68%[11]	32%[11]
1908	42%[5]	58%[5]	....	....	....	....	....	....
1914	34%[6]	66%[6]	....	....	29%[10]	71%[10]	78%[12]	22%[12]

In the earlier tables, the number of men holding the degree of Doctor of Philosophy has been noted. Not only men engaged in strictly academic work held this degree but a good many business men, lawyers, officials, etc. Moreover, it stamps the members as belonging largely to the so-called "educated" classes and may perhaps help to account for the theoretical and academic attitude which the League assumed toward many matters. Though the business men vie with the teachers for first place, yet the fact that the so-

[1] *Alldeutsche Blätter*, 1894, p. 16.

[2] *Alldeutsche Blätter*, 1897, pp. 93 *et seq.*

[3] *Alldeutsche Blätter*, 1898, pp. 117 *et seq.*

[4] *Handbuch*, 1906, pp. 8 *et seq.*

[5] *Handbuch*, 1908, pp. 8 *et seq.*

[6] *Handbuch*, 1914, pp. 18 *et seq.*

[7] *Alldeutsche Blätter*, 1897, pp. 95 *et seq.*

[8] *Alldeutsche Blätter*, 1898, pp. 119 *et seq.*

[9] *Handbuch*, 1906, p. 6.

[10] *Handbuch*, 1914, pp. 16 *et seq.*

[11] *Handbuch*, 1906, pp. 5 *et seq.*

[12] *Handbuch*, 1914, pp. 14 *et seq.*

called professional classes—the medical men, lawyers, technical men, and officials—are so well toward the top of the list, makes the League on the whole representative of these professional classes rather than of the business men.

But who were these " business men " and what type of " business " did they represent? There seems to have been absolutely no connection before the war between big business and the Pan-German League, either financially or in the League's membership. The business men were for the most part small merchants, salesmen, a few manufacturers and bankers, and quite a number of publishers and booksellers. There were bank clerks, druggists, florists, printers —but no large industrialists with interests all over the world.

The " officials ", comprising in each case the third largest category, were the usual members of the German bureaucracy, federal, state and municipal—burgomasters, *"Räte"* [1] of all sorts, officers of justice, and the innumerable petty *" Beamter "* [2] of a bureaucracy.

Medical men have the fourth place in the membership lists, and technical men, that is, engineers of all varieties, are close behind in the fifth place, with the legal profession ranking almost as high. For the rest, the church, the army and navy, the titled nobility and the landowners make a very poor showing.[3] It is true that a few military men like General Keim, General von Liebert, and Admiral Breusing, held positions high in the the inner circles of the League and made a great many noisy speches at League conventions and meetings. But it would seem that in the rank and file of League members, army and navy men were not very numerous. The official table (V) showing professions of all members for 1901 does not even have a military divi-

[1] Councillors.

[2] Officials.

[3] The Reichstag members have been treated separately.

sion.[1]   However, a few sabre-rattling generals on the executive council were probably worth a good many lesser
military lights.   On the whole we find that the membership
of the Pan-German League was recruited largely from the
educated classes and was very decidedly bourgeois.

[1] See *supra*, p. 65.

CHAPTER IV

THE FINANCES OF THE PAN-GERMAN LEAGUE

THE question of whence the funds of the Pan-German League came, what these funds were used for and how much money the League actually had, is an interesting and important part of the history of the organization. For the first thirteen years (1894-1907), the financial reports were published annually in some detail in the *Alldeutsche Blätter* together with some explanation concerning the status of the League. A study of League finances falls automatically into two parts: the actual moneys of the League used to further directly its own aims and ideals, and the sums collected through its agency for certain specific purposes.

The accompanying tables show the annual income and expenditure of the League from 1894 to 1907 inclusive, and give an accurate idea of its financial condition.

In order to enroll the largest possible number of people in the League, the annual dues had originally been placed at the very nominal figure of one mark.[1] This was raised to two marks in 1899, for the League felt that it did not wish to be so largely dependent upon gifts from its members for actual current expenses.[2] This accounts for the fact that the amount of dues collected in 1899 was almost double the amount collected in 1898 (see income table). By payment of one hundred marks or more, one could become a life member. The dues of the local branches were fixed by them at

[1] *Alldeutsche Blätter*, 1895, p. 77.
[2] *Ibid.*, 1900, p. 232.

about the same rate, and it was through the local branches that most of the dues to the central organization were collected. That is, the local branches sent two marks per capita to the central office,[1] retaining the amount of their local dues, which usually amounted to two or three marks also, for the use of the local branch.[2] There was a good deal of trouble in collecting the dues and the *Alldeutsche Blätter* published table after table of arrears. For instance, the arrears amounted to:

1901	13,600.00	marks	[3]
1902	13,221.51	"	[4]
1903	15,097.00	"	[5]
1904	21,500.00	"	[6]
1906	16,507.00	"	[7]
1907	13,324.00	"	[8]
1908	11,121.00	"	[9]
1909	11,409.00	"	[10]

These arrears included membership dues, subscriptions to the *Alldeutsche Blätter,* payments for badges, pamphlets, handbooks, etc., and in the case of the year 1904, 8,000 marks of the 21,500.00 marks listed represented membership dues of people who had resigned or dropped out without paying their dues.[11]

The publication of the *Alldeutsche Blätter* was made pos-

[1] *Alldeutsche Blätter*, 1898, p. 90.

[2] Grell, *Der alldeutsche Verband, seine Geschichte, seine Bestrebungen, seine Erfolge,* (*Flugschriften,* no. 8) pp. 5 *et seq.*

[3] *Alldeutsche Blätter*, 1902, p. 553.

[4] *Ibid.,* 1903, p. 19.

[5] *Ibid.,* 1904, p. 31.

[6] *Ibid.,* 1905, pp. 157, *et seq.*

[7] *Ibid.,* 1906, pp. 122 *et seq.*

[8] *Ibid.,* 1907, pp. 123 *et seq.*

[9] *Ibid.,* 1908, p. 139.

[10] *Ibid.,* 1909, p. 151.

[11] *Ibid.,* 1905, pp. 157, *et seq.*

sible at the start by the collection of a Guaranty Fund,[1] to which individual members contributed small amounts over several years in order to underwrite the publication of the weekly. This fund, which was continued until 1899, amounted to:

1894	8742	marks [2]
1895	8742	" [2]
1896	8905	" [3]
1897	2780	" [3]
1898	5176	" [4]
1899	1864	" [5]

The subscription rates to the *Alldeutsche Blätter* were 2.50 marks a year for members of the League and 4 marks for non-members at first, but in 1895 they were raised to 4 marks for members and 6 marks for non-members.[6] Advertisements published in the *Alldeutsche Blätter* helped to put it on a self-supporting basis.

The subscriptions to the *Alldeutsche Blätter* were swelled to a slight extent by the Diederichs Fund, the gift of August Diederichs, long the oldest member of the League,[7] and a staunch supporter of *das Deutschtum*. He arranged in 1897 for a gift to the League of 20,000 marks in Imperial German bonds, bearing interest at $3\frac{1}{2}\%$. Four-fifths of the income from this capital was to be used for League purposes and the remaining fifth was to be reinvested in government securities. At least three of the four-fifths designated for League purposes, Diederichs

---

[1] *Ibid.*, 1895, p. 77.

[2] *Ibid.*, 1895, p. 77.

[3] *Ibid.*, 1897, pp. 8 *et seq.*

[4] *Ibid.*, 1899, pp. 161 *et seq.*

[5] *Ibid.*, 1900, pp. 182 *et seq.*

[6] Grell, *op. cit.*, p. 5.

[7] He died in October, 1917, at the age of 98.

directed should be used to distribute free copies of the *Alldeutsche Blätter*. He desired that the organ of the League should reach the people who might most effectively spread its doctrines—teachers and students for the most part. At the same time that he made this gift of 20,000 marks to the League, Diederichs gave 15,000 marks to the *Allgemeiner deutscher Schulverein* and a like sum to the *Allgemeiner deutscher Sprachverein*.[1] But he was most interested in the work of the Pan-German League, and by virtue of his gift eighty copies of the *Alldeutsche Blätter* were sent free to various institutions annually.[2]

In September 1909, Herr Diederichs added another 5,000 marks to the capital of the fund and thus increased its annual yield from 700 to about 900 marks.[3] Of this amount, 525 marks covered the cost of sending out two hundred free copies of the *Alldeutsche Blätter* and the rest went into the League's treasury.

In examining the tables further, one is struck by the fact that the League spent relatively little in the publication of pamphlets and received very little from their sale. This bears out the conclusions reached before concerning the mythical character of the " masses of Pan-German pamphlets " spread broadcast through the world. Another interesting item concerns the League badges. These were in the shape of oak-leaves and their popularity is evidenced by the fact that for several years the income from their sale rivaled and even surpassed the returns from pamphlets.

In general, the financial tables show that the League lived within its income but had no surplus. Its annual expenditures were not of an alarming size; in fact they were surpris-

[1] *Satzungen des Diederichsstiftungs des alldeutschen Verbandes,* pp. 10 *et seq.*

[2] See *infra* p. 119 for actual working of the fund.

[3] *Alldeutsche Blätter,* 1909, p. 320; 1911, p. 79; 1912, p. 7; 1913, p. 31; 1914, p. 15.

ingly small. Had the League really been the author of all that has been attributed to it, its annual budget must have far exceeded the rather modest sums shown in these tables.

The League was not on a particularly firm financial basis during the first decade of its existence. Some money was raised by annual contributions to a " fund for aiding the work of the League," [1] and a sum of 10,000 marks was collected in 1898 in memory of Bismarck.[2] The former, the so-called *Betriebs und Werbeschatz* amounted in all to 13,538 marks by January 1903, and had been collected slowly and built up from small individual contributions.[3]

In November 1903, the League was incorporated as a company with limited liability, and capitalized at 20,000 marks,[4] Dr. Hasse assuming responsibility for 10,000 marks and Dr. Class for 10,000.[5] The same year the *Alldeutscher Wehrschatz* was started. This was a fund to be used only for *das Deutschtum* and not for any running expenses of the League.[6] J. F. Lehmann, the Munich publisher who published all the League pamphlets and handbooks, started the movement to found such a *Wehrschatz* by circulating a petition at a League convention. The petition received eighty signatures at once and the fund was launched by flowery articles and appeals in the *Alldeutsche Blätter*. By December 1904, 19,424.49 marks had been collected [7] and the Leaguers were using all sorts of means to popularize the fund and raise money for it. Pan-German seals were advertised for sale in the *Alldeutsche Blätter*, Pan-German

[1] *Alldeutsche Blätter*, 1896, p. 102.

[2] *Ibid.*, 1898, p. 158, p. 171.

[3] *Ibid.*, 1901, pp. 554 *et seq;* 1902, pp. 19, 35, 54, 79, 99, 159, 335; 1903, p. 63. *Der alldeutsche Verband im Jahre 1901*, pp. 60 *et seq.*

[4] *Alldeutsche Blätter*, 1903, p. 417.

[5] *Handbuch*, 1906, pp. 27 *et seq.*

[6] *Alldeutsche Blätter*, 1903, p. 330, p. 346.

[7] *Alldeutsche Blätter*, 1904, p. 438.

stamps were sold,[1] one local instituted social evenings for bowling and skat, the proceeds to go to the *Wehrschatz;*[2] Dr. Hasse went without his New Year's cards and contributed five marks to the fund, a fact which he announced in the *Alldeutsche Blätter*[3] in order to inspire other members to follow his example.

In four years, 91,122.68 marks had been collected, of which 45,518.66 marks were capitalized, leaving over 45,-000.00 marks available for "national purposes", as the League expressed it.[4]   By June 1909, a total of 182,854.51 marks had been reached, of which 86,820.00 marks were capitalized under the name of the Hasse fund, in memory of Dr. Hasse who died in January 1908; 24,124.15 marks had been given away for various purposes to aid in the work of the League; and 51,026.21 marks had been appropriated by the business managing committee over the period of these same six years, for various relief funds, etc., in which the League was interested.[5]   Part of the remainder, which was deposited in the *Mainzer Volksbank*, had been put to the following uses:

1. German press	2242.95	marks
2. Support of People's League [6] and of individuals	3000.00	"
3. Loans	600.00	"
4. Gifts of books	204.10	"
5. Burg Persen [7]	1000.00	"
6. Miscellaneous	566.92	"
7. Expenses	35.70	"
Total	7649.67	"

[1] *Alldeutsche Blätter,* 1905, p. 27.

[2] *Ibid.,* 1904, p. 416.

[3] *Ibid.,* 1905, p. 10.

[4] *Ibid.,* 1907, p. 365.

[5] *Ibid.,* 1910, pp. 19 *et seq.*

[6] *Völkischer Verein.*

[7] A health resort in South Tyrol.

The general financial aid of the League was given for the most part to such causes as the other so-called " national associations," on account of the restrictions of their constitutions, could not serve.

By January 1911, the latest date for which official figures are available, 206,948.43 marks had been collected in the *Wehrschatz*.[1] ·Mention is made, however, of the fact that during the first half of the year 1912, over 40,000 marks were collected [2] in gifts, aside from the regular contributions, and in 1913, one member willed the League 20,000 marks.[3] Wenck gives a total of 413,808 marks collected for the *Wehrschatz*, from 1903 through 1913, and there seems no reason to doubt his figures.[4]

The money in the *Wehrschatz*, for the most part, however, was raised by voluntary self-taxation on the part of the Leaguers. A " constitution " was drawn up in September 1909, at a League convention in Schandau,[5] the provisions of which were as follows:

1. The *Alldeutscher Wehrschatz* is to be built up through voluntary self-taxation on annual incomes, as well as through other means.

2. The resources of this *Wehrschatz* are to be used exclusively for militant *Deutschtum*, in the aid of German national endeavors; they are not to be used to defray the costs of running the Pan-German League.

3. The assessments for the *Wehrschatz* (through self-taxation) shall take place from January first to March first. The control of the *Wehrschatz* lies in the hands of the business managing committee of the League.

[1] *Alldeutsche Blätter*, 1911, p. 125.

[2] *Ibid.*, 1912, p. 263.

[3] *Ibid.*, 1913, p. 242.

[4] Wenck, Martin, *Alldeutsche Taktik*, p. 15.

[5] *Alldeutsche Blätter*, 1910, p. 45.

4. Gifts and payments of all kinds are accepted for the *Wehrschatz* in all amounts. . . . . A person pledging annually at least ½ per cent of his cash income shall be designated as a *Zeichner* (subscriber). Any clubs, etc. regularly pledging a fixed annual amount to the *Wehrschatz* shall be called *Förderer* (promoters).

5. The book-keeping for the *Wehrschatz* shall be done separately from that of the League.

6. Thirty per cent of the *Wehrschatz* is to be invested. This capital stock of the *Alldeutscher Wehrschatz* shall bear the name *Hasse Stiftung* (Hasse fund) from February 1906 on, in honor of the League's president, Professor Dr. Ernst Hasse.

7. The subscribers and promoters of the *Wehrschatz* shall receive each February an annual report of its condition.

The stated uses for the *Wehrschatz* were " to strengthen and fortify *das Deutschtum* on the borders of the Empire and outside; to help settlers, students, schools, book-stores, newspapers, and commercial undertakings; and to support orphans in the Eastern provinces and to work for the settling of German colonies oversea."[1]   The 400,000 odd marks collected for these purposes over a period of ten years, meant in our money about $100,000. Thus the average annual amount of money available for purposes of League propaganda, aside from running expenses, was about $10,000.

After the establishment of the *Wehrschatz*, the League seems to have been in much better financial condition. There was a flurry of strict economy after Dr. Hasse's death in 1908, and the central business office was moved to Mayence at that time.[2]   Mayence was the home of Dr. Class, Hasse's successor as president of the League, which accounts

[1] *Alldeutsche Blätter*, 1910, pp. 25 *et seq.*

[2] *Ibid.*, 1909, pp. 274 *et seq.*

for the choice of that city.   Count Ernst zu Reventlow was
placed in charge of a Berlin office to attend to political
affairs of the League, and a new business manager took
charge in Mayence, reorganizing the office thoroughly.
Further notices of the financial state of the League, made
in the *Alldeutsche Blätter* after 1909, were to the effect
that everything was quite satisfactory.   In June 1910, it
was entirely free from debt,[1] and it seems to have remained
so.   On the whole, the League officers showed themselves
very energetic and self-sacrificing in financial matters and
the organization was conducted with cautious economy.
In its entire financial aspect, the history of the League
shows a certain " family " spirit and naïve belief in the
cause for which it was working, which only real sincerity
could motivate.   The other phase of League finances—the
collection of money for various and sundry " causes "—
bears this out.   The contributions were many and small
and probably cost the donors considerable pinching at
times.

The funds which the League raised, or which the Leaguers
aided through the agency of the *Alldeutsche Blätter* and the
central office, were many and varied.   One was the support
of an orphanage for German children at Neu Zedlitz in
Posen.   A gift to it of 10,000 marks from a Baron Hoff-
man of Leipzig, through the League,[2] very small contributions from various locals and Christmas gifts made by the
wives of men in the League, helped to support it.   A
sewing circle under Frau Dr. Lehr sent gifts of books,
pictures, fans, pencils, toys, clothes, and odds and ends, as
well as very small sums in cash,[3] but it must have been
very hard sledding for the institution.   It was reported in

[1] *Ibid.*, 1909, pp. 274. *et seq.*
[2] *Ibid.*, 1898, p. 108.
[3] *Ibid.*, 1905, p. 9.

the *Alldeutsche Blätter* at one time [1] that Dr. Hasse had donated twenty marks won from a bet which he had made.

A collection of money to enlarge the German navy was started by Dr. Wislicenus [2] at a meeting of the Leipzig local branch in 1896. This was, of course, some time previous to the general agitation for an increase of the German navy. Dr. Wislicenus's suggestion met with immediate response and 10,802 marks were raised by the League, including 1,000 marks from a Guatemala local branch. [3] The League addressed an inquiry to the Secretary of State for the Navy as to just what to do with the money in order that it might go directly towards the building of a battleship. The minister, in reply, deeply regretted that it was impossible for his department to accept the money and suggested that it be sent to an institution for the care of sailors' widows and orphans. This quite incensed the League, but as there was no other alternative, it was decided to use the money to agitate for the enlargement of the navy. The fund had been raised entirely by small contributions from a good many members. [4] The money was actually used for twenty-five lectures on the need for a larger navy, given at various local branches by a retired naval *Kapitän— Leutnant* Weyer, and for the publication of a pamphlet, (one of the regular series) *Genügt Deutschlands Wehrkraft zur See?* [5]

The most significant collection made by the League and the most successful, was the Boer fund raised for relief work among the Boers during and after the Boer War. The Leaguers' Anglophobia at that time amounted to a sort of

[1] *Alldeutsche Blätter*, 1903, p. 63.

[2] See *supra*, p. 35, note 2.

[3] *Alldeutsche Blätter*, 1896, pp. 205 *et seq.*

[4] *Ibid.*, 1897, p. 32, p. 96.

[5] *Ibid.*, 1897, pp. 90 *et seq.*

frenzy, and contributing to a fund to relieve the Boers must have given tangible relief to their emotions at the same time. The list of contributors is a tremendous one, the amounts sent ranging from tiny sums to good-sized gifts, and 634,-111.24 marks were collected in all.[1] The collection was not confined to members of the League alone, for it was advertised in newspapers throughout Germany,[2] and coming at a time when public opinion in general was stirred, the response was considerable. The money was used in many different ways. Support was given to a German-Belgian ambulance corps sent out from Antwerp; the widows and orphans of Boer soldiers killed in action were aided;[3] prisoners of war were helped. A good deal was done through the local branches of the League in Cape Town and Johannesburg in the Transvaal to help needy Boer families and Germans and to aid the German school in Johannesburg. There were many reports of British atrocities, and stories of this sort added greatly to the hatred of England and consequently to the fund. People sent in money to the fund from all over the world. The League itself was moved primarily because of its feeling that the Boers were Low-Germans, but it was impossible to know how far such a feeling motivated the numberless small subscribers who swelled the total with their tiny gifts.

Through the fund, Boer soldiers and Germans who had fought in the war were helped to return to their homes after the war was over and supplies and goods were sent out in kind to be distributed in South Africa.[4] Germans stranded there were helped to return to the fatherland and general relief work was carried on in the concentration camps.

[1] *Ibid.*, 1911, p. 125.

[2] *Ibid.*, 1899, p. 390.

[3] *Ibid.*, 1900, pp. 41, 114, 184, 522.

[4] *Ibid.* 1902, pp. 381, 205.

The 634,111.24 marks were spent entirely for relief work of the kind indicated.[1]

The Pan-German League's interest in South Africa did not wane after the Boer War and from 1904 to 1909 it collected 192,135.15 marks for gifts for the German troops in German Southwest Africa fighting the Hereros.[2] Christmas gifts of all sorts were sent out, the usual cigarettes, chocolate, comfort kits, etc., as well as money, and in this way the Leaguers endeavored to make life a little easier for the men who were fighting for *Deutschtum* against the barbarians of Southwest Africa.

Another fund, the responsibility for which can scarcely be laid at the door of the League, was the *Liebermann Ehrengabe*— a collection made in honor of the twenty-fifth anniversary of Liebermann von Sonnenberg's entrance into political life. Long a foremost anti-Semite and member of the *Deutsch Soziale Partei*, which he represented in the Reichstag, Liebermann von Sonnenberg was a member of the Pan-German League as well. He was a fluent orator and an intensely emotional person; the announcement of the collection in his honor spoke of his spirit as a " clear flame of inspiration ".[3] The money raised amounted to 17,709.17 marks, and since the collection was advertised in

[1] *Alldeutsche Blätter*, 1902, p. 381.

A considerable sum was spent as follows:

Cash sent to League agents in South Africa	145,000	marks
For clothes, etc. sent to South Africa	15,000	"
For prisoners of war in St. Helena, Ceylon, etc.	40,000	"
For returning German soldiers	30,000	"
For South African refugees	45,000	"
For the German-Flemish ambulance	45,000	"
Relief work among suffering Boers and Germans in and outside of South Africa	70,000	"

[2] *Ibid.*, 1911, p. 125.

[3] *Ibid.*, 1904; p. 343, 1905, p. 11.

the pages of the *Alldeutsche Blätter,* the Leaguers must be held responsible for some part of it at least.

An annual fund to which the Leaguers contributed was collected by Karl Pröll, one of the founders of the League and a member of the executive council. The purpose of the fund was to buy Christmas trees for poor German children living along the borders of Germany, especially in Austria-Hungary, Saxony, Transylvania, Bohemia, South Styria, Carinthia and the Ukraine.[1] After 1908, the fund was carried on by the *Verein für das Deutschtum im Auslande,* and the League seems to have had little or nothing to do with it. This fund amounted to:[2]

1894	....		724.60	marks ⎫					
1895	....		1281.50	” ⎪		Total amount collected by			
1896	....		1716.40	” ⎬		Pröll and the League			
1897	....		2247.37	” ⎪					
1898	....		1592.02	” ⎭					
1899	The League collected		816.50	marks	out	of	total	of	2634.15
1900	”	”	” 745.05	”	”	”	”	”	3720.45
1901	”	”	” 391.55	”	”	”	”	”	3720.20
1902	”	”	” 393.55	”	”	”	”	”	3192.85
1903	”	”	” 224.20	”	”	”	”	”	2023.90
1904	”	”	” 384.80	”	”	”	”	”	3793.35
1905	”	”	” 418.35	”	”	”	”	”	3960.50
1906	”	”	” 208.05	”	”	”	”	”	3608.55
1907	”	”	” 427.00	”	”	”	”	”	5909.40
1908	”	”	” 116.00	”	”	”	”	”	4308.15

Aside from the funds already enumerated, the League collected the following money:

[1] *Ibid.,* 1902, p. 379.

[2] *Ibid.,* 1895, p. 12; 1896, p. 44; 1897, p. 16; 1897, p. 276; 1899, p. 16; 1900, p. 14; 1900, pp. 534 *et seq.*; 1901, p. 563; 1903, p. 475; 1904, p. 451; 1905, p. 446, p. 416; 1908, p. 14; 1908, p. 447.

1896—For navy agitation .... 39,000.00 marks [1]
1899—for suffering Germans in Graslitz
     (Bohemia) [2] .... 227.75   ,,
1899—For Austrian and Bavarian flood sufferers [3] 2,049.75   ,,
1901—For the German soldiers in China [4] .... 9,076.29   ,,
1903—For German sufferers from a fire in
     Windischgrätz [5] .... 250.00   ,,
1904—For German sufferers from a fire in
     Winterberg [6] .... 100.00   ,,
1905—For German sufferers from the Russian
     Revolution [7] .... 6,346.50   ,,
1911—For German sufferers in Lusern
     (South Tyrol) [8] .... 2,436.62   ,,
1911—For flood victims in South Brazil [9] .... 3,905.75   ,,
1913—For the family Welker [10] .... 5,930.13   ,,
1914—For the family Kempf [11] .... 7,537.11   ,,

Of these collections, the last two demand some explanation. Welker was a German who lived in Cservenka in Hungary and published the *Südbatschkaer Zeitung* in defense of *das Deutschtum*. He got into trouble, however, with the Magyars and was tried and convicted for " inciting against the Hungarian government ".. " His only sin ", said the *Alldeutsche Blätter,* " was that he remained true to his German people." As a result of his conviction, he was faced with bankruptcy and his family were in desperate straits, and though the League had never had any previous

[1] *Alldeutsche Blätter,* 1911, p. 125.

[2] *Ibid.,* 1899, p. 367.

[3] *Ibid.,* 1899, p. 351.

[4] *Ibid.,* 1901, p. 473.

[5] *Ibid.,* 1903, p. 319.

[6] *Ibid.,* 1904, p. 295.

[7] *Ibid.,* 1905, p. 343.

[8] *Ibid.,* 1911, p. 274.

[9] *Ibid.,* 1911, p. 448.

[10] *Ibid.,* 1914, p. 35.

[11] *Ibid.,* 1914, p. 243.

connection with Welker, it appealed for financial aid for his family.   Indeed it had never even heard of him before the news of his trial.

Kempf had been maltreated by an anti-German Alsace-Lorraine manufacturer named Heyler who had profiteered on some government business and been detected.   As a result, Heyler lost the government's business.   He vented his wrath on Kempf, a poor publisher in Grafenstaden where both men lived, because the latter had reprinted an article from the *Rheinisch-Westfälische Zeitung* severely censuring Heyler for his anti-German acts.   Kempf was forced to move to Frankfurt-am-Main and was absolutely without money. The Pan-German League, wishing to help this patriot who had suffered from the profiteer, raised a fund to help his family.   Many small contributions were made by sympathetic people and 7537.11 marks were raised.

CHAPTER V

The Aims and Ideals of the Pan-German League

THERE are in German two terms, *Pangermanisch* and *Alldeutsch,* both of which are translated in English by the word " Pan-German " and in French by " *Pangermaniste* ". It is always difficult to express the full value of words when translating them into another language, and confusion is likely to result. In this case, the danger is augmented, for *Pangermanisch* and *Alldeutsch* are not synonymous, and it is essential to an understanding of the Pan-German League that the use of this term " Pan-German " be fully explained.

The roots of the words *Pangermanisch* and *Alldeutsch* differ; *Pangermanisch* comes from *Germani* and has the connotation of " Germanic " or " Teutonic ", which in its extended ethnic sense embraces any member of the races or peoples speaking a " Germanic " or " Teutonic " language—i. e., Gothic, the Scandinavian tongues, low German high German and English.[1] *Alldeutsch,* on the other hand has the connotation of " *Deutsch* " which is said to be derived from the root " Thiod ", meaning " people ", which appears in Gothic, Anglo-Saxon, and other comparatively early Germanic languages.[2] The word *Deutsch* was prob-

---

[1] Murray's *New English Dictionary,* vol. 9, pt. 2, p. 236.

[2] " The Old High German adjective, *diutisk*—"pertaining to the people "—which was written *theodiscus* in the Latin of the ninth century, became the *diutsch* or *tiutsch* of Middle High German, and the *deutsch* of Modern German." Hayes, C. H., *Sources of the Germanic Invasions* (New York 1909), pp. 16 *et seq.*

ably not written until the ninth century A. D. As to the words *Germani* and *Germania,* Tacitus wrote about 100 A. D :

The name " Germania ", they say, is modern and of recent application, since those who just crossed the Rhine and ex-pelled the Gauls, and who are now called " Tungri ", were then named " Germani ": thus what had been a tribal name, not a national name, spread little by little, so that later they all adopted the newly-coined appellation that was first em-ployed by the conquerors to inspire fear and called themselves " Germani ".

An analogy might be drawn in the case of the terms " Anglo-Saxon nations " and " English-speaking nations "; the former is a broader, more indefinite expression, while " English-speaking " is a more definite term. In the Ger-man language, the terms *Germane* and *Germanisch* have broad connotations and are very elastic. They may be used historically to designate early Germany and its inhab-itants, or they may refer to the great racial and linguistic group which includes Germany, the Netherlands, Switzer-land, Austria, England, Scandinavia, the Baltic provinces, Iceland, and any other place in the world where there is a preponderance of Germanic blood or Germanic speech.[1] *Deutsch,* on the other hand, refers only to Germany and Germans of today.[2]

In order that this study may be as clear as possible, it is necessary to translate *Germane* by the rather arbitrary word " Teuton ", inasmuch as even " Germanic " might be confusing. *Deutsch* is translated in the usual fashion by

[1] Grundzweig, Armand, *Activism in Belgium,* p. 38.

[2] In this connection it is interesting to note the Norwegian, Danish and Swedish word for German which is *Tysk,* the Dutch which is *Duitscher,* the Italian which is *Tedesco,* and our own term " Dutch ", all of which obviously have the common root *Thiod.*

" German ".   Therefore *Alldeutsch* becomes Pan-German
or Pan-Germanic and *Pangermanisch* is Pan-Teutonic.
Alldeutsch has generally been translated by Pan-German and
it would seem that a good deal of the force of the study
might be lost were this familiar appellation changed.   The
trouble in the past has been that *Pangermanisch* too has been
translated by the same word.

With this in mind, it is now possible to proceed with an
explanation of the *Pangermanentum* (sometimes written
Allgermanentum) as opposed to the *Alldeutschtum*.   An
understanding of the difference between the two will be of
value in dealing with the actual platform of the Pan-German
League.

The *Pangermanentum* means, in accordance with the
usage adopted, the collectivity of all the Teutonic peoples.
These comprise the Scandinavian peoples, the peoples of
Iceland, and of the Baltic provinces, the English, the
Germans in Germany, Austria and Switzerland, the so-
called low-Germans in the Netherlands, the Boers in
South Africa, the Flemings in Belgium.[1]   Such a grouping
was a nebulous thing that lent itself admirably to after-
dinner speeches, indefinite flowery essays and glittering generalities.   The Pan-German League called it a " cultural
ideal taken from the past and to be regarded with an eye to
the future." [2]   On the other hand, in the Pan-German
scheme, the cultural ideal was second to the political.   The
members of the League felt this to be the case, largely because for them the emphasis in Pan-Teutonic was on the
" Teutonic ", while in Pan-German, it was the Pan—the
" All "—that counted.   Teutonic was thought to be entirely
a cultural ideal which conflicted in no way with the Pan-
German ideals for the future.   A union of all Teutonic

[1] *Alldeutsche Blätter*, 1901, p. 214; 1902, pp. 46 *et seq.*
[2] *Ibid.*, 1902, pp. 114 *et seq.*

peoples might be desirable for the purpose of establishing the supremacy of the Teutonic race in the world, or preparing defense against a common danger, or of securing and nurturing common cultural ideals. The Pan-German League felt that there was no definite way of knowing just what this so-called Teutonic culture embraced, and that the many different theories advanced as to what comprised its component parts were rather unsound and certainly conflicting.

It may seem that the Leaguers were splitting hairs in their attempts to differentiate between the *Pangermanentum* and the *Alldeutschtum*. The former was considered as having a more or less direct relationship to the growth of nationalism in Germany during the nineteenth century and its connotations were broad and cultural. The latter was intimately related to the development of German nationalism, and was narrower; it was essentialy political; it could be swallowed by the *Pangermanentum* and would scarcely be missed; its very name was the chance invention of an old man unknown outside of the narrow circle in which he moved.

The Pan-German League struggled valiantly against losing its identity in the nebulous Pan-Teuton movement. Because it was organized and because it spoke out fearlessly and loudly on all subjects at all times, it became notorious. For the layman, it embodied not only its own specific aims but the broader aims of the Pan-Teutonic movement, and in the resulting ambiguity the purposes of the two movements were popularly confused. Outside Germany this was particularly true, and it was easy for scaremongers in all countries to seize on the nebulous Pan-Teuton movement and turn it into a gigantic plot—the " Pan-German plot ". Thus the League had greatness more or less thrust upon it; nor was this an unmixed blessing, for motives entirely outside of its own aims were ascribed to it.

The Pan-German League was founded as a direct result of intense anti-English feeling. The Pan-Teutonic movement, on the other hand, urged the union of all the Teutonic races in the world, including the English. Obviously the Pan-German League desired no such union, cultural or otherwise, except perhaps in the extreme case of an actual Slavic invasion. In the matter of mere " Slavic peril ", they were not yet ready to unite with their Teutonic brothers, the English. They felt that Pan-Slavism was encroaching upon other non-Slavic peoples, and they regarded the growth of the British Empire in the same light.[1] The Boer War seemed to bear this theory out; and it is important to note that most of the articles in the *Alldeutsche Blätter* on the subject of the differences between the *Pangermanentum* and the Pan-German League's ideals for *das Deutschtum* appeared during the Boer War period. It leads one to suspect that a good deal of the strong feeling about Pan-Teutonism on the part of the Pan-German Leaguers was rationalization.

The development of nationalism in Germany has been indicated, and the Teutonic paeans of Houston Stewart Chamberlain and the Count de Gobineau have been mentioned in an earlier chapter.[2] They were a part of the Pan-Teutonic movement; we are almost tempted to say that they were the movement. They represent the extreme of the nationalist movement, and a large part of its cultural background. The Pan-German League, on the other hand, was more strictly political in its work, nebulous and vague as its ideals were.

An official handbook of the League gives the following statement of its purpose:[3]

[1] *Alldeutsche Blätter,* 1901, pp. 129 *et seq.*

[2] See Chapter I.

[3] *Handbuch des alldeutschen Verbandes,* 1908, p. 30.

It is an organization of all German-minded people of different shades of opinion, who aim, without respect to the pleasure of the government and the great mass of the people, independent of political parties and factions, to oppose everything which is un-German and to stretch a helping hand to all those Germans, whether at home or abroad, who are oppressed. It believes that the national development of the German people is not completed.

The League's official constitution is a bit more explicit. It states that:[1]

1. The Pan-German League strives to quicken the national sentiment of all Germans and in particular to awaken and foster the sense of racial and cultural kinship (*Zusammengehörigkeit*) of all sections of the German people.
2. These aims imply that the Pan-German League works for:
   1. Preservation of the German people (*Volkstum*) in Europe and oversea and its support wherever threatened.
   2. Settlement of all cultural, educational and school problems in ways that shall aid the German people (*Volkstum*).
   3. The combating of all forces which check the German national development.
   4. An active policy of furthering German interests in the entire world. The League is particularly interested in working for practical results in the German colonial movement.

The basic plank of the Pan-German League's platform was the vigorous enlivenment of German national sentiment.[2] It was felt that this was the foundation upon which all else might be built. Therefore the League was, as it said, primarily an organization for agitation and for education. Educationally, it was to work to teach people to prize national interests above the machinations and squabbles

[1] *Handbuch,* 1914, p. 7. For text of document see appendix no. 1.
[2] *Kampf um das Deutschtum,* title page.

of political and commercial organizations; it was to work to preserve German folkways and customs in Europe and oversea and for the union of *Deutschtum* entire over the whole earth. In its capacity as agitator, the League held itself ready to enter the lists anywhere that German comrades might be struggling to maintain their own individuality against the domination of foreign people. Further it felt it to be its task to see that the German people was not cheated of its rightful share in world domination and world commerce. " For ", said the League, " the German people is a dominant people;[1] it must be considered and respected as such by other powers throughout the entire world."

This statement is very reminiscent of Gobineau, and when Dr. Hasse takes the Social Democrats to task in the Reichstag for their theories concerning the equality of man, and announces that his point of view is the exact opposite—that there is nothing more unequal than the human races[2]—we seem to hear the very voice of Gobineau himself. Upon this inequality of races Dr. Hasse makes a plea for the Boers, low-Germans, as he considered them to be, and makes some derogatory remarks concerning the English, the Poles, the Danes, and the French. Here too the difference between Pan-Teutons and Pan-Germans is clearly shown, for the former included the English and the Danes in the Teutonic race and did not feel superior to them as the Pan-Germans did.

Dr. Hasse's theory of the state is of prime importance to us here, for in taking him as its leader, the Pan-German League took over too his ideas and general philosophy of life. That the German national development was not entirely completed as a result of the war of 1870-71 was one of

[1] *Herrenvolk.*

[2] *Stenographische Berichte des Reichstags, X. Legislaturperiode, 2te Session, (1900-1903) 157te Sitzung,* (Mar. 4, 1902), pp. 559 *et seq.*

the main points in Hasse's theory. His belief in this was based upon his conception of a nation. " We understand by a nation ", said he, " a community of people of the same descent, who speak one and the same language, have gone through a common political and cultural development together, and have a consciousness of belonging together." [1] The community of language was considered by Hasse the most important single factor. Furthermore, the formation of a nation could only be deemed complete when at least the majority of the people speaking one language, etc., were gathered together into a single state. Such is his ideal state—the *Nationalstaat* or national state. He defines it as follows: " It is a state in which the boundary lines correspond exactly with the boundaries of nationality; though we consider that a state in which there are racial minorities besides the ruling race, may be termed a *Nationalstaat* if it pays no especial attention to these minorities." [2]   On the other hand, according to Hasse, there is the *Völkerstaat*, a state of peoples, in which peoples belonging to different nationalities live together as a nation. He gives Switzerland and Austria-Hungary as examples of this type. But to him the *Nationalstaat* was the ideal, and it was his life work to aid Germany to become such a state. Millions of non-Germans lived in Germany and millions of Germans lived outside the Empire, said Hasse, and therefore the German Empire was not a *Nationalstaat*.[3]   He gives the following figures to show the distribution of Germans in the world: [4]

[1] Hasse, Ernst, *Deutsche Politik,* vol. i (*Das deutsche Reich als Nationalstaat*), (Munich, 1905), pp. 10 *et seq.*

[2] *Ibid.,* p. 14.

[3] *Ibid.,* p. 31.

[4] *Ibid.,* p. 38.

In Germany	52.1 million	=	58.35%
” Austria	9.4 ”	=	10.53%
” Hungary	2.1 ”	=	2.35%
” Switzerland	2.3 ”	=	2.57%
” Luxemburg	0.2 ”	=	0.22%
High Germans	66.1		74.02%
In Belgium	3.4 ”	=	3.80%
” the Netherlands	5.1 ”	=	5.71%
Low Germans	8.5 ”		9.51%

Total High and Low Germans in the so-called German language area	74.6 million	=	83.55%
Total in the rest of Europe	2.9 ”	=	3.24%
Total in Europe	77.5		86.79%
In America, Africa, Asia, Australia	11.0 ”	=	13.21%

Grand total of 90 million Germans in the world.

It is these Germans that the Pan-German League wished to unite by fostering their consciousness of being Germans and by keeping their patriotism at fever heat. We find Hasse protesting in the Reichstag that that representative body was more interested in the relatively few Danes, Poles and Alsace-Lorrainers within the confines of the Empire than in the millions of Germans who lived just outside its borders.[1] This is easily explicable when one considers his definition of the *Nationalstaat* and his desire for Germany to continue her expansion. His was a veritable " Will to Power " for Germany, though he was not a disciple of the Nietzschian philosophy as a whole.[2]

[1] *Stenographische Berichte des Reichstags, X. Legislaturperiode, 2te Session (1900-1903), 157te Sitzung,* Mar. 4, 1902, pp. 4559 *et seq.*

[2] The common conception of Nietzsche's influence on extreme chauvinism in Germany might make it seem probable that he was a hero of the Pan-German League. The following statement of Bonhard in his

The racial minorities within the Empire were considered a source of grave danger to the fatherland — the Poles, the Danes, the Alsace-Lorrainers, all must be subdued and

(official) *Geschichte des alldeutschen Verbandes* (pp. 186 *et seq.*) will set all doubts at rest on that score. Nietzsche himself could have wished for nothing stronger had he been interested in such trivial matters: .... "There is a philosophy which falsely turns heroes into 'Supermen' and contrasts the slave-morality of the masses with the moral excesses of master-morality. It is the natural exaggeration of the inequality (of races) idea as opposed to the excesses of its opponents who have allowed the idea of the similarity and equality of races to degenerate into utter silliness. It leads, as we have said, to the master-morality of the "blond beasts" and in the final analysis to immorality. And here we perceive the crux of the matter—why Nietzsche, the creator of this *Weltanschauung,* has been connected with Pan-German teachings. People have wished to show that the Pan-Germans themselves are the exponents of these immoral teachings. For that reason, the difference between the pure hero-worship of the Pan-Germans and this Nietzschian master-morality must be shown as clearly as possible, precisely because their common origin in the study of races leads to much confusion. It is not the function of this exposition to side with or against Nietzsche's position. Everyone must do that for himself after careful study. But we must absolutely deny the doctrine of master-morality, for we Pan-Germans will have as our future leaders only heroes whose moral greatness is unmistakable. 'Time is great and powerful. But woe unto us if our hearts are not clean! How then shall we endure in battle?' And our future followers can only be a free, self-conscious race of heroes, and no slaves. ... In order to prove the absolute independence of Pan-German doctrine from Nietzsche, another point must be made—viz: his lack of fatherland. This half-sane thinker has abused our German Empire rancorously and thinks little enough of our people: 'We good Europeans do not want to hear anything of national differences', says he. He adds to his offences against the German people still further by insults of unbelievable lack of taste and vulgarity, and when he ceases from such ugly abuse, he degrades *Deutschtum* by blindly interchanging it with Latins, French, Jews and Slavs. We really have nothing in common with such a line of thought. Nor is it a fact that any of the Pan-German leaders followed Nietzsche's teachings. It is evident that the Pan German League could not have had any connection whatsoever with the ideas of Nietzsche and since he himself became insane in 1889, the year before the foundation of the League, it obviously had nothing whatever to do with him personally."

Germanized, and racial minorities in the Austro-Hungarian Empire should receive as much attention as those within the German Empire itself. The League had a very strong anti-Semitic bias, feeling that the Jews were non-Germans and therefore as much a racial minority to be reckoned with as the Poles or the Danes. But the fear of Pan-Slavism was the most potent factor in the minds of the leaders of the League.

We cannot do without those Germans living on our borders if we wish to preserve our world-position in the future. It is a duty of self-preservation that we do not look on with folded arms at the battle that is being waged there for *Deutschtum*. " Slavization " of the Germans in Austria, Magyarisation in Hungary is threatening; the Germans stand there as the vanguard in the struggle against Pan-Slavism, whose victory would mean the downfall of the German people and all *Kultur*.[1]

Thus the League aimed to transform Germany into a true *Nationalstaat* in which the racial minorities were to be entirely disregarded, and the ruling race was to be united with the Germans living on the borders of the Empire. The stated aims of the League operated directly to further Hasse's ideal.

We want to strengthen the feeling of relationship between all Germans in order to protect our people (*Volkstum*) against dangers which will threaten the very roots of its being during the coming century; in order that we may present as solid a front as possible and at the same time be able to oppose the united commercial power of our enemies, the Anglo-Saxons upon the one hand and the Russians on the other. . . . The Germans are opposing these great masses of Anglo-Saxons and Russians with a relatively small population, and the re-

[1] Lehr, *Zwecke und Ziele des alldeutschen Verbandes* (*Flugschriften,* no. 14), p. 77.

sult of this threatening development will be that a greater part of the world will be closed to us commercially if we do not speedily take up the gauntlet through the exertions of a greater mass of the German people (*Volksmassen*) and by the creation of a central European commercial sphere solely under German protection.

It is all this that the Pan-German League understands by bringing together all the Germans in the world (*Zusammenfassung aller Deutschen auf der Erde*). We dare not limit ourselves to the fifty-two million Germans [1] in the Empire, we must join together the entire German people (*Volkstum*)—all the Germans that there are, including the twenty-millions (ten millions in Austria-Hungary, two millions in Switzerland, eight millions in the Netherlands) who live on our borders in other countries, but who speak our language (*Sprachgebiet*) ; and the other eight millions who are scattered over the rest of the world. These, above all, it behooves us to help to maintain their German individuality in order that they do not become absorbed by some other people (*Volkstum*) and thus be entirely lost to us!" [2]

The League was interested in the economic aspects of *das Deutschtum* as well as in its racial aspects; indeed, aside from the sentimental satisfaction which the leaders felt in their super-patriotism, an undercurrent of fear seems to have greatly influenced their opinions. "How can the fifty-three million Germans in the German Empire", asks Hasse, "hope to compete with more than one hundred million Anglo-Saxons, Yankees and Russians?" [3] The answer to this question was to be found in the formation of a closed mid-European commercial area,[4] an idea which

[1] Written 1895.

[2] Lehr, *op. cit.*, p. 76.

[3] Hasse, *op. cit.*, p. 48.

[4] *Mittel-europäisches Wirtschaftsgebiet; cf. Alldeutsche Blätter*, 1898, pp. 266 *et seq.* Bonhard, *op. cit.*, pp. 127 *et seq.*

is reminiscent of Fichte's *Geschlossener Handelsstaat.* This mid-European plan embraced Germany and Austria-Hungary primarily and was directed mainly against the British Empire, Russia, and " Pan-America ". The idea was nebulous and hazy and the means by which it was to be carried out were limited to a customs' union and closer railway connections. Friedrich List, during the first half of the nineteenth century, had written a good deal in favor of such a plan, and Dr. Hasse was much influenced by his work. As a result we find Hasse writing considerably on the subject in the *Alldeutsche Blätter,* and in his *Deutsche Politik* he treats it very fully. However, it was obviously such a nebulous scheme and the hopes of its fullfilment were so far in the future that the treatment of the whole matter was decidedly academic.

The emigration of many thousand Germans each year to other countries was a source of great anxiety and concern to the Pan-German League. That Germans for one reason or another should leave the fatherland and go to live elsewhere was, of course, more or less incomprehensible, but even such a rash step should not cut them off from the advantages of belonging to an elect people. The League was particularly desirous that they should not become Americanized or Russianized, and thus lost entirely to *das Deutschtum* commercially and nationally.[1] The *Alldeutsche Blätter* is full of naïve anecdotes, such as the following [2] about the visit of Prince Henry, the Kaiser's brother, to St. Louis, Missouri. The Prince benevolently spoke to an old German veteran and asked him whether he still thought of the old fatherland; whether his children had been raised in the faith of his forefathers; whether he spoke German at home to his family and sent the children to a German

[1] Lehr, *op. cit.,* p. 76.
[2] *Alldeutsche Blätter,* 1902, p. 150.

school. The old man was able to answer " Yes " to all the questions and shed a tear at the mention of Prince Henry's father. From all of which the *Alldeutsche Blätter* points a moral and adorns a tale; here is exemplary behavior on the part of an emigrated German. The naïveté of the Pan-German League in general and of the *Alldeutsche Blätter* in particular would be most amusing, if it had not been taken so seriously by many Germans and non-Germans too.

With the problem of German colonial policy the Pan-German League had been concerned from the outset. Founded as a direct outgrowth of the trend towards colonial expansion in Germany,[1] the League espoused in its official constitution " an active policy of fostering German interests in the entire world, in particular the furtherance of the German colonial movement to practical results ".[2] Its members desired to assure the prestige and power that were supposed to accrue from the possession of a mighty empire; to make Germany commercially independent of the rest of the world and self-sufficient; and to create new outlets for German commerce and industry,[3] and thus to remove the necessity of having German capital invested in the service of a foreign nationality. Last but not least, was the desire to have German emigrants settle in German-owned colonies instead of going to some foreign country where they might soon become assimilated to an alien nationality and be entirely lost to *das Deutschtum.* Hand in hand with an aggressive colonial policy, the League maintained, must go a national emigration policy, one which would really take care of the emigrating Germans and work for the closest national and commercial ties between them and the fatherland. The fact that, unless an emigrant were registered in the records

[1] See Chapter II.
[2] *Handbuch,* 1914, p. 7.
[3] Lehr, *op. cit.,* p. 80.

of a German consulate, he automatically lost his German citizenship after ten years unbroken absence from his native land, was an added thorn in the side of the League, for many people were lost to *das Deutschtum* in that way. It made the need for German colonies where German emigrants could settle without losing their German citizenship seem even more imperative. Directly in line with its colonial policy was the League's agitation for the protection of German nationals in foreign lands. The well-known cry of all imperialists in all countries had no different sound when issuing from Pan-German lips.[1] In general, it may be said that the colonial policy of the League set forth very directly the goal of binding together all Germans in the world—the unity of the German *Volkstum*.

"*Volkstum*", "*Deutschtum*" are indefinite terms, capable of many and varied interpretations, and, like the ideals of the Pan-German League, they have many connotations and great elasticity. National feeling, a purely emotional thing, seems to thrive on glittering generalities and the leaders of the Pan-German League felt that in working towards their goal, they must not be hampered by anything definite, but must be free to agitate on any and every question. Dr. Adolph Lehr made this very clear in an address delivered before various local branches of the League during 1895 and 1896,[2] on the " Aims and Ends of the Pan-German League ":

[1] Their calling upon the " German national honor "; as is always usual in such cases, brings the following to mind: " The sense of national honor is at bottom simply another name for the deep emotional reaction of the social group toward anything which affects its egotism, its longing for prestige." A. H. Hanlius, in the *Journal of International Relations,* April 22, p. 156. Also Veblen's definition of patriotism as a " sense of partisan solidarity in respect of prestige ". (*An Inquiry into the Nature of Peace,* New York and London, 1917, p. 31).

[2] Lehr, *op. cit.,* p. 73.

I have often heard the criticism that the League in its constitution has set an entirely too sweeping, general, and indeterminate goal before itself. Exactly the contrary is true! The wording of our constitution is exceedingly fortunate, as experience since the League's foundation has proved. The constitution must be drawn up in as general a fashion as possible because unforeseen things may occur at any moment and we may then take action upon them without being nailed tightly to the words of the constitution. It is the very generality of the terms of the constitution which constantly enables us to step in wherever the national interests, the national honor — *das Deutschtum* in general — seem to be threatened, without being hampered and hobbled by the constitution in a way that those who drew it up never intended. Other associations, which like us are striving for the preservation of *Deutschtum,* have imposed handicaps of this sort upon themselves. For instance, the German School Association [1] may deal only with matters concerning the furtherance of education—and indeed only outside of Germany; at this moment when the battle against *das Polentum* ("Polishism") is raging in our Eastern provinces, the support of German schools there would be more than desirable. The *Kolonialgesellschaft* is restricted to work solely outside of Germany and is forced to hold aloof from any colonial activity within the German state or language area. [2]

The Pan-German League, on the other hand, was free to agitate on any and all questions which had bearing on the " fostering of German national sentiment, racial or cultural kinship "—surely a mandate broad enough to allow complete freedom of action. As a result the scope of its activities was very large, and the *Alldeutsche Blätter* developed into an organ for the expression of Pan-German opinion on the current issues of the day. At the same time issues more

---

[1] *Deutscher Schulverein.*

[2] *Sprachgebiet.*

or less peculiarly Pan-German were not allowed to lapse;
and the state of *das Deutschtum* in Belgium, in Austria-
Hungary, in South America, etc., was reported on frequently. In the main, however, it can be said that the
history of the Pan-German League's particular policies,
both domestic and foreign, involved the main German political issues of the entire period with which we are concerned,
from 1890 to 1914. The Pan-German mirror reflects a
tiny portion of German opinion over two and a half decades
which were all-important in the history of Germany and of
the world. In the formation of this opinion, the broad
general principles of the Pan-German League were used
as foundation stones upon which its agitation was based.

The scope of the League's interests is well illustrated by
the following list of problems with which it expressed itself
as primarily concerned: The Polish question; Navy question; Anglo-German relations; reform of the citizenship
law; conditions in Alsace-Lorraine and North Schleswig;
the entire foreign policy of the Empire, particularly in relation to Austria-Hungary.[1] At the 1898 League convention, it gave forth the following more definite list and the
action it wished taken upon each item:[2]

1. Adoption of bill for reorganization of the navy.
2. Laying of a cable from Kiao-chau to Port Arthur, with
   connection with the Russian-Siberian cable.
3. Strengthening of the German foothold in Kiao-chau.
4. German coaling and cable stations in the Red Sea, the
   West Indies and near Singapore.
5. Complete possession of Samoa.
6. More subsidized German steamship lines to Kiao-chau
   and Korea.

[1] Class, *Zwanzig Jahre alldeutscher Arbeit und Kämpfe*, p. v.
[2] *Alldeutsche Blätter*, 1898, pp. 17 *et seq.*

7. Understanding with France, Spain, Portugal and the Netherlands about the laying of an independent cable from West Africa through the Congo to German East Africa, Madagascar, Batavia, and Tongkin to Kiao-chau.
8. Development of harbor of Swakopmund (German Southwest Africa) and railroads to Windhoek (German Southwest Africa).
9. Securing of concessions for commerce and industry in Asia Minor.
10. Raising of the fund for German schools in foreign countries to 500,000 marks (had been 150,000 marks), division in foreign office to be created to deal with these schools; creation of pension fund for their teachers; standard German textbooks to be supplied to these schools.
11. Further endowment of the Colonization Commission by 100 million marks, the Polish Commission to be under the general commission.
12. Transference to the west of all officials (local, etc.) and military men of Polish race.
13. Guarantee of increase of pay to the German officials in the Polish parts of the East Province.
14. Acquisition of imperial holdings on the French border in Alsace-Lorraine and of Prussian royal holdings on the Danish border in Schleswig.
15. Employment of only German labor in imperial and state possessions and domains.
16. Prohibition of immigration of less worthy elements into the German Empire.
17. Possession of German citizenship by all Germans from the Empire in foreign countries.
18. Taxation of foreign-language-speaking firms, projects and advertisements.
19. Prohibition of the use of foreign languages in clubs and meetings.
20. Germanization of all foreign place-names in the German Empire.

21. Establishment of a German consulate general for Bohemia in a German town in Bohemia.

22. Increase in the number of German commercial consuls in the Levant, Far East, South Africa, Central and South America.

23. Increase in the number of German public libraries in the Eastern provinces, in Schleswig and in Alsace-Lorraine. State and imperial subsidies ought to support them.

24. Setting aside of a sum of money in the colonial office treasury to be used to pay for the attendance of the sons of Germans living in foreign countries at German schools in the fatherland.

25. A lessening of the obligation to military service of Germans living in foreign lands.

26. Germanization of foreign words in official language:
    1. *Gouverneur* to *Landeshauptmann*.
    2. *Gouvernement* to *Landesregierung*.
    3. *Kommandant* to *Befehlshaber*.

The most important of the foundation stones upon which the agitation of the League was based was the development of a truly national spirit.[1]   The League stood unequivocally for " 100% Germanism" and combated with all its might everything that it considered to be un-German.   A weekly column in the *Alldeutsche Blätter* was devoted to *Deutsches und Undeutsches*,[2] and nothing was too insignificant or petty to escape the notice of the energetic editors.   If a Berlin soap manufacturer advertised in French, his advertisement was quoted and he was roundly berated; if a Vienna leather merchant put out an English sign he received his full quota of abuse; children were taken to task for counting in English on the tennis courts; hostesses for placing French menus upon their tables.   The League supported the efforts of the

[1] *Handbuch*, 1914, p. 7.
[2] German and un-German.

Allgemeiner deutscher Sprachverein (General German Language Association) to purify the German language of all foreign words and carried this to extremes as it did everything else. It has been said that as there was once a religious fanaticism so now there is a *national* fanaticism.[1] The leaders of the Pan-German League were more emotional than intellectual and the powerful virus of superpatriotic nationalism intoxicated them to the point of fanaticism. Though for the most part they carried their agitation to such extremes as to be too patriotic for the government itself, and were therefore almost always in the position of criticizing the government in no uncertain fashion, the Pan-German League did not consider itself an opposition party in any real sense. It wanted only to work for a " *deutsch-national* " (German national) public opinion—either for or against the government as the case might be and not as a political party. " *Das Vaterland über die Partei* ",[2] was its aim.[3]

Here and there, (said Lehr),[4] people have believed that we should be styled a party opposing the government. Nothing is further from the truth than that! Certainly, we fight everything that is contrary to our national feelings and philosophy, or contrary to our national interests, but we joyfully acclaim it whenever these national feelings and interests are sufficiently guarded. No rank pessimism, no bitter looking on the dark side of things, but joyful cooperation! Where it must be, earnest warning and sharp blame; where it can be, recognition and thanks! Therefore, we offer no fundamental opposition to the government—no opposition for its own sake. We want much more to have a German national public opinion

[1] Nippold, Otfried, *Der deutsche Chauvinismus* (Berne, 1917) p. v.
[2] Fatherland above party.
[3] Bonhard, *op. cit.*, p. 132.
[4] Lehr, *op. cit.*, p. 74.

which will lay bare the soul of the people to the government, which will strengthen the hand of the government in its outside dealings, and which will allow it to say to strangers: " See, that is the will of the German people with which alone we must reckon, and with which you also must learn to reckon whether you want to or not! " And as we are no opposition party, we are not even a political party. We neither desire to be one nor could we be, nor do we wish to found a new party. There are enough already! Standing outside of all organized political parties, we may go our own purely national way; we do not ask: Are you conservative? Are you liberal? We do not ask: Are you a Protestant or a Catholic? We ask only: *Are you German?* The German nation is the meeting point upon which all parties can make common cause.

It was the cement of pure, unadulterated nationalism that solidified the aims of the Pan-German League. If they could awaken the German people to a complete realization of the advantages and responsibilities of being Germans and citizens of the German Empire, *das Deutschtum* would be saved and unified and the Empire would emerge into a truly national state.

CHAPTER VI

Methods of Action of the Pan-German League

The constitutional structure of the organization created for the purpose of realizing the aims of the Pan-German League has already been described. The meetings of the local branches, the work of the executive, the League convention, and the publications of the League were the chief means employed to further its ends, and a closer study of these mediums must now be made.

" The local branches must see to it that they become the center of the national life in the community ",[1] said the League's leaders. As means to this end, the League suggested that great public demonstrations be held on the anniversary of Bismarck's birth and death; that so-called *" Deutsche Abenden "*[2] be held in cooperation with other national societies; and that above all the personal interest of each member in the League be kept lively and vigorous. The Cassel local branch held in May, 1901, a Pan-German and naval exhibition, according to the account of which [3] thousands of visitors were stirred by the range of embattled *Deutschtum,* and stimulated to demand an explanation of the German naval policy. This is typical of the League's ideal of the activities of its local branches. Furthermore,

---

[1] *Der alldeutsche Verband im Jahre 1901,* p. 22.

[2] German evenings.

[3] *Der alldeutsche Verband im Jahre 1901,* p. 11.

the League was desirous that each local branch should exert all possible influence upon the local and provincial press and seek to influence local and imperial representatives, those in the Reichstag and in the Landtag.

The *Alldeutsche Blätter* published a monthly announcement of the meetings of the various local bodies for the ensuing month; such meetings were usually announced for certain fixed days of the week—fortnightly, monthly, and now and again weekly, and normally at a " *Ratskeller* " or " *Bierhaus* " or restaurant where a " Pan-German table " was reserved. A branch—at Eisleben—reserved the first Monday of each month as an " Alldeutscher Bierabend ",[1] and several branches had bowling clubs. It does not take much imagination to see these jovial, middle-class Germans enjoying their evening away from home, consuming many a " *Grosses Helles* " or a " *Grosses Dunkeles* " and discussing the political situation at home and abroad, as they pulled at their pipes and knocked on their glasses for the waiter to bring another stein. Patriotism waxed warm as the evening advanced and everyone went home in a comfortable glow of self-satisfaction and commendation, congratulating himself on the fact that he was a member of that race of heroes— the Germans—and feeling that he had done his bit for that month toward saving *das Deutschtum*.

Lectures were arranged by the local branches which dealt, either with matters upon which the League was momentarily concentrating all its efforts—the Boer War, the Navy Bills, the Moroccan question, etc.—or with matters less timely perhaps, but always of interest to the Leaguers—the state of *Deutschtum* in various parts of the world and kindred subjects. For instance, the Leipzig branch held the following lectures during the year 1900:

[1] (Pan-German beer-evening). *Alldeutsche Blätter*, 1902, p. 6.

1. Professor Dr. Otto Hötzsch.[1]
   German world commerce.
2. Herr Müller, a Leipzig business man.
   Old and new ideas concerning the navy question, from my own experience.
3. Herr Siegfried Moltke, a Leipzig journalist.
   Deutschtum in Austria and particularly in Tran-
   sylvania.
4. Dr. Armin Tille, Leipzig.
   The conception of perpetual peace and the mean-
   ing of war in international law.
5. Professor Dr. Hasse, Member of the Reichstag.
   Pan-German impressions of a journey to Brussels,
   Paris, the French battlefields and the Vosges
   Mountains.
6. Dr. (medicine) Otto Schmit of Porto Alegre.
   German settlements in Rio Grande do Sul and
   Brazil.[2]

During the year 1901 almost two hundred lectures were
given in the local and district branches in an endeavor to
broaden the scope of the League's work.   The subjects of
these lectures may be summarized as follows:

106 dealt with the Boer War.
14   ”   ”   China.
2   ”   ”   the fleet.
31   ”   ”   colonial and world policies.
25   ”   ”   the Austrian question.
16   ”   ”   the Polish danger.[3]

[1] Professor Hötzsch is an authority on the Near East and Russia, and
is teaching at the University of Berlin at present.   He is well-known there
as a fanatic on the subject of nationalism.

[2] *Jahresbericht der Ortsgruppe Leipzig des alldeutschen Verbandes
über das Jahr 1900,* pp. 3 et seq.

[3] *Der alldeutsche Verband im Jahre 1901,* p. 11.

The officers of the League delivered more than eighty lectures during the year 1901, Professor Samassa speaking in twenty-five places, and the business-manager, Herr Geiser, in sixty.[1] It is a good index to the energy and activity of the leaders of the League.

The president of the Pan-German League exercised the greatest influence of any single person connected with the organization. Well might he have said " *L'état c'est moi* ", though according to the constitution, the business managing committee was to pass upon " complaints of the League's officers concerning the instructions of the president." [2] Dr. Hasse had originally been elected president by the executive committee of the old *Allgemeiner deutscher Verband* and remained president of the Pan-German League until his death in 1908. He was followed by Heinrich Class [3] who was still in office in 1914. Hasse had wished to resign his position before his last term because of failing health and because he wanted to devote himself to the writing of his *Deutsche Politik,* but had finally consented to serve one more three-year term. Bonhard says in this connection: [4]

Looking toward the coming change, Hasse had carefully thought over the question of who should be elected as his successor. He knew from his own experience in 1893, when he had decided to take over the leadership of the League, how important it was for the success or failure of the League that the man who headed it not only be fitted for the position but that he be able to merge his own personality entirely in his work. . . . In Heinrich Class, Hasse believed that he had found the man who possessed the requisite qualifications—

[1] *Der alldeutsche Verband im Jahre 1901,* pp. 15 *et seq.*

[2] *Handbuch,* 1914, p. 10.

[3] *Alldeutsche Blätter,* 1908, p. 52.

[4] Bonhard, *Geschichte des alldeutschen Verbandes,* p. 24.

glowing enthusiasm for the German people and political far-sightedness, strong character and independent position. For that reason he had already brought him into the executive committee, and in that way brought him nearer to the work in order that when he (Hasse) retired, the continuity of the work should be assured during the period of transition. Unprejudiced as he always was, he took no offense at the fact that Class had in general assumed a more sharply defined policy than he had done. In that way it came about that during Hasse's last years, especially in matters dealing with foreign relations, Class took a directing position within the League. In particular, this was shown by his coming to the fore in the Moroccan question. So that his election to the presidency of the League occurred with great unanimity of spirit, and the change of leadership which usually leads to internal difficulties and shake-ups in associations of this sort, was accomplished entirely without friction.

It seems clear from the above that the power in the Pan-German League was pretty much in the hands of the few at its head. Yet one can not believe that the red-tape which the elaborate constitution tied around the League's functioning was designed to throw sand in the eyes of the members and lead them to think that the organization was based on more or less democratic principles. The tradition of the members was against democratic control and the president of the League, practically unhampered by the constitution, was able to dominate and control its destinies. In patriotic societies of this sort, as in almost any activity outside the actual sphere of earning one's daily bread, the entire work and responsibility of the organization falls naturally rather upon the shoulders of the few people who are actively engaged in conducting it as a full-time occupation (whether as a vocation or an avocation), than upon the many whose names appear on paper as members of this council or that committee.

The annual conventions were important events in the life

of the Pan-German League, and according to the accounts in the *Alldeutsche Blätter,* the meetings were always well attended and a good time seems to have been had by all. Moreover, a good deal of business was transacted; the council and the business managing committee met as the constitution prescribed, and the convention itself attended to the routine business that came under its jurisdiction. Reports were made by the council and the business managing committee, and the general ideals of the League were iterated and reiterated. Petitions were signed, and resolutions drawn up and passed, and the members listened to speeches on various subjects. The president spoke at length upon the state of *das Deutschtum* and on the political situation in the Empire; representatives from Austria were frequently present to report on conditions in the Dual Monarchy, and other speakers delivered orations on subjects connected with the work of the League. There was usually an excursion to some neighboring point of interest and a reception given by the local branch, and in general the spirit seems to have been one of holiday merrymaking and good comradeship. The beer flowed freely, a *Männerchor* or a *Gesangverein* performed, and members of the League enjoyed themselves with the full assurance that they had earned their pleasure and aided their country.

If the annual convention served to unify the Pan-German League and give its members a feeling of solidarity and comradeship for the rest of the year, the *Alldeutsche Blätter* was the connecting link between the central office and the local and district branches. Costing six marks a year, it had appeared regularly every week since 1894, and all members of the League were urged and exhorted to subscribe. Hasse once characterized the publication as the " best agitator the League possessed." [1] Through the

---

[1] Wenck, Martin, *Alldeutsche Taktik,* p. 20.

Alldeutsche Blätter the members were appraised of the
course of the League's routine business—the meetings of
the council and business managing committees, the annual
report of the League, and the financial notices of collections
of funds to be devoted to specific causes.   The information
concerning business affairs was not imparted in a brief paragraph or two but was commented upon editorially.   In this
fashion the news of the activities of the League's governing
bodies was made vital to the individual members, and the
League's conventions in particular were fully reported in
order that those members not lucky enough to have been able
to attend, should not lose their feeling of solidarity.   The
League was, of course, responsible for everything published
in the *Alldeutsche Blätter,* articles, notices, etc., and according to the constitution (article 33), the editor was responsible to the business managing committee.   The *Alldeutsche
Blätter* was thus truly the mouthpiece of the League.

Besides the news which dealt directly with the machinery
of the League, the *Alldeutsche Blätter* always carried longer
or shorter articles calculated to stimulate the " consciousness of racial and cultural kinship of the entire German race
both within and without the German borders."   Under this
head may be cited the numberless articles dealing with the
" support of *das Deutschtum* in Europe and oversea ",
" educational and school problems of the German race, and
the struggle against all forces seeking to limit or cramp the
national development."   However, the subjects which received the largest space were the questions of German foreign policy and those dealing with the racial minorities
within the Empire (Poles, Alsace-Lorrainers, and Danes).
Almost invariably the articles on these subjects criticized
the action of the government in the sharpest and most caustic
manner.

Polemics occupied a considerable place in Pan-German tac-

tics. Before everything else, they directed their fire against
the imperial government wherever and whenever the latter did
not direct its policies along Pan-German lines, and that according to Pan-German judgment had almost never been the
case since Bismarck's resignation from the government. Although it is very easy to prove that what the *Alldeutsche
Blätter* presents as Bismarck's point of view shows considerable divergence from Bismarck and that the Pan-Germans are
not always in agreement as to what Bismarck's policies would
have been under new circumstances, yet they invariably appeal
to the authority of the old chancellor. In his name they desire to be the conscience of the government and of the parties,
and especially to play the rôle of political whip to the so-called
" national " parties. . . . On the whole, the tone in which the
Alldeutsche Blätter is written is one of overbearing presumption as though they held political wisdom in all fields by hered-
itary tenure, and above all as though they alone can decide
what politics and action are truly German and patriotic.

This explains to a large extent the impression made by the
Alldeutsche Blätter outside of Germany. There one is apt
to confuse presumption with reality and to accept as the opinion of the German people what is merely a Pan-German idea.
Out of this is constructed a picture of the world as the German
people supposedly conceive it, while in reality the picture is
only the fantasy of a political sect.[1]

In order that the *Alldeutsche Blätter* should reach as
many non-members of the League as possible, the members
of the League were requested to ask for it at all hotels, inns
and news-stands and thus give the paper and the League a
bit of free advertising. Under the terms of the " Diederichs Fund ", free copies were distributed annually to institutions of learning in Germany and outside of the Empire.
From 1901 [2] until 1910, eighty such institutions received

[1] Wenck, *op. cit.*, p. 22.

[2] *Alldeutsche Blätter*, 1901, p. 351.

free weekly inspiration; in 1910, due to an increase in the amount of capital of the fund established by Herr Diederichs, the League was enabled to send the *Alldeutsche Blätter* to two hundred recipients. The list of the favored, revised every two years,[1] was composed chiefly of normal schools in Germany,[2] until 1906 when the publication was sent to eighty schools located outside of Germany.[3]

[1] *Alldeutsche Blätter*, 1907, p. 430.

[2] *Alldeutsche Blätter* 1901, p. 351.

[3] *Alldeutsche Blätter*, 1906, p. 7; 1909, p. 27; 1912, p. 7. German schools in the following places outside of the German Empire received the *Alldeutsche Blätter* at one time or another between 1906 and 1914 under the terms of the Diederichs' Fund; (those marked * are on more than one list)

Antwerp	Milwaukee, Wis.	Rustchuk (Bulgaria)
Hoboken (Belgium)	Addison, Ill.	Athens
Brussels	Seward, Neb.	Belgrade
Verviers	Concordia, Mo.	Haifa
Amsterdam	* St. Paul, Minn.	Jaffa
Rotterdam	New York City	Yokohama
Copenhagen	Nepperhan, N. Y.	Cairo
Genoa	New Ulm, Minn.	Columbus, O.
* Rome	Mexico City	Woodville, O.
Naples	Havana	Dubuque, Ia.
Messina	Guatemala	Brenham, Texas
Madrid	Caracas	Clinton, Ia.
Barcelona	Valparaiso	Concepción
Porto	Santiago (Chile)	Victoria (Chile)
Lisbon	Temuco (Chile)	Joinville, (Brazil)
Bukharest	Valdivia (Chile)	Blumenau (Brazil)
Craiova (Rumania)	* La Unión (Chile)	Santa Cruz (Brazil)
Turn-Severin "	Osorno (Chile)	Dorpat
Galatz "	Puerto Montt (Chile)	Fellin
Jassy "	* Buenos Aires	Wenden
Constanza "	Palermo (Argentina)	Werro
Sofia	Belgrano "	Reval
* Constantinople	Barracas al Monte	Goldingen (Courland)
Salonika	(Argentina)	

In 1908 and 1909 thirty-eight normal schools in Germany and forty-two German schools outside of Germany received it.[1] When in 1910 the number of recipients was raised to two hundred, several Austro-Hungarian libraries and reading-rooms in small provincial towns were similarly favored,[2] and clubs, *Turnvereine,* societies, associations, casinos, lodges of all sorts in Germany and a few in Austria-Hungary were put on the list. In 1912 and 1913 the Pan-German League sent the *Alldeutsche Blätter* to sixty libraries and reading-rooms and to some schools and one hundred and eighteen associations; and clubs of various sorts received the weekly, among them a number of National Liberal clubs and such associations as the *Beamten-Kasino der Gerwerkschaft des Steinkohlberggwerkes Zollverein,*[3] Canterberg, near Essen; the *Beamten-Kasino der Gerwerkschaft des Steinkohlberg-*

* Riga	Rosario de Santa Fe	German societies in
* Smyrna	(Argentina)	the following places
Sarona	Romano (Argentina)	received the *Alldeut-*
* Jerusalem	Montevideo	*sche Blätter* gratis:
Tsingtau	Asuncion	Rosario (Argentina)
Hongkong	Rio de Janeiro	Belgranio "
Shanghai	Petropolis (Brazil)	Philadelphia, Pa.
Alexandria	Curityba (Brazil)	New York City
Wynberg	Porto Alegre, Brazil	Pretoria
(Cape Colony)	São Goão Montenegro	Bloemfontein
Port Elizabeth	(Brazil)	Pietermaritzburg
(Cape Colony)	Rio Grande do Sul	(Natal)
Pretoria (Transvaal)	(Brazil)	Durban (Natal)
St. Louis, Mo.	São Paulo	Adelaide
Springfield, Ill.	Venice	Melbourne
Fort Wayne, Ind.	Braila (Rumania)	Huancayo (Peru)

[1] *Alldeutsche Blätter,* 1909, p. 271.

[2] In 1910-11 thirty town libraries in Germany and forty-two town libraries and reading rooms in Austria-Hungary received it, particularly the local branches of the *Bund der Deutschen in Böhmen* (Association of Germans in Bohemia). *Alldeutsche Blätter,* 1910, p. 110.

[3] Club for the officials of the customs union of collieries.

werkes,[1] Langenbrahm, Rüttenscheid; *Kaufmännescher Verein,*[2] Hall, Swabia; and to *Jünglingsvereine,*[3] soldiers' clubs and agricultural associations, besides the usual *Turnvereine* and singing societies.[4]   In 1914-1915, the entire mailing-list consisted of clubs, schools, libraries, etc., within Germany.[5]   By such means the League hoped to reach various sections of German society.

The following table shows the number of subscribers to the *Alldeutsche Blätter*:

Year	Number	Source				
1894	2,507	*Alldeutsche Blätter,* 1896, pp. 101 *et seq.*				
1895	3,586	"	"	1896, pp. 101 *et seq.*		
1896 (April 1)	3,759	"	"	"	"	"	"
1896 (end of year)	4,098	"	"	1897, p. 89.		
1897 (April 10)	4,367	"	"	1898, p. 90.		
1897 (Dec. 10)	5,304	"	"	1898, p. 90.		
1898 (Apr. 10)	5,955	"	"	1898, p. 255.		
1898 (Nov. 1)	6,664	"	"	1899, p. 161.		
1898 (end of year)	6,746	"	"	1900, p. 182.		
1899	8,215	"	"	1900, p. 182.		
1900 (Apr. 1)	8,279	"	"	1900, p. 182.		
1900 (end of year)	8,151	"	"	1901, p. 35.		
1901	8,046	*Alldeutscher Verband im Jahre 1901,* p. 19.				
1902	No figures available					
1903	6,109	*Alldeutsche Blätter,* 1905, pp. 160 *et seq.*				
1904	6,055	"	"	1905, pp. 160 "		
1905	5,811	"	"	1906, p. 208.		

The general curve indicated by these figures is much the same as that of the membership statistics.[6]   Though no information is available after 1905 concerning the number of

---

[1] Club for officials of the colliery at Langenbrahm, Rüttenscheid.

[2] Salesmen's Association.

[3] Young men's clubs.

[4] *Alldeutsche Blätter,* 1912, p. 7.

[5] *Alldeutsche Blätter,* 1914, pp. 15 *et seq.*

[6] For tables concerning number of members, distribution, etc., see *supra,* pp. 54 *et seq.*

subscriptions to the *Alldeutsche Blätter,* it may be assumed from the known membership figures that the number of subscribers remained about the same or if anything decreased slightly. At any rate these figures do not indicate a very wide distribution of the weekly.

Next in importance among the publications of the Pan-German League comes the official *Handbuch des alldeutschen Verbandes,*[1] (Handbook of the Pan-German League) which appeared annually and was sold to the members. It contains a full account of the League's work, organization and aims, as may be seen from the following table of contents of the 1914 edition:[2]

1. Aims and purposes of the Pan-German League.
2. Constitution.
3. Membership.
   - a. Executive committee
   - b. Business managing committee
   - c. Council
   - d. District organizations
   - e. Local branches and agents
4. Members of the Reichstag who are members of the League.
5. Treasury and Hasse Fund.
6. Diederichs Fund.
7. Business affairs.
8. Suggestions for work of the local branches.
9. Short review of the work of the League.
10. Books recommended for reading.
11. German societies and associations.
12. For travelers and " hikers ".
13. Speech commemorating the centennial of the War of Liberation.

[1] Published by J. F. Lehmann, Munich.

[2] *Handbuch des alldeutschen Verbandes,* 1914.

14. Statistics of *das Deutschtum.*
15. Extent of the projected Central European Customs' Union.
16. The European peoples according to their geographical extent.
17. The European peoples according to their nationality.

From the handbooks it is possible to ascertain who the leading members of the League were, and thanks to the German love of titles and the custom of designating every one by some term that announced his profession or business, the occupations of these leaders are also given. The complete list of local and district branches is given and the handbooks form a very valuable source of information concerning the League's organization and the details of its work. It is almost impossible to find copies of them however, and after a search through all the main libraries in Germany,[1] the 1916 number was located in the library of the University of Bonn, and the 1905 and 1908 numbers in the *Preussische Staatsbibliothek* in Berlin. The 1906, 1908 and 1916 numbers are in the New York Public Library, while the 1914, 1917 and 1918 numbers were discovered in a private collection in Germany and are now in the Columbia University Library (New York City).[2]

The literature issued by the Pan-German League, besides the weekly *Alldeutsche Blätter* and the annual *Handbuch des alldeutschen Verbandes,* was very scant. There are

[1] Such a search is possible and definitive through the *Auskunftsburo der deutschen Bibliotheken*, Unter den Linden 38, Berlin W. 7.

[2] The publisher (J. F. Lehmann of Munich) writes as follows in answer to a request for the publications of the League in general and the Handbooks in particular: "In answer to your inquiry of May 2, 1921, I am sorry to state that various publications of the Pan-German League are out of print. We have so few copies of the remaining publications that these must be kept for members of the League."

two collections of League pamphlets—the *Flugschriften des alldeutschen Verbandes* and the series entitled *Der Kampf um das Deutschtum.*[1] These deal with various phases of League interests and are written in the usual exaggerated style of chauvinist works. Paul Langhans edited a so-called *Alldeutscher Atlas* for the League, which was published by Justus Perthes (Gotha, 1900). It contains maps and statistics concerning the number of Germans in the world and their geographical distribution. A very occasional reprint of a speech or an article was issued by the League but in almost every case the same document was printed in the *Alldeutsche Blätter.*

The following table shows the amount of mail handled by the office of the League over a fairly representative period of eight years. Viewed in the light of the general growth and development of the League, it is interesting to compare it with the previous table (page 121) giving the number of subscribers to the *Alldeutsche Blätter,* and with Table I, (page 54) which gives the League's membership statistics. The curves represented in all three tables are about the same. From the point of view of the general importance of the League, this particular table shows conclusively that the great mass of propaganda about which one hears so much was largely mythical.

The two official histories of the League's work are *Zwanzig Jahre alldeutscher Arbeit und Kämpfe,*[2] edited by Heinrich Class, and *Geschichte des alldeutschen Verbandes*[3] by Otto Bonhard. The first of these was issued in 1910 to celebrate the twentieth anniversary of the League's foundation. Aside from a short historical foreword by Heinrich Class,

---

[1] For complete list of titles under each, see Bibliography.

[2] Dieterich'sche Verlagsbuchhandlung, Theodore Weicher, Leipzig, 1910.

[3] Theodore Weicher, Leipzig, Berlin, 1920.

MAIL HANDLED BY THE OFFICE FORCE OF THE PAN-GERMAN LEAGUE

Year	Incoming	Outgoing	Printed Matter [1]
1898 [2]	8,876 pieces	15,124 pieces	124,800 pieces
1900 [3]	10,017 "	11,893 "	141,672 "
1901 [4]	11,571 "	114,876 [10]	
1903 [5]	9,864 "	11,632 "	88,722 "
1904 [6]	10,719 "	12,903 "	80,678 "
1905 [7]	10,750 "	11,824 "	86,965 "
1906 [8]	10,104 "	10,993 "	80,554 "
1907 [9]	10,153 "	9,328 "	81,602 "

the volume is merely a compendium of the most important actions taken by the League during its twenty years of existence and reprints of accounts of League conventions or leading articles which had appeared in the *Alldeutsche Blätter*.

Bonhard's *Geschichte* is more pretentious.[11] Written after

[1] *Alldeutsche Blätter* and all other printed propaganda.

[2] *Alldeutsche Blätter, 1899*, p. 162.

[3] *Alldeutsche Blätter, 1901*, p. 350.

[4] *Alldeutscher Verband im Jahre 1901*, pp. 15 *et seq.*

[5] *Alldeutsche Blätter, 1905*, p. 161.

[6] *Alldeutsche Blätter, 1905*, p. 161.

[7] *Alldeutsche Blätter, 1906*, p. 208.

[8] *Alldeutsche Blätter, 1907*, p. 174.

[9] *Alldeutsche Blätter, 1908*, p. 216.

[10] This figure includes outgoing letters and printed matter.

[11] The following letter was received by the author from the Pan-German League's office in Berlin in answer to a request for material on the League's history:

JULY 2, 1921.

" In answer to your inquiry of June 21, we beg to inform you that the *Geschichte des alldeutschen Verbandes* by Lieutenant Colonel Bonhard (Theodore Weicher, Berlin W. 9, Potsdamerstrasse 134 b.) is the best source from which you can learn the incontestable (*einwandfrei*) history of our League. I do not believe that you will find it necessary

the war, it gives the external chronological history of the
League from the beginning until 1920, and then launches into
a defense and exposition of its work for *Deutschtum* inside
and outside the Empire. Written from the point of view
of a member and sincere supporter of the League, the
Geschichte is a valuable reference book, and since it is based
entirely upon source material, is sound and reliable. Greatly
in its favor is the fact that the author's style is direct and
to the point and that his book is less emotional than the
other publications of the Pan-German League.

In almost every number of the *Alldeutsche Blätter* there
is a column headed " *Beachtenswerter Lesestoff* "—reading
matter that is worthy of notice. Under this, one finds books
mentioned and briefly reviewed or described, that should be
of interest to members of the Pan-German League.[1] In
the same category may be put the list of books recommended
in the annual *Handbuch,* though these are for the most part
more serious works dealing with race, *Volkstum* and politics (as the heading states) of the type of Gobineau's
works, Paul de Lagarde's *Nationale Schriften* and Houston
Stewart Chamberlain's *Grundlagen des neunzehnten Jahrhunderts,* etc., besides a complete list of the League's own
Flugschriften and *Kampf um das Deutschtum* series. The
books recommended by the *Alldeutsche Blätter,* since there
are many more of them, are selected less carefully and are
almost entirely of the worst type of yellow jingo literature,

to compile such a history after you have read the aforementioned
work. However, if you should really still have greater interest in
our Pan-German League, as I must presume from your letter that you
have, we would like to suggest to you that you circulate the above-
mentioned *Geschichte des alldeutschen Verbandes* in America as widely
as it lies in your power to do so. You will surely find German-Ameri-
cans who would spend the necessary money for the book, presuming of
course that they still love their old home."

[1] For partial list of these books see appendix no. 3.

inciting to war and weaving romantic tales of victories won on land and sea in imaginary wars or exposing the terrible weakness of the fighting forces of the nation. Books dealing with the need for patriotism and exuding the " my country right or wrong " spirit and lauding the German people to the skies; descriptions of other peoples and comparisons with the Germans—always depreciating the non-Germans; books urging the German people on to *Weltpolitik;* pamphlets against the Poles and Czechs and the French; descriptions of the remote corners of the earth which Germans have colonized or should colonize; in a word all that mass of literature which is loosely termed " Pan-German ". In reality the counterpart of this type of literature may be found in every language indigenous to every country. Its volume increases alarmingly during a war and it becomes much more strident and noticeable, but it should be taken for what it is—the irresponsible vaporings of over-emotional persons. The members of the Pan-German League were exhorted by their leaders to read this type of literature, and the League's own publications were written in the same colorful style and belong distinctly in this category.

The tales that one has heard of the masses of Pan-German propaganda spread broadcast over Germany, the surrounding countries and the world in general[1] would lead one to

---

[1] Under the headline " Pan-German League Out to Defy Allies; Revived Society Enters Election Fights," the *New York Times* of April 29, 1924, prints a wireless dispatch from its Berlin correspondent, T. R. Ybarra, which is typical of the kind of report that has given the Pan-German League its mighty reputation abroad: " The Pan-German League, that sinister organization whose program was the best expression of Imperial Germany's lust for world domination, whose agents worked even in remote corners of the world . . . has suddenly leaped forth as arrogant as ever after a period of sullen rest.

" In a ringing manifesto, . . . the League calls upon Germans to vote at the coming elections in favor of the extreme nationalistic parties who

believe that it would be very easy to find sources of information concerning the Pan-German League. Just the opposite is true. Switzerland, one of the countries that the Leaguers felt was racially akin to Germany and therefore a part of *das Deutschtum,* has almost none of the League's publications in its libraries. The *Zentralbibliothek* in Zürich contains the *Alldeutsche Blätter* from 1911 to 1915 and one pamphlet on the League (published in 1916), and the *Schweizerische Landes-Bibliothek* in Berne has the *Alldeutsche Blätter* from January, 1914, to November 10, 1917. The librarian of the Berne library took great pains to explain that these had been donated gratis by the League. The central catalogue of Swiss libraries revealed no other literature concerning the League, and the head of the Swiss library association [1] vouched for its reliability and added that he knew of no other material on the League in Switzerland.

are against the German government's 'fulfillment policy' so that the way may be paved for German defiance of the Entente, suppression of parliamentary government in Germany, elimination, if necessary, of the German President, refusal by Germany of payments under the terms of the report by the 'so-called experts' and the provocation of Germany's foes to do their worst. . . .

"All German statesmen seeking reconciliation with the Entente, it continues, must vanish from public life, 'which refers particularly to Jews and those who are inspired by the Jewish spirit, namely Marxian Socialists, Democrats and the Stresemann group.'

"Pan-German fury is especially directed against Foreign Minister Stresemann, who is held largely responsible for Germany's woes. . . . .

"'We hail the rapid and powerful awakening of the Völkisch movement which is sweeping through Germany like a Spring storm. To it belongs the future—the very near future. Germany for the Germans!'

"The manifesto was issued following a big meeting of the Pan-German League at Jena yesterday, where fiery speeches were made by Councilor Class, head of the League, and other Pan-German leaders, including Dr. Bang and Baron von Vietinghoff Scheel."

[1] Dr. Herman Escher, of Zürich.

In the Netherlands, the public library of Rotterdam and the University Library of Amsterdam report that they do not possess any of the publications of the League. The Royal Library of Copenhagen (Denmark) has the *Alldeutsche Blätter* 1909-1922, Bonhard's *Geschichte* and Class's *Zwanzig Jahre alldeutscher Arbeit und Kämpfe.* The University Library in Christiania (Norway) has numbers 3, 10, 11, 13, 15 of the *Kampf um das Deutschtum* series, while the Royal Library of Stockholm (Sweden) has none of the League's publications. The Royal Library of Belgium (in Brussels) possesses the 1916 *Handbuch* but otherwise, to quote its librarian: " It has not a single other book about the Pan-German League or published by that Association." The University Library of Brussels is even more vehement. It " does not possess the publications mentioned, nor has it ever had any relations at all with the Pan-German League."

In Central Europe, the University Library and the library of the National Museum in Budapest (Hungary) reported that they have no publications of the League whatsoever. The University Library in Vienna (Austria) has the following: *Alldeutsche Blätter* (1911-1915, incomplete), a gift to the library; *Der Kampf um das Deutschtum* (numbers 1, 2, 6, 7, 8, 9), bought by the library; Bonhard's *Geschichte* and Class's *Zwanzig Jahre alldeutscher Arbeit und Kämpfe,* donated by the League; and *Der alldeutsche Verband, eine Aufklärungsschrift* (1916), a gift to the library. The library of the University of Prague (Czecho-Slovakia) has no League publications.[1]

[1] Information about Switzerland and the British Museum in London was gathered by the author personally; the Dutch, Hungarian, Austrian, Danish, Swedish, and Norwegian libraries gave the desired information by mail. The situation in Prague was personally investigated by Dr. Ernst Salz of that city. In Germany, the author worked

In Germany proper, the *Preussische Staatsbibliothek* in Berlin has a complete set of the *Alldeutsche Blätter* and the *Mitteilungen des allgemeinen deutschen Verbandes,* the *Flugschriften* and *Kampf um das Deutschtum* series, besides the *Handbücher* for 1905 and 1908. The *Deutsche Bücherei,* which is the main library of Leipzig, has all the League's publications since 1913, but nothing earlier, and the University Library in Leipzig has Class and Bonhard but nothing else, though one of their under-librarians has been for years the treasurer of the Leipzig local branch of the League and knows a great deal about it. The *Bayerische Staats-Bibliothek,* the main library in Munich, has nothing dealing with the League before the war; and the new collection of all material in any way dealing with the war, which is being made by the *Kriegsbücherei* in Stuttgart, has one small pamphlet—*Der alldeutsche Verband, ein Aufklärungsschrift.* In Mayence, the home of Heinrich Class, there is a real depository of League publications, and books and pamphlets recommended by the League. This was the library of the Mayence local branch of the League and was given to the Mayence *Stadtbibliothek* by that organization. The librarian repeated this statement again and again in order to make sure that his library should not be thought to have had any part in collecting this type of material. He said further that no one ever used the collection, and many uncut pages seemed to verify his statement.

The British Museum in London has no material dealing with the Pan-German League except numbers one to thirty-four (1897-1913) of the *Flugschriften.* In the United States, the New York Public Library has the *Alldeutsche*

in the *Preussische Staatsbibliothek* in Berlin, the University Libraries in Berlin and Leipzig, the library of the Reichstag in Berlin, and the Mayence *Stadtbibliothek.* She also looked through the *Kriegsbücherei* in Stuttgart and interviewed its librarian.

Blätter from 1894 to 1920, the *Flugschriften,* the *Kampf um das Deutschtum* series, the *Handbücher* for 1906, 1908, 1916, and the *Alldeutscher Atlas.* These were gifts of the New York local branch of the League. Besides, the New York Public Library has Bonhard's *Geschichte.* The Columbia University Library in New York has the *Alldeutsche Blätter* from 1902 through 1917, and most of the *Flugschriften* and *Kampf um das Deutschtum* series, as well as the 1914, 1917 and 1918 *Handbücher* and a few odd pamphlets published by the League.

CHAPTER VII

THE PAN-GERMAN LEAGUE AND THE REICHSTAG

IT was always the boast of the Pan-German League that it placed the fatherland before party affiliations. On this point it expressed itself forcibly many times in its publications. It did not feel that political parties were to be combated save in specific instances and in so far as they denied the truth of the League's basic principles. On the other hand, it did not definitely support the political parties with whose aims it was more in sympathy, any more than it directly worked against those—notably of the center and left—in which international currents incompatible with Pan-German aims were operating. Bonhard says in this connection:[1]

Naturally we Pan-Germans do not desire to reproach individual members of certain parties, apart from Social Democratic and Jewish exponents of the world brotherhood of man, with having worked against the expansion of Germany as a great power. Nevertheless, individual party members do not realize the international danger or do not wish to recognize it. Party discipline and blind attachment to party principles perform their part; but, consciously or unconsciously, there are definite leanings toward internationalism. Because of such conditions, it may easily be explained why the Pan-German members of these parties were soon restricted to a few men who placed the importance of the German people

[1] Bonhard, *Geschichte des alldeutschen Verbandes*, p. 89.

[382

above the demands of party and in spite of all attacks remained true to the Pan-German flag. This also explains why no member of the so-called opposition parties could be counted among the Pan-German members of the law-making bodies of the Empire.

During the twenty-odd years covered by the present study, the Pan-German League boasted a number of Reichstag members among its own members. The accompanying table (I) lists them and gives their party affiliations and the length of their tenure.

A further analysis of the party affiliations of the members of the Reichstag who belonged to the Pan-German League shows that:

47% belonged to the National Liberal Party
15%   ”   ”   ” Conservative Party
15%   ”   ”   ” *Deutsch Soziale* and *Reform Partei*
14%   ”   ”   ” *Reichspartei*
 9%   ”   ”   ” *Wirtschaftliche Vereinigung*

Table (II) gives the total number of Reichstag representatives of the parties to which the Leaguers belonged and the number of Pan-German League members in each group.

TABLE I

MEMBERS OF THE REICHSTAG WHO BELONGED TO THE PAN-GERMAN LEAGUE [1]
(1894–1914)

Name	Party	Number of Terms
Dr. Arendt	*Reichspartei*	1898 through 1912–
Count von Arnim-Muskau	*Reichspartei*	1887 to 1906
Dr. Heinrich Arning	National Liberal	1907 to 1912
Eduard Bartling [2]	National Liberal	1903 to 1906; 1912–
Ernst Bassermann [3]	National Liberal	1893 to 1903; 1904 through 1912
Anton Beck [4]	National Liberal	1898 through 1912–
Dr. Jakob Becker [5]	National Liberal	1903 to 1906; 1912–
Dr. Beumer	National Liberal	1901 to 1907
Dr. Karl Böhme	*Reform Partei*	1907 to 1912
Dr. Böttger [6]	National Liberal	1903 to 1906; 1912–
Eugen von Brockhausen	Conservative	1898 through 1912–
Count Dohna-Schlodien	Conservative	1893 to 1906
Otto Everling	National Liberal	1907 to 1912
Ernst Froelich	*Reform Partei*	1903 to 1906
Fuhrmann	*Reform Partei*	1907 to 1912
Emil Gäbel	*Reform Partei*	1907 to 1912
Baron von Gamp [7]	*Reichspartei*	1884 through 1912–
Dr. Giese	Conservative	1889 to 1893; 1907 through 1912
Dr. Görck	National Liberal	1907 to 1912
Dr. Dietrich Hahn	Conservative	1893 to 1903; 1907 to 1912
Friedrich Hanisch	*Reform Partei*	1907 to 1912

[1] The sources for this list of members:

Alldeutsche Blätter from 1894 to 1906.

Handbuch, 1906, pp. 20 *et seq.*; 1908, p. 21; 1914, p. 38.

The statistics concerning the terms which these members served in the Reichstag were compiled from the following:

Wer Ist's? 1905, 1906, 1908, 1909.

Kürschner's *Deutscher Reichstag*, 1912-1917 (Berlin and Leipzig).

The official *Alphabetisches Verzeichniss der Mitglieder des deutschen Reichstags*, 1893, 1898, 1904, 1907, 1912.

After 1912, no general election was held in Germany until 1917, so that members elected in 1912 were sitting in 1914, the last year covered by this study.

[2] First appears in a League list of Pan-German Reichstag members in 1914.

[3] Not listed as a League member after 1908.

[4] Listed as a League member only in 1906 and 1908.

[5] Listed as a League member only in 1906.

[6] Not listed as a League member until 1914.

[7] Listed as a League member only in 1906 and 1908.

r. Ernst Hasse	National Liberal	1893 to 1903
riedrich Heck	National Liberal	1912–
r. Heinze	National Liberal	1907 to 1912
aron Heyl of Herrnsheim[8]	National Liberal	1874 to 1881 ; 1893 through 1912
ɔuis Heyligenstaedt	National Liberal	1903 to 1906
rofessor Dr. Hieber	National Liberal	1898 to 1912
tto Holtz	*Reichspartei*	1887 to 1897 ; 1898 to 1906
ermann Horn	National Liberal	1898 to 1906
tto Traugott Keinath	National Liberal	1912–
einrich Krämer	National Liberal	1890 to 1906
ʾilhelm Lattmann	*Wirtschaftliche Vereinigung*	1903 to 1912
r. Lehr	National Liberal	1898 to 1901
ɔuis Leinenweber	National Liberal	1898 to 1906
hilipp Lichtenberger	National Liberal	1898 to 1906
ebermann von Sonnenberg	*Deutsch Soziale Reform Partei*	1890 to 1911
eneral von Liebert	*Reichspartei*	1907 through 1912–
riedrich List [9]	National Liberal	1912–
ichard Löscher [10]	*Reichspartei*	1907 through 1912–
riedrich Linz	*Reichspartei*	1907 to 1912
ubert von Michaelis [10]	Conservative	1903 through 1912–
ɔunt Mirbach von Kardorff	*Reichspartei*	1888 to 1906
duard Müller	National Liberal	1907 to 1912
riedrich Mumm	*Wirtschaftliche Vereinigung*	1912–
riedrich Raab	*Wirtschaftliche Vereinigung*	1904 to 1912
ɔunt Ludwig Reventlow	*Wirtschaftliche Vereinigung*	1903 to 1906
ʾilhelm Schack	*Reform Partei*	1906 to 1912
chrempf	National Liberal	1898 to 1903
eorge Schulenburg	National Liberal	1912–
ɔn Staudy	Conservative	1893 to 1912
einrich Stauffer II	Conservative	1903 to 1912
ɔunt Udo Stolberg-Wernigerode	Conservative	1877 intermittently ; 1903 to 1912
r. Gustav Stresemann	National Liberal	1907 to 1912
r. Friedrich Wagner	Conservative	1907 to 1912
r. Karl Weber	National Liberal	1907 to 1912
. Werner	*Wirtschaftliche Vereinigung*	1911 through 1912–
. Werner [10]	*Deutsch Soziale Reform Partei*	1890 through 1912–
lbert Wetzel	National Liberal	1907 to 1912
swald Zimmermann	*Deutsch Soziale Reform Partei*	1890 to 1898 ; 1904 to 1912

[8] Listed as a League member only in 1906, 1908 and 1914.

[9] Kürschner's *Deutscher Reichstag* gives List as a member of the Pan-German League.

[10] Not listed by the League as a member in 1914.

TABLE II

PARTY AFFILIATIONS OF PAN-GERMAN MEMBERS OF THE REICHSTAG [1]

	1893	1898	1903	1907	1912
Total membership of Reichstag..........	397	397	397	397	397
Total number of Pan-German Leaguers belonging to Reichstag	15	23	28	34	15
National Liberals in the Reichstag	49	48	51	49	44
Pan-German Leaguers in the National Liberal faction.....................	4	11	11	12	7
Conservatives in the Reichstag..........	61	52	53	56	44
Pan-German Leaguers in the Conservative faction	4	5	6	8	3
Reichspartei representatives in the Reichstag	27	22	21	20	13
Pan-German Leaguers in the *Reichspartei*	4	5	4	6	2
Deutsch Soziale Reform Partei representatives in the Reichstag.............	13	9	......	......	......
Pan-German Leaguers in the *Deutsch Sozial* faction	3	2	......	......	......
Reform Partei representatives in the Reichstag	......	......	7	6	3
Pan-German Leaguers in the *Reform Partei* faction	......	......	4	4	1
Wirtschaftliche Vereinigung representatives in the Reichstag..............	......	......	13	19	8
Pan-German Leaguers in the *Wirtschaftliche Vereinigung*	......	......	3	4	2

It will be seen from the above tables that the League members were to be found as far to the right in the Reichstag as it was possible to get. The *Deutsch Soziale Partei* and its successor the *Reform Partei* were violently anti-Semitic, while the Conservative party itself had a strong

[1] The following sources have been used in preparing this table:

Alldeutsche Blätter, 1894 to 1906.

Handbuch, 1906, pp. 20 *et seq.*; 1908, p. 21; 1914, p. 38.

Alphabetisches Verzeichniss der Mitglieder des deutschen Reichstags, 1893, 1898, 1904, 1907, 1912.

Kürschner's *Deutscher Reichstag*, 1912-1917 (Berlin and Leipzig).

Wer Ist's? 1905, 1906, 1908, 1909.

anti-Semitic leaning. The National Liberal party was notoriously the party of extreme patriotism, and the *Reichspartei* had much in common with both the National Liberal and Conservative parties. The *Wirtschaftliche Vereinigung* was composed for the most part of anti-Semitic agrarians.

However, almost all of the Reichstag members listed as members of the Pan-German League were good party-men first and Leaguers secondarily. Their speeches in the Reichstag deal with the matters of the moment and do not concern the League or its work. The mere fact that they were members of the League brands them, of course, as super-patriots and anti-Semites of the first water, and this could not but tinge their actions within the counsels of their parties. Their exact influence as Leaguers on governmental policy can not be estimated, but it may be said that their voices not only swelled but often rose above the clamor in Germany for a vigorous world policy. However, the details of the Pan-German League's program seem not to have been of much immediate concern to the Leaguers in the Reichstag with the exception of Professor Dr. Hasse, the president of the League. Dr. Hasse sat [1] for a Leipzig constituency from 1893 until 1903 when he was defeated by a Social Democrat.[2] An indefatigable worker, he took his duties in the Reichstag very seriously and spoke on all occasions when he thought that the cause of *Deutschtum* might be aided. Often he spoke of himself as a " Pan-German ", and not as a representative of his party, the National Liberal.[3] He never let a chance slip to defend the Pan-German League or to introduce its name or platform into the debate, and almost might it be said that after his retirement in 1903, the League was without its own representative in the

[1] *Hasse als Politiker* (Leipzig, 1898), p. 41.

[2] *Alldeutsche Blätter*, 1903, p. 234.

[3] *Ibid.*, 1906, p. 361.

Reichstag,[1] though numerous Reichstag members still belonged to the League.

For instance, in the midst of an impassioned plea to the Reichstag in the name of the National Liberals, demanding protection for all Germans outside the Empire, Hasse managed to inject the fact that the Pan-German League, the president of which he had the honor to be, had been the recipient of many complaints from Germans in foreign parts concerning the lack of protection afforded them by their mother country.[2] Subsequently he offered the file of these complaints to the secretary of state for foreign affairs (Baron Marschall von Bieberstein), at the same time taking occasion to quote a particular complaint from the Bogotá (Colombia) local branch of the League.[3]

The secretary of state for foreign affairs replied politely that he inferred from this that organizations for the acquisition of complaints against the foreign office had been founded not only, as he had thought, within Germany, but also outside the Empire. He went on to say that he expected Dr. Hasse would be able to collect a great quantity of such complaints, but added that what the foreign office desired was quality and not quantity.

This sally could not go unchallenged by the League, and Count von Arnim, a member of the League's executive council and the Leaguer who, next to Hasse, generally had the most to say in the Reichstag, rose to his feet to answer Baron Marschall von Bieberstein. He explained how the Pan-German League had grown out of opposition to the policies of Caprivi and from the feeling that the latter was not supporting and strengthening the nationalism of the

[1] Bonhard, op. cit., p. 23.

[2] Stenographische Berichte über die Verhandlungen des Reichstags, IX Legislaturperiode, 3te Session (1894-5) 14te Sitzung (Jan. 14 1895), pp. 322 et seq.

[3] Ibid., 34te Sitzung (Feb. 11, 1895), pp. 81 et seq.

state as a large portion of the nation wished. Then he went on to describe the purpose of the League. " It does not exist merely to work within Germany, to protect the Germans from the onslaughts and aggressions of citizens who speak only foreign tongues—in Posen, in the north and the west of the Empire. It exists also to strengthen the feeling of unity among the Germans outside the Empire, and to preserve their sense of common kinship; for it is recognized, sad to say, that the Germans who emigrate to foreign parts lose such feeling all too readily." The speaker went on to explain that as a result, the League had local branches in Australia, Asia and America which were in close touch with the central office, and that naturally along with their annual reports, etc., complaints were made now and again concerning the general condition of the German emigrants. The tendency of the League he affirmed to be good, patriotic and valuable.

Von Bieberstein, in reply to von Arnim, declared that he did not doubt or deny the value of the League, but he insisted that the organization caused the foreign office a good deal of trouble through these very complaints; for after the formation of the League, people whose claims had been denied earlier by the foreign office, thought that their day had come and put in further complaints and claims through the League. The latter, not differentiating between complaints made prior to 1890 and those of later date, had taken the foreign office to task about them.

The work of our representatives in foreign lands was thus made much more difficult and the gentlemen of the Pan-German League are not at all in a position to judge whether complaints coming to them are justified or not. The foreign office must cable for information and it often takes weeks before the matter can be cleared up. In the meantime the organ of the

Pan-German League is waging a strenuous battle against the foreign office. . . . I merely wish to show Dr. Hasse that in spite of all the patriotism which I am sure the founders and leaders of the Pan-German League feel, yet the methods they employ may cause a great deal of confusion.

Dr. Hasse, moreover, spoke on all occasions when matters relating to foreign policy were on the docket. Thus we find him the only speaker on a treaty concerning Tunis and he did not lose the opportunity to argue for an aggressive German *Weltpolitik*.[1] Further League tenets were set forth when Dr. Hasse spoke against the Poles, though no mention was made of the League.[2] When a few days later,[3] he made a lengthy speech on general foreign policy, he managed to ask for larger appropriations for German schools outside the Empire, and to speak on military service for Germans living in foreign countries, and concerning his pet subjects of emigration and loss of citizenship, ending by a defense of German world policy and world commercial interests. The question of emigration soon came up again and Hasse made another long speech supporting the bill under debate.[4] He said that he rose to speak because the project corresponded with Pan-German [5] wishes:

But I ask you *not* to confuse this movement which continues to interest ever widening circles of people with the Pan-Teutonic [6] movement. It (Pan-Germanism)[7] does not in any way

---

[1] *Stenographische Berichte des Reichstags, IX Legislaturperiode, 4te Session* (1895-97), *148te Sitzung* (Dec. 16, 1896), pp. 3937 *et seq.*

[2] *Ibid., 169te Sitzung* (Feb. 6, 1897), p. 4522.

[3] *Ibid., 182te Sitzung* (Feb. 22, 1897), pp. 4852 *et seq.*

[4] *Ibid. 192te Sitzung* (Mar. 16, 1897), pp. 5093 *et seq.*

[5] *Alldeutsch.*

[6] *Pangermanisch.*

[7] *Alldeutsch.*

concern itself with the union of all Teutonic peoples—Scandinavians and English—with the Germans. No, this movement is limited entirely to the German people in the narrower sense of the word; however, it does include both the high-German and the low-German peoples. It results from the feeling that the Empire as such does not absorb our interest; that, along with our love for the Empire, we also have other interests in the entirety of the German people regardless of territorial limitations through empire and state boundaries. Into this come not only those Germans who live as our neighbors outside the confines of the Empire, but also all those who have left these regions and struck out for lands across the sea—not only the emigrants from the German Empire proper, but also those from German Austria, the German Netherlands, from the land of the Flemings; for we believe that the Empire has the *nobile officium* to care for these peoples as well.[1]

This speech is an excellent example of how the Pan-German in Dr. Hasse transcended the National Liberal. In similar fashion, he talked at length on his ideas of nationalism and the national state, saying that his own ideas were exactly opposed to those of the Social Democrats. In the same speech he took occasion to talk about the danger to *das Deutschtum* that lay in the situation in Hungary. For since the Magyars were not a Germanic race, he had no patience with their national aspirations. The subject occupied his attention at a later date when he was speaking on Germany's foreign policy. He felt that the uneasiness in Hungary was a distinct menace to the Triple Alliance [2] and that the major reason for the uneasiness was Magyar ambition for a "Greater Hungary".[3] He summarized the Magyar demands:

---

[1] *Stenographische Berichte des Reichstags, X. Legislaturperiode, 2te. Session (1900-1903), 157te Sitzung* (Mar. 4, 1902), p. 4560.

[2] *Ibid., 287te Sitzung* (Mar. 19, 1903), pp. 8722 *et seq.*

[3] *Gross-Ungarn.*

In the river plain in which Hungary is situated, only one people may live; all other peoples must be crowded aside. And as though this were not enough, the Magyars claim half of the Balkans and a large portion of the Danube countries. It is madness, but there is method in their madness, for through the handling of it in the official Hungarian press, the matter has really assumed a political significance.

But Dr. Hasse had introduced his speech by protesting against the fact that the liberal German press had taken him to task for a speech he had made earlier on his favorite subject of German world policy. The Pan-Germans were accused, through him, of shaking a mailed fist in the face of the world. The only saving thing, perhaps, was the fact that Hasse said very clearly that he was not speaking in the name of his National Liberal faction but as the president of the Pan-German League.

The fact that he spoke often in this latter capacity made it necessary for Dr. Hasse to defend the League and the so-called " Pan-Germans " from attacks on all sides in the Reichstag. The passage at arms between Marschall von Bieberstein and Dr. Hasse has already been mentioned. Herr Rickert of the *Freisinnige Vereiningung,* using the convenient term of Pan-German [1] as a slogan covering a multitude of chauvinists and reactionaries, took the Pan-Germans to task for a meeting held in Hamburg (on October 23, 1899) which passed resolutions supporting the Boers in South Africa and condemning England in a rather foolish telegram to His Majesty, the Kaiser.[2] Rickert's reference to the Pan-Germans was made in the midst of a very long speech on finances and *Weltpolitik,* and consisted of the following short remark: "It is a fact that anti-Semitic and Pan-German [3] meetings in Hamburg and wherever else they have

[1] *Alldeutsch.*

[2] *Alldeutsche Blätter,* 1899, pp. 394 *et seq.*

[3] *Alldeutsch.*

been held have strenuously opposed the Kaiser's trip to England." [1] However, even this was enough to bring an impassioned retort from Dr. Hasse [2] to the effect that it had again and again been declared that the Pan-German League had had nothing whatever to do with the Hamburg meeting in question. [3] On the other hand, Dr. Hasse said that he wanted it understood that he felt that the gentlemen who had arranged the meeting had a perfect right to do so, and after uttering a few deprecatory remarks about Caprivi he launched into a typically National Liberal speech on colonial policy which was heartily applauded by his party.

During the discussion of the Navy bill, Karl Liebknecht [4] berated the " Pan-Germans " soundly for their wish to enter into naval competition with England—for that was his interpretation of their desire for a large German navy—and said that had these gentlemen (" Pan-Germans ") been in the government they would have declared war on England within twenty-four hours because of questions arising from the Boer War. [5] The result would have been that in another twenty-four hours the German navy would have disappeared from the high seas and her few colonies would have been lost. " For England ", said Liebknecht, " has and needs the largest navy in the world."

[1] *Stenographische Berichte des Reichstags, X Legislaturperiode, 1te Session* (1898-1900), *112ten Sitzung* (Dec. 14, 1899), p. 3378.

[2] *Ibid.*, pp. 3391 *et seq.*

[3] The *Hamburger Correspondent* and the *Hamburger Fremdenblatt* had reported that this meeting had been arranged by Pan-German, German-national and anti-Semitic associations. This was copied by the *Berliner Neueste Nachrichten.* The League and its Hamburg local branch denied all part in the meeting but they were unsuccessful in making the Berlin paper retract, for the latter merely replied that it had received its information from supposedly well-informed Hamburg papers. *Alldeutsche Blätter,* 1899, pp. 394 *et seq.* ; p. 434.

[4] A member of the extreme left of the Social Democratic party.

[5] *Stenographische Berichte des Reichstags, X Legislaturperiode, 1te Session* (1898-1900), *209te Sitzung* (June 12, 1900), pp. 6025 *et seq.*

Hasse's answering speech was made in the name of his " Pan-German " friends and was hot in its frenzy against England. He said that he was speaking at that time only because Liebknecht "had reproached his Pan-German friends and himself with having aroused the present anti-English feeling among the German people. I am not so unreasonable as to suppose that the influence of the Pan-German League is large enough to have inspired such a feeling in the ninety-five per cent of the German people who have it. No, the feeling which we have is the result of a long historical development in which the English state, the English people, must bear the blame, and not the German people and the German Empire." [1]   Then followed a violently Anglophobe speech with a vigorous plea for the enlargement of the German navy.

Upon the occasion of the attempted visit of President Krüger of the Transvaal to Germany, Hasse was called upon to defend before the Reichstag the action of the Pan-German League in sending him a memorial of respect. It had been reported in the *Kölnische Zeitung* that Dr. Hasse and Dr. Lehr had gone to The Hague and presented Krüger with an address in which in the name of the German people, the Pan-German League had strongly condemned the foreign policy of the Kaiser and his chancellor.[2]   On the very day that Hasse and Lehr (and thirteen other representatives of the League [3]) were calling upon President Krüger at The

[1] *Stenographische Berichte des Reichstags, X Legislaturperiode, 1te Session* (1898-1900), *209te Sitzung* (June 12, 1900), p. 6037.

[2] *Stenographische Berichte des Reichstags, X. Legislaturperiode, 2te Session* (1900-1902) *18te Sitzung* (Dec. 10, 1900), pp. 413 *et seq.*

[3] Among those who went were Heinrich Class of Mayence, Hasse's successor as president of the League, Dr. Fick of Zürich, one of the original founders of the League, J. F. Lehmann, the publisher of the League's *Flugschriften*, Geiser, the business manager of the League, and Dr. Samassa, the editor of the *Alldeutsche Blätter. Alldeutche Blätter,* 1900, pp. 503 *et seq.*

Hague, Chancellor von Bülow defended the policy of the government in not receiving Krüger in Berlin.[1] Though Krüger had been received by M. Delcassé in Paris, the chancellor did not feel that this had helped him in any way, and told the Reichstag that he felt very decidedly that the same would have been true of a reception in Berlin.

Though Dr. Hasse had left the representation of the League in the Reichstag temporarily in the hands of Count von Arnim, Count Stolberg and von Kardoff,[2] he found upon his return from The Hague after forced night traveling, that the task of defending the League and of speaking out strongly against the chancellor had as usual been left to himself. On December 12, 1900, he made an impassioned speech, again taking the government to task and explaining his pilgrimage to The Hague.

We could not help it, (said he), that it had been made impossible for us to address President Krüger in Berlin; we would much rather have done that, but we had to turn our steps to The Hague. . . . Holland is outside of Germany in the legal sense; but I ask you to remember that the Pan-German League is an organization that is spread over the entire world. [Shouts of " Hear, hear," from the left.] No, not an international organization, but a national one; for the German people live not only within the German Empire but outside its borders, and Holland to the Pan-German League is low-German territory.[2]

He then went on to explain that the delegation had not addressed Krüger in the name of official Germany but had very definitely stated that it was there in the " name of the Pan-German League ". They had added that the latter had

---

[1] *Stenographische Berichte des Reichstags, X. Legislaturperiode, 2te Session* (1900-1902) *16te Sitzung* (Dec. 10, 1900), pp. 413 *et seq.*

[2] *Ibid., 18te Sitzung* (Dec. 12, 1900), p. 470.

the support and sympathy of the majority of the German people. After defending the League, Hasse turned to the task of proving that von Bülow's Boer policy was entirely wrong, Anglophobia forming the mainstay of his speech.

So vehement was Dr. Hasse's speech that the chancellor felt called upon to defend his policy in another speech, this one aimed directly at Hasse and showing a slightly sarcastic vein at times:

Public opinion is a strong stream which should turn the wheels of the state mill. However, when danger threatens this mill and the wheels seem likely to be turned in the wrong direction, it is the duty of any government which is worthy of the name, to try to regulate the misdirecting stream, uninfluenced by its own unpopularity. There are higher crowns than those which the Pan-German League can distribute, namely the consciousness of allowing oneself to be influenced solely by real and lasting national interest. . . . It is an honor to the good Dr. Hasse that he sees as our first and foremost task the deliverance of foreign peoples. However, that is good only in private life; in international relations one does not get very far in that way. The desire to rescue foreign peoples has not always brought good fortune, and history furnishes numerous examples to prove this. . . I do not wish to chide Dr. Hasse for his journey to The Hague; I respect his idealism. . . . But he must not disturb the well-being and the future of the nation through his idealism.

A touch of humor was added to the situation a bit later in the sitting when Eugen Richter referred to Dr. Hasse as the " world president of all Germans ",[1] but the whole incident is a striking example of how the small and relatively uninfluential body of men comprising the League, at times came near to embarrassing the German government.

In view of subsequent events, several of Dr. Hasse's

[1] *Stenographische Berichte des Reichstags, X. Legislaturperiode, 2te Session* (1900-1902) *16te Sitzung* (Dec. 10, 1900), p. 489.

statements in the Reichstag are of major interest. Speaking of the conduct of the war in South Africa, he said:[1]

It is a peculiar coincidence that just at the time when the worst news of the conduct of the war in South Africa reached Germany, the Hague agreement concerning rules and regulations of land warfare (of July 29, 1899) was published in the *Reichsgesetzblatt. I maintain that the English have violated every point in this agreement.*[2] But I wish to lay even more stress upon a book entitled *Hunnen in Süd Afrika,*[3] which I will place upon the table of the House.

And again, while talking at a later date on the foreign policy of the government, he made this statement:[4]

We " Pan-Germans " are ready at any time to offer the French our hand in friendship across the Vosges. . . . However, not alone the " Pan-Germans ", but all Germans feel that they can treat with the French only after the latter have recognized the permanence of the Frankfort peace in all its consequences; and have ceased thinking that a change of the western border to their advantage is possible.

When in the election of 1903 Dr. Hasse lost his seat in the Reichstag to a Social Democrat, the Pan-German League may really be said to have lost its representation in the National legislature. It is true that other Reichstag members belonged to the League, but Hasse was the only one who was a Leaguer first, last and all the time, and a member of the Reichstag more or less secondarily.

However, the fame of the Leaguers with the government

[1] *Stenographische Berichte des Reichstags, X. Legislaturperiode, 2te Session* (1900-1903) *116te Sitzung* (Jan. 13, 1902), p. 3339.

[2] Italics are the author's.

[3] Huns in South Africa.

[4] *Stenographische Berichte des Reichstags, X. Legislaturperiode 2te Session* (1900-1903) *244te Sitzung* (Jan. 22, 1903), p. 7493.

as super-patriots was not diminished, and Hasse's memory was green even after three years of absence from the Reichstag. Thus in November 1906, following an interpellation by Bassermann, the National Liberal leader, on Germany's international relations, von Bülow took the Pan-German League to task for its attitude, just as he had done during Hasse's term in the Reichstag. The chancellor first spoke of Bismarck as the great idol and comfort of the German people, but said that a nation must learn to rely upon itself and not to lean upon such Titans as the gods might see fit to send every few hundred years.[1] And as patriots they must all strive to see that the work of the great chancellor be not undone:

Gentlemen, it is the Pan-German League which brings forward for me the boots and the broadsword of Prince Bismarck. I know well that the aims of the Pan-German League have the good points of keeping national feeling fresh and that its members work against that inclination of the German Philistines to gravitate toward indistinct cosmopolitanism on the one hand, and narrow church politics on the other. I regret for myself that the president of the Pan-German League has not been returned to this House. [Great merriment expressed by the House]. I know well that, besides their president, other warm-hearted patriots belong to this League; but when it comes to foreign affairs, clear-headedness is more essential than warmth and goodness of heart. The heart of the patriot should not show itself only in indiscriminate disputes with all foreigners—English and Russians, North Americans and Brazilians, Hungarians and Italians; still less should it display itself in bold dreams for the future which serve only to make the problems of the present more difficult and cause us to be mistrusted everywhere. [Great applause]

[1] *Stenographische Berichte des Reichstags, XI. Legislaturperiode, 2te Session* (1905-06), *117te Sitzung* (Nov. 14, 1906), pp. 3629 *et seq.*

Naturally enough, the Pan-German League felt called upon to answer the chancellor, and this it did in a long, detailed open letter which was published in the *Alldeutsche Blätter.*[1] The letter acclaimed as the League's ideal a "leader with a clear head whose policies warmed the hearts of the people," and then reviewed the aims and accomplishments of the League.   Entire credit was taken for the government's naval policy and for whatever firmness had been shown in the treatment of the Poles.   An attempt was obviously made to impress the chancellor with the fact that the League was a really powerful and influential organization which had already accomplished much, but which had much more work to do.   The letter went on to say:

We agree with Heinrich von Treitschke that the future of the German peoples rests upon how many million people on this earth will speak German in the future.   We see in this such an important and tremendous goal for the future that we consider ourselves more than ever bound to put our entire strength to this task, for the government seems entirely occupied with the problems of the present.

The respect which we feel for the most responsible position in the Empire has made it our duty to present these facts to your Excellency, for it arouses our patriotic zeal to find you conversant with only part of the aims of the Pan-German League.   No desire for public recognition prompts this action.   The complete independence of the League from the government seems necessary to the fulfilment of our purposes. Nevertheless, an exact knowledge of our ends and a just evaluation of them do not seem inconsistent with the interest of our people whom we wish to serve even as do your Excellency and the imperial government.

But von Bülow had already expressed himself, and this typically "Pan-German" answer could not alter the official

---

[1] *Alldeutsche Blätter*, 1906, pp. 377 *et seq.*

opinion concerning the Pan-German League which he had thus publicly announced. Dr. Hasse's answer merely went to prove the chancellor's point and to drive it home to those already unsympathetic to the League. To League sympathizers, Hasse's words were as the law and the prophets, and in these circles von Bülow and the government did not gain in popularity by their criticism. The exigencies of party politics and the complications of international politics meant nothing to such terribly sincere and earnest patriots as the Pan-German Leaguers.

In the election of 1907 the League made its usual statement about being above mere party interests, but it lost no time after the dissolution of the old Reichstag in saying how glad it was to see the country rid of such an unpatriotic body.[1] Nor did it mince words in registering its hope for the victory of the national parties over the Center, the Poles and the Social Democrats. The election itself was greeted as a great victory for nationalism,[2] which indeed it was. The return of a super-patriotic Reichstag sent a glow through the hearts of the Leaguers and gradually, as time went on, the parties of the extreme right became a bit less caustic at mention of the " Pan-Germans ".[3] The term itself was used more and more as a slogan (comparable to our " one hundred per cent Americans ") covering extreme patriots of all descriptions. For instance, a Social Democrat, commenting upon a warlike speech which had been made against Germany at a banquet in London, said that it was the " Pan-Germans " who were the most likely to push Germany into greater danger because of their belief that Germany must " devour the whole world ".[4]   General von

[1] *Alldeutsche Blätter*, 1906, pp. 409 *et seq.*

[2] *Ibid.*, 1907, p. 33.

[3] *Die Alldeutschen.*

[4] *Stenographische Berichte des Reichstags, XII. Legislaturperiode, 2te Session* (1909-10), *24te Sitzung* (Jan. 26, 1910), vol. 259, p. 823.

Liebert of the Pan-German League answered at once that " The League has in no place and at no time incited to war [laughter among the Social Democrats]. It has the noble and distinguished duty of aiding and furthering *Deutschtum* both in and outside Germany ".[1]

Perhaps the best example of the sensitiveness of the Leaguers may be found in the large-sized tempest which was raised in the German tea-pot by a speech made in Philadelphia (Pennsylvania) by Count von Bernstorff, the German ambassador to the United States. Speaking before the American Academy of Political and Social Science on November 6, 1909, on " The Development of Germany as a World Power," the Ambassador said in part:[2]

In speaking of Germany as a world power, I am obliged to begin by saying that our world policy has often been intentionally or unintentionally misrepresented abroad, and this particularly because foreign authors and journalists have taken or pretended to take seriously the flights of fancy of the so-called Pan-Germanists who are of no importance at all. They have hardly any representatives in our parliament, and not the slightest influence on the government. By the latter the Pan-Germanists are even considered a very undesirable element of German journalism, because they stir up ill-feeling abroad against Germany by putting forth questions and aims which are quite beyond the scope of practical politics. Even Mr. Coolidge[3] whose book (*The United States as a World Power*) is written in a very impartial and friendly spirit for Germany, believes " that the Pan-Germanists express freely the extreme of ambitions which many quieter patriots cherish in some degree ". That erroneous assumption leads him further to believe that the interests of Germany and the United States might some day clash, and this without fault of anyone.

[1] *Ibid.*, p. 832.

[2] *Annals of the American Academy, suppl.*, vol. 35, p. 8.

[3] Professor Archibald C. Coolidge.

Here I must again differ with Mr. Coolidge. In the quite improbable case that a clash should ever occur between Germany and the United States, this would in my opinion be the result either of a foolish policy or of an outburst of unbridled popular jingoism.

This speech of von Bernstorff caused considerable comment in the German press,[1] those papers which inclined toward conservatism and a nationalistic view-point for the most part taking the ambassador to task for his remarks about the " Pan-Germans ".   In the Reichstag the government was forced to defend its accredited representative.

Bassermann of the National Liberal party, in view of the rather general newspaper comment on the speech, said that even though Pan-German policies were not to the taste of everyone in the Reichstag, nevertheless the "Pan-Germans" were good German patriots and he wished to protest against the unfavorable criticism of these good German patriots by a German ambassador in a foreign country.[2]   His statement was heartily applauded by the National Liberals and the extreme right.   The Reichstag had been elected on this very plank of " patriotism ", and by calling the " Pan-Germans " good German patriots, Basserman made the government's task of defending the ambassador rather difficult.   Baron von Schoen, the secretary of state for foreign affairs, tried to soothe the ruffled patriots by explaining that von Bernstorff had been doing his utmost to help German-American relations, which were not of the best.   Part of the trouble was due to the fact that the Americans were very quick to seize upon publications which they considered to be of a " Pan-German " character, and which led them to believe that Germany was trying to pick a quarrel with England and then expected to fall upon America.

[1] See *infra*, chap. ix.

[2] *Stenographische Berichte des Reichstags, XII Legislaturperiode, 2te Session* (1909-1910), *7te Sitzung* (Dec. 9, 1909), vol. 258, p. 189.

But, [said the secretary,] I wish it well understood that I differentiate between the activity of the Pan-German League as such and Pan-Teutonic expressions for which this League is not responsible. The Pan-German League cannot be identified with everything that has appeared under the Pan-German flag, and I wish to point out in this connection that Count Bernstorff did not refer specifically to the Pan-German League.[1] It is to the honor of Pan-German writers that nothing is farther from their thoughts than harming our interests outside Germany or making the difficult task of our diplomats more difficult. Nor can the Pan-Germans be held responsible for the fact that a large part of the anti-German press relies on the so-called " Pan-Teutonic " literature for its ammunition, and that plans set forth in such publications are given as the official policy of the Empire. When the imperial government or its representatives outside of Germany are singled out as open or secret adherents and promoters of such exaggerated ideas, the line must be drawn again between fantasy and reality. It was against such ideas that the imperial ambassador in Washington was speaking when he endeavored to lay the ghost of a German colonial Empire in South America, which had haunted American public opinion. Therefore I can find nothing to condemn in Count Bernstorff's speech, and everyone who knows the Count, must know that he can not be accused of enmity toward good German patriots.

Herr Zimmermann [2] of the Reichstag and the Pan-German League remained unconvinced that von Bernstorff's " Pan-Germanists " were not the *Alldeutsche,* nor did Liebermann von Sonnenberg who also belonged to both the Reichstag and the League [3] agree with Baron von Schoen.[4]

[1] *Ibid., 8te Sitzung* (Dec. 10, 1909), p. 209.

[2] *Reform Partei.*

[3] *Stenographische Berichte des Reichstags, XII Legislaturperiode, 2te Session* (1909-10), *9te Sitzung* (Dec. 11, 1909), vol. 258, pp. 257 *et seq.*

[4] *Ibid.,* p. 237.

Herr Gröber, a member of the Center party, tried to convince Liebermann von Sonnenberg that von Bernstorff had not referred specifically to the Pan-German League,[1] and at the same time took occasion to talk about jingo propaganda and tried to show its evil effects on Germany's international relations. The word " patriot " held no terrors for him, and amid the applause of the Centrists he told the truth which the Leaguers never recognized—that " the patriot must not develop ' patriotic ' ideas which are bound to have unpatriotic consequences."

The debate convinced no one, of course, but it served to show tenderer feelings toward the Pan-German League on the part of the government. Conciliation rather than direct criticism seemed to have become the latter's policy, even though the League annoyed the government and made the international relations of Germany more difficult to handle. This newer attitude toward the League was no doubt due to the rising tide of nationalism in Germany. The League took a great deal of credit to itself for this very tendency; it is impossible to estimate how far the assumption was justified. The Pan-German League was small, relatively unimportant but very noisy, and in the development of strong nationalism noise counts for a great deal.

The more conciliatory attitude toward the League on the part of the parties of the right may be seen, too, in the Moroccan question. Ever since the first excitement in 1904, the League had been untiring in its efforts to awaken the German people to the great need for a foot-hold in Morocco. Very closely connected with the question of Germany's supposed international isolation, the matter lent itself admirably to super-patriotic propaganda. The *Alldeutsche Blätter* printed numberless articles on Morocco, its advantages, the

---

[1] *Stenographische Berichte des Reichstags, XII Legislaturperiode, 2te Session* (1900-10), *9te Sitzung* (Dec. 11, 1909), vol. 258, p. 240.

necessity of protecting Germany's large interests there, the perfidy of France and Great Britain in treating Germany as a *"quantité négligeable"* in the whole affair. Pamphlets were published and the local branches passed resolutions. Every fresh Moroccan crisis gave the League new impetus in its work. Moreover, the "cause" was a popular one, and public opinion throughout Germany was somewhat worked up about the fact that the fatherland seemed internationally isolated and was losing its just share in the partition of the backward regions of the globe in general and Morocco in particular. As always, the Pan-German League was far in the van in its demands; but to those who were against a strenuous German colonial policy, the convenient slogan "Pan-German" as usual covered the larger part of the patriotic propaganda, even though the actual part taken by the League itself was relatively a minor one.

However, it was not until late in 1911 that members of the Reichstag accused the government of any connection with the "Pan-Germans". Then, in the debate on the Franco-German Moroccan aggreement, Dr. Weimar of the *Freisinnige Volkspartei,* described a meeting held by the Pan-German League in Berlin, at which many fiery speeches were made against the government's Moroccan policy, and war-hymns and songs were sung to arouse the people present to war fervor. And in the same speech he accused the government of dealings with the "Pan-Germans", which the chauvinist press of the country had hinted at, viz. a meeting on July eighth at which the seizure of southwest Morocco by Germany was demanded with the knowledge and consent of the Foreign Office; and the reception at the Foreign Office[1] of Dr. Class, the president of the Pan-German League and the author of *Westmarokko deutsch!* There

---

[1] *Stenographische Berichte des Reichstags, XII Legislaturperiode, 2te Session* (1911), *202te Sitzung* (Nov. 10, 1911), vol. 268, p. 7743.

was the usual parliamentary fencing in the course of the debate, no one particularly representing the League itself, though Herr Lattman (of the *Wirtschaftliche Vereinigung*), a member of the League, said that he could not but feel flattered that the League should be considered the keeper of the national conscience,[1] in that it was made the butt of all derogatory remarks concerning the agitation to annex as large a portion of Morocco as possible. Herr Bruhn (*Reform Partei*) tried to show that there was no connection between Class's visit to the Foreign Office and the German demand for "compensations", since Class had demanded west Morocco in his pamphlet and Germany's compensations from France were in the Congo.[2]

Count v. Brudzewo-Mielzynski, of the Polish party, accused the Pan-German League of trying to incite the country to war[3] just when the internationl situation was at the greatest tension; but nothing really important was said about the visit of Dr. Class to the Foreign Office until Ledebour of the Social Democratic party made a fiery speech which compelled the foreign secretary, Herr von Kiderlen-Wächter, to explain and defend his policy before the Reichstag.[4] Ledebour accused the foreign secretary of insinuating to Herr Class that he (von Kiderlen-Wächter) thought more or less along Pan-German lines. Further, he was reported to have said that the Pan-German Moroccan demands were absolutely justified and that Dr. Class might rest assured that concerning Morocco "he (von Kiderlen-Wächter) stood on Pan-German ground just as firmly as Class did". Later Dr. Class was reported to have been received again

[1] *Ibid.*, p. 7757.

[2] *Ibid.*, p. 7762.

[3] *Ibid., 203te Sitzung* (Nov. 11, 1911), pp. 7784 *et seq.*

[4] *Stenographische Berichte des Reichstags, XIII Legislaturperiode 1te Session* (1912), *8te Sitzung* (Feb. 17, 1912), vol. 283, pp. 96 *et seq.*

at the Foreign Office, this time by an under-secretary, Herr Zimmermann, and informed that just at that moment the " Panther " had appeared at Agadir. These charges of Ledebour were serious, and he tried to drive his point home still further by saying that there was indirect evidence to the effect that the Pan-German movement, which seemed to have been unchained by sending the " Panther " to Agadir, was not at all unwelcome to the imperial chancellor. The government had made use of the enthusiasm of the super-patriots to support them in this move. Ledebour felt very strongly that the government should not have delayed announcement of the fact that it really did not mean to seize Morocco. As a matter of fact, it was three weeks after the " Panther " reached Agadir—and then only because of pressure from the Powers—that the government made the announcement. And in the meanwhile, of course, the Pan-Germans were clamoring and no one knew whether their noise was more or less officially led or whether it was what a member of the Reichstag once called the " delirium tremens of the Pan-Germans ".[1]

The foreign secretary answered Herr Ledebour's charges more or less in detail. He reported his conversation with Dr. Class as follows: " We will do something to bring Moroccan affairs to a head. But I beg of you to see to it that there is not too much noise about it. Please be careful." About this time, von Kiderlen-Wächter said that he had begun negotiations with the French ambassador concerning " compensations ", and when Dr. Class wanted to talk to him again he was absent on this mission. It was left to the under-secretary, Zimmermann, to tell the president of the Pan-German League that Germany did not want part of Morocco and why no settlements could be made there, or

---

[1] *Stenographische Berichte des Reichstags, XIII Legislaturperiode 1te Session* (1912-13), *78te Sitzung* (Dec. 5, 1912), vol. 286, pp. 2590 *et seq.*

war-harbor acquired that would be a help rather than a hindrance. Dr. Class said at the close of the interview, " that is a shame ", and published his pamphlet, *Westmarokko Deutsch!*, just the same. Herr von Kiderlen-Wächter went on to report still a third interview which Class had at the foreign office, this time with him (the secretary), saying:

This meeting was in September when the Franco-German treaty was practically drawn up. Moreover at that time there was a particularly strong chauvinistic spirit rampant in the French press, and it was greatly to be desired that the French should see that there were some patriotism and national feeling in Germany as well, which demanded just rights for the fatherland. Dr. Class wanted an interview with me at this time because he said there was soon to be a Pan-German meeting, and he was very desirous of being able to say exactly what the government's views on the situation were. I said to him: " The matter is thus and so; we want compensations but the time has not come yet when we can say that things are finished. However, it would be excellent if some patriotic spirit were shown, even if you do not entirely agree with my Moroccan policy."

It must be quite obvious from this that I never told anyone that we wanted to take part of Morocco or that propaganda supporting that view should be started. That movement was entirely unaided by the government.

It can scarcely be said that there was official support of the Pan-German League's propaganda; on the other hand, there is a wide gulf between this last speech and von Bülow's chiding the Leaguers for their want of intelligence. Nevertheless, though more in favor than formerly with the parties of the right, the Pan-German League was too violent in its demands to be over-popular and the term " Pan-German " was distinctly a derogatory one. The general status of the

League was well summed up by Herr Wendel of the Social Democratic party during a debate on the Polish question :[1]

The small but noisy group comprising the Pan-Germans are the wildest Pole-baiters. These Pan-Germans do not stand on very familiar terms with the government,[2] for the latter is too weak in its handling of domestic politics and too retiring in foreign affairs, and does not show the mailed fist often enough to suit them. These Pan-Germans are still sad that we did not wage war in 1911, with half the world, over Morocco; they are disgruntled now (1913) that the German Empire shows no will to conquer in the crisis in the Near East.

Dr. Hasse's was a voice crying in the wilderness, when he first entered the Reichstag, but gradually the virus of extreme nationalism worked itself into the blood of the majority parties even as it spread through the German people. It is absolutely impossible to calculate how much this was due to the efforts of the League, and how much to more important factors. Certainly the League was always well in the van of extreme patriots, and on the whole its main contribution seems to have been the term " Pan-German "— *Alldeutsch*—that all-embracing slogan which was used so glibly by everyone. The League might be considered a symptom of the disease of extreme nationalism rather than a *major* contributing factor. That there was any vital connection before the War between the League and the imperial government is entirely preposterous. However, the fact remains that small and unimportant as the League was, its noise carried far.

[1] *Stenographische Berichte des Reichstags, XIII Legislaturperiode 1te Session* (1912-13), *100te Sitzung* (Jan. 29, 1913), vol. 287, p. 3344.

[2] " *Stehen mit der Regierung durchaus nicht auf Du und Du.*"

CHAPTER VIII

The Major Activities of the Pan-German League
1894-1914

A complete survey of the activities of the Pan-German League would be nothing more nor less than a detailed history of the German Empire from 1894 to 1914 as seen through Pan-German eyes. A sample of the myriad issues upon which the League felt itself competent and constrained to take a stand has already been given.[1] But it is desirable, nevertheless, to indicate the attitude of the official publications of the League toward the most significant phases of German development during the two decades of its existence prior to the outbreak of the Great War. The *Alldeutsche Blätter* contain the most complete and illuminating account of League sentiment as expressed in special articles, editorials and appeals, as well as full descriptions of all the activities of the League. The 1914 *Handbuch*[2] gives a brief chronological summary of what the League itself considered the most significant developments from 1894 to 1914; the following summary is based on this, as representative of the League's view of what comprised the most significant phases of German development during the period, on Class's *Zwanzig Jahre alldeutscher Arbeit und Kämpfe* and on the *Alldeutsche Blätter*. The League conventions served to crystalize opinion among the members in the form of resolutions and many of these are conveniently collected in the two sources mentioned.

[1] The year 1898, see *supra* p. 106.
[2] Pp. 44-51.

The objects of Pan-German agitation during the decade 1894-1904 fall naturally into three main groupings: colonial affairs; the navy; and a more or less strictly "Pan-German" division which might be called *"der Kampf um das Deutschtum"*.[1]

In matters of colonial policy, the League's interest was untiring. The Zanzibar treaty of 1890 directly motivated the foundation of the League; the Franco-German treaty of 1894 delimiting boundaries in the hinterland of the Kamerun; the civil strife in Samoa and the tripartite treaty between Great Britain, the United States and Germany under which the government of the territory functioned until 1898—the League felt that Germany was slighted in each transaction, and that German interests and German honor were unprotected. The question of the possession of Delagoa Bay occasioned much bitter Anglophobia as did the Samoan difficulty. And the policy of the German government in the colonies, notably in German Southwest Africa, as it concerned settlement and land-concession policies and the building of railways, was under a constant fire of criticism from the League. The latter was very much against the granting of large individual land concessions in the colonies and very desirous of governmental encouragement for small farmers and settlers. Resolutions were passed, articles written and many speeches made urging the acquisition of more colonies, protectorates where Germans could settle and German industry could procure necessary raw materials and markets for goods. In fact, agitation on colonial matters formed a very large part of the activities of the League, and the Leaguers were loud in their protestations that Germans and German interests in foreign countries must be protected. It was the old cry of imperialists the world over and one of the most potent factors, especially

[1] The battle for *das Deutschtum*.

when backed up by extreme nationalism of the Pan-German variety, in causing strife.

The Boer War aroused the Leaguers tremendously, both before the actual breaking out of hostilities and during the war, and a large fund to aid the suffering Boers was raised under the League's auspices. Its hatred for England and all things English was surpassed by no emotion except its patriotic love for Germany, and the Boer War gave ample scope for exercise of its anti-British feeling and vocabulary.

A good deal of relief work was done among the Boer prisoners of war with the aid of the League's Boer fund, as well as in the notorious concentration camps in South Africa. Individual Germans and Boers were helped to leave South Africa and to emigrate and find occupation elsewhere; and the League also endeavored to press German claims at the *Wilhelmstrasse* for damages from the English. The Leaguers considered the Boers to be their blood-brothers—the low Germans of South Africa. Though the official German position was one of neutrality in the war, yet the League felt that the German people were perfectly justified in entertaining sympathetic feelings for their bitterly persecuted brothers. And though the German Empire could do nothing directly to aid the Boers, yet the League exhorted the people to work hard and to make their country strong on land and on sea. For it was of the opinion that were Germany well armed, she could step into the breach and demand that German interests in South Africa be untouched and the advance posts of *das Deutschtum* on the dark continent be preserved. " Preparedness is everything!" said the League.

During the decade from 1894 to 1904, as in the succeeding period, the League's steady demand for a larger and a still larger German navy comprised a big share of its efforts. When a naval bill was before the Reichstag, it worked hard for its passage; when none was on the docket, it agitated unceasingly for the drafting of another bill. Scarcely an issue of the *Alldeutsche Blätter* appeared during those years which did not contain some sort of article on the subject. There are forty-two articles indexed in the *Alldeutsche Blätter* for 1897, for instance, and some fifty for 1900. Lectures were held under League auspices at many local branches and no chance was lost to keep the question a burning one. There seemed to be no limit to the naval desires of the League.

In the *Kampf um das Deutschtum* class of Pan-German objectives, come such matters as the Polish question and the nationality problems throughout the world wherever a German was directly or indirectly concerned. The Polish question, that thorn in the side of Prussia, was considered to be a most pressing problem. The rising tide of Polish nationalism in the Eastern Marches especially was viewed by the League as a force which, if it was not checked, would undermine the very foundations of the German Empire. Commercially, socially, politically, the Poles must be pressed back and oppressed until they should leave Germany to the Germans or become Germanized themselves. Schemes for strengthening the middle-class Germans in the Polish east and guarding as far as possible against the inheritance of land by Poles were advised by the League, and scarcely a number of the *Alldeutsche Blätter* appeared which did not contain an article or note dealing with some phase of the Polish problem. Innumerable resolutions were passed at League conventions calling for complete Germanization of schools, theatres—even names of places; prohibition of immigration of Russian-Polish migratory workers; and much emphasis was laid on the necessity for recognizing disparity and inequality between Prussian and Polish officials and people. The final expropriation of Polish landowners was strongly urged upon the government.

The struggle of the Germans in the Austro-Hungarian Empire to maintain the supremacy of their language and customs against the encroachments of Czechs, Magyars and South Slavs was adopted by the League as its own concern. The League's resolutions were particularly fervent and numerous concerning the Dual Monarchy, where the question of the rights and privileges of Germans and the German language was an especially burning one. The Flemish nationalist movement in Belgium, to the disgust of its leaders, was also of interest to the League. The maintenance and improvement of German schools in Alsace-Lorraine agitated it during this first decade,Germans who had emigrated from the fatherland, and immigrants coming into Germany —all were considered by the League as within its special province. For years Dr. Hasse and Count von Arnim attempted unsuccessfully to put a bill through the Reichstag, making German citizenship more difficult for Germans to lose and for non-Germans to acquire. After many petitions, memorials, speeches and editorials on the part of the League, at all events the bill was finally passed in 1913.

In 1903, at the League convention in Plauen, Heinrich Class made a speech which he called "The Balance Sheet of the *neuer Kurs*".[1] In it he reviewed the successes and failures of the *neuer Kurs,* enumerating in detail the glowing promises made by the young Kaiser and then showing how little had actually been accomplished since Bismarck had been forced out of office and the Kaiser had presumed to act largely as his own chancellor. This speech throws a good deal of light on the feelings which the Pan-German League entertained for the Kaiser and must once for all lay the ghost of the tale of the direct relationship between the

---

[1] The speech may be found in full in *Alldeutsche Blätter,* 1903, pp. 331 *et seq.* Class, *Zwanzig Jahre alldeutscher Arbeit und Kämpfe,* pp. 157-189; *Flugschrift,* no. 16 of the Pan-German League.

League and the Kaiser. The balance sheet of achievement from a Pan-German standpoint was drawn up as follows:[1]

In order to see how this policy of the imperial chancellor together with that of his two predecessors has guarded the lasting interests of Germany, we shall draw the balance of the *neuer Kurs*. First in regard to foreign affairs:

Before 1890, the saying was: "We are not running after anyone"—since then we are making bows to everyone. We flatter everyone and make enemies of all, since no one believes in our honesty and steadfastness any longer.

We have cut the lines leading to Russia; the efforts to join them together again were unsuccessful and so spasmodic as to lower us still further in the estimation of Russia.

The attempt to readapt the principles of Bismarck, that is, to have two or more irons in the fire—and the fear of falling into dependence on Russia, threw us unconditionally into the arms of England. There also we achieved only distrust and humiliation.

The flattery of North America only increased the arrogance of that country and did not remove the distrust which had been conjured up at Manila.

Our attitude in South Africa has ruined our hopes there, has delivered South Africa to the English, has estranged the *Afrikanders* from us, has injured the growing confidence of the Dutch, has endangered our colonies and has brought about the disappointment of the Delagoa Treaty.

In Morocco and Fernando Po we have missed our opportunity.

The enterprise of the Bagdad Railway, provided it materializes, has depreciated so far as German world policy is concerned.

The Triple Alliance has lost its importance and permits the gagging and combating of *das Deutschtum* in Austria and Hungary.

We have won neither naval, coaling, nor cable stations and have not gotten beyond the beginnings of a world cable.

[1] Translated by Rüdiger Bilden.

We have acquired neither oil wells nor cotton-fields, and above all no real territories for colonization.

We have, moreover, incurred the growing enmity of England and America; we are looking upon France irreconcilable as of old, and upon a distrustful Russia, and we are thrown back upon the Triple Alliance, that is, upon our own resources.

As acquisitions of those years we bring back:—Heligoland, Kiao-chau, the Carolines and Samoa.

The result of our policy in contrast to that of the other powers will be most evident when we compare in square kilo-meters the areas of the territories acquired in the years from 1890 to 1903.

	1890	*1903*
German Empire, Europe	540,596	540,743 (*sic*)
" " colonies	2,234,860	2,656,620
France, Europe	536,408	536,464 (*sic*)
" colonies	3,112,797	6,087,203
Great Britain, Europe	314,951	314,869 (*sic*)
" " colonies	23,685,688	29,073,316
Russia (without Manchuria) Europe .	5,389,993	5,389,985 (*sic*)
Russia, Asia	16,495,949	16,545,520
United States, America	9,068,271	9,381,159 (*sic*)
" " colonies	———	425,174

But what about the result in the realm of internal policy?

In social policy great progress has undoubtedly been made through the enlargement of legislation; in the field of national policy we have only retrogressed, if one excepts the pacification of the *Nordmark* by Köller and the small successes in Alsace-Lorraine.

As for our Polish policy, we stand where we stood in the be-ginning.

Nothing, really nothing has been done to convert the German Empire into a national state, because the government has let itself be governed by the *Centrum* and the Social Democrats instead of conducting, as Bismarck did in 1863-1864, a strong German national policy, if necessary, against the majorities in the Reichstag and the Diet. The power of ultramontanism has reached the peak; that of the Social Democrats is in rapid growth.

The particularistic forces are strengthened and the gap between the Empire and the individual states is widened.

The prestige of the imperial crown, of the dynasties, and of the monarchy has decreased; the German Reichstag has lost the respect of the people; and the office of the imperial chancellor has been deprived of its essential meaning.

We have heard speech after speech through which hopes were aroused and anxieties were dispelled; the deeds were not forthcoming.

Pageants and festivals, parades and unveilings of monuments, as well as an influencing of the press as has never been conducted on such a scale heretofore, corrupts the picture of our public life, but cannot deceive intelligent persons as to the fact that we have in reality no government.

Great aims are unknown; when they are talked of, they are vague; we live from hand to mouth. . . . .

This is the total result of the official German policy since Bismarck's dismissal. It is fortunate only that the political life of a nation is not exhausted with the doings of its government. Otherwise woe to the German Empire.

During the first decade of its existence the League did seem to pay more attention to purely philosophical tenets of faith; during the decade from 1904 to 1914 the field of practical politics seemed crowded with events of the greatest import, and the development of an intensely national public opinion within the German Empire to deal with the pressing problems of the day occupied the League almost to the exclusion of the more theoretical questions. Working along much the same lines as those which it had followed from 1894 to 1904, it agitated unceasingly for a larger navy, passing numberless resolutions demanding that this or that arm of the service be strengthened, that the life of battleships be shortened in order to intensify their efficiency; that work be rushed so that no time should be lost in making the German Empire second to none on the seas. It joined in the hue and cry for better and more land armaments, and strongly urged the passage of the 1913 army bill, congratulating the government upon the introduction of the measure.

In colonial affairs, the interest of the League was unflagging. It advocated stern suppression of the Herero uprising in German Southwest Africa and collected money for Christmas gifts for the German colonial troops there. The League severely censured the government's land-concession policy in the colonies and engaged in agitation for the reparation of property damages incurred by German settlers during the Boer War and the Herero uprising. The government was urged to show more zeal in colonial affairs and the German people were exhorted to awaken from their apathy. Nor was the League lacking in concrete suggestions for the improvement of the colonies: self-government schemes, an independent colonial office, financial reorganization for the colonies, stricter selection of colonial officials, the building-up of railways and further opening-up of the interior regions, all manner of plans were put forth and advocated by the League.

In the more strictly "Pan-German" division of the League activities which we have called *"der Kampf um das Deutschtum"*, the eternal Polish problem was as usual well to the fore. The League agitated upon much the same lines as it had worked during the earlier period and was particularly anxious that the Prussian policy of expropriation be strictly enforced. The Russian revolution (1905) caused the League some worry as to the plight of Germans in Russia and the Ukraine and it aided in the raising of a relief fund for the German sufferers. The effects of the revolution on Baltic *Deutschtum* were also the cause of some apprehension on the part of the League. *Deutschtum* in Austria-Hungary was of especial interest during the decade from 1904 to

1914 because of the agitation in the Dual Empire for universal suffrage. The troubles in the Tyrol between Italians
and Tyrolese, and the annexation of Bosnia and Herze-
govina to the Dual Monarchy were matters of natural
concern to the Pan-Germans. And as German land armaments increased and the disparity between those of Austria-
Hungary and those of the German Empire became more and
more marked, the League took occasion to urge upon the
ally of Germany the necessity for enlarging her armaments.

The Flemings received some attention and the encroachments of the Danes in North Schleswig were a cause of
great worry to the League, but the language question in
Alsace-Lorraine and the granting of a constitution to the
Reichsland in 1911 were of primary concern to it. The
League felt that the imperial government had acted in the
most foolhardy and dangerous way possible in granting a
constitution to Alsace-Lorraine and expressed forebodings
for the outcome just as it had agitated unceasingly against
the step before it became a *fait accompli*.

Foreigners studying at German universities and technical
schools were made the object of many resolutions passed by
the League. It was felt that they were crowding out the
German students and benefiting from what should have been
a strictly all-German system of education designed to train
the German youth. But the world situation in general in its
relation to Germany, and the Moroccan question in particular, occupied the center of the Pan-German stage during
the period from 1904 to 1914.[1]

A pamphlet under the title of *Marokko verloren?*, by
Heinrich Class, was published in the League series of *Flug-*

[1] The late Kurt Eisner in a pamphlet entitled *Treibende Kräfte,*
Verlag " Neues Vaterland," Berlin, 1915, speaks of the theoretical " Pan-
German " fantasies of the League as a mere sideshow to their aims in
the realm of *Realpolitik*.

schriften early in May, 1904.[1] Here the League's Moroccan policy is clearly set forth. The first part of the pamphlet was prepared before definite news of the Anglo-French Moroccan agreement had been received, and Herr Class explains in detail the German claim to Morocco and Germany's great need of just that portion of the globe, the very last of the backward regions of the earth in the temperate zone that was as yet unclaimed. Class dismisses the Near East—Asia Minor, Syria, Mesopotamia—as a possible area where the surplus German population might settle, by saying that were she to consider that as a possible sphere of influence, Germany would need a Mediterranean fleet which she did not possess. Furthermore, she would antagonize both England and Russia in the process. "Therefore," says Herr Class, " these countries (in the Near East) are not to be considered." [2]

In 1896 the League had published a pamphlet entitled *Deutschlands Ansprüche an das türkische Erbe.* Both the richness and the weakness of the Ottoman Empire were described, and opinions of Moltke, Sprenger, de la Garde, List, Rodbertus and others quoted to show Germany's interest in the Near East. The pamphlet was not made much of even by the League and is of no particular importance. Though German capital had been interested in the Anatolian railway since 1888 and had received important concessions in 1899 and 1903 from the Turkish government for building the Bagdad Railway, the Pan-German League in 1904 did not consider the Near East — the section of the world opened up by the Bagdad Railway—as a possible field for German colonization or exploitation. Thus Herr Class's

---

[1] Class, Heinrich, *Marokko Verloren? Ein Mahnruf in letzter Stunde* (Munich, 1904). *Flugschrift*, no. 17.

[1] *Ibid.*, p. 7.

[3] Germany's claims to the Turkish inheritance (Munich, 1896).

pamphlet on Morocco dismissed the Near East with a sentence and devoted many pages to showing why Germany must have west Morocco—the entire Atlantic coast of Morocco. Surplus population, the need for coaling and naval stations, markets, raw materials, all the arguments of all imperialist agitators were sincerely employed. The second part of the pamphlet was prepared after the Anglo-French pact had been announced and is so choked with rage over the fact that Germany had been treated as a *quantité négligeable* that it is almost incoherent. Class goes so far as to say that the matter is worth going to war over, for it injures the sacred honor of the fatherland and impairs the interests of its citizens.

The League continued, by means of articles, speeches and resolutions, to urge on the government a strong German policy in Morocco, and when the Kaiser made his entry into Tangier, it rejoiced that at last something was to be done to protect German interests in the Sherifian Empire. But when no further move was made, and Germany's position of isolation was made obvious at the Conference of Algeciras, the League chafed and fretted and demanded that drastic measures be taken. Finally in 1911, Class published another pamphlet, *Westmarokko Deutsch!,* which had a wider circulation than most League publications and was commented upon in the Reichstag.[1] The pamphlet went into some five editions, reaching between fifty and sixty thousand copies, which was the largest circulation of any of the League's pamphlets.

In *Westmarokko Deutsch!* Class brings events in the dealings of the Powers concerning the Sherifian Empire up to date from the point where the 1904 publication stopped. He accuses France of deliberately stirring up trouble in Morocco in order to keep troops there and of desiring posses-

[1] See *supra,* p. 155.

sion of all Morocco in order to be able to draw freely on the country for black troops in case of war with Germany. Class takes a firm stand against any " compensation " for Germany in lieu of a portion of Morocco.

The Leaguers became so noisy on the subject of Germany's claims to a large section of Morocco that after the Agadir incident the government was accused in the Reichstag of some official connection with the Pan-German League. The explanation and denial of the foreign secretary, von Kiderlen-Wächter, in the Reichstag has already been described.[1] This took place in February, 1912. In November and December, 1911, Class had reprinted and answered in the *Alldeutsche Blätter* a statement made by von Kiderlen which had been given out by " Wolff's " news agency.[2] In the statement, the foreign secretary, speaking before the budget committee of the Reichstag, was reported to have said:

One of the chief reasons why the idea has spread that we must gain a foothold in Morocco lies in the brochure of Dr. Class. This brochure was known to me before it was made public, but that does not mean that I agreed with it. On the contrary, Herr Class was advised not to print it. The brochure would have been judged differently had it appeared in full, for it recommended the peaceful annexation not only of Morocco but also of the Department of the Rhone.

Class pronounced the last sentence as an absolute untruth, and described how the foreign secretary had very hastily glanced the brochure over and urgently requested that it should not be printed. He went on to say that the pamphlet had contained a recommendation to the effect that in case of war, victorious Germany should demand not gold but

[1] See *supra,* p. 156.
[2] *Alldeutsche Blätter,* 1911, pp. 406 *et seq.*

territorial reparation in the form of the country from Nancy northwest to the mouth of the Somme river and southwest to Toulon. This idea was put forward, Class explained, merely to frighten England and show her how much better it would be to allow Germany undisputed possession of the west coast of Morocco. However, the section in question was omitted from the pamphlet.

Class's defense and explanation was printed in most of the chief newspapers and copies were sent to the imperial chancellor and to the Foreign Office. No answer was received by Herr Class from the foreign secretary. On the other hand, he was informed by a member of the Reichstag that von Kiderlen-Wächter had said more before the Budget Committee than had been reported by Wolff. The further statement read:

I specifically told Herr Class *before* [1] Agadir that we wanted only a sort of ' dead pledge ' in order to make the French amenable. We wanted only guarantees for our commercial interests and desired no foothold in Morocco.

Class commented (in italics) on this as follows:

I maintain that this statement, too, if it really was made by the foreign secretary, is untrue. Neither the foreign secretary nor anyone else in the Foreign Office made any such statement to me before Agadir.

Class then said that two weeks *after* Agadir, von Kiderlen-Wächter made such a statement to a political friend of Class, who showed the foreign secretary Class's *Westmarokko deutsch!*. Moreover an item in the *Deutsche Tageszeitung* announced, just as Class's article in the *Alldeutsche Blätter* was going to press, that von Kiderlen-Wächter had entirely repudiated the Wolff despatch.

The business managing committee and executive coun-

---

[1] Italics are Class's.

cil of the League supported Class in a resolution, praising his patriotic stand in the controversy with von Kiderlen-Wächter and condemning the government's settlement of the Moroccan question as a great triumph for France and a defeat for Germany. After the foreign secretary made his defense in the Reichstag, the following resolution, which was the last word in the matter, was passed in February, 1912: [1]

The business managing committee of the Pan-German League, which met today in Berlin, busied itself at once with the announcement which had just been made concerning the speech of foreign secretary von Kiderlen-Wächter in today's session of the Reichstag. The speech dealt with his interview with *Rechtsanwalt* Class about Morocco and the committee, basing its reply upon incontestable material, makes the following answer:

The conference between the foreign secretary and the president of the Pan-German League did not take place a few days before Agadir but upon the nineteenth of April. On July first an interview between *Rechtsanwalt* Class and under-secretary Dr. Zimmermann took place, Herr von Kiderlen-Wächter being away on leave.

No further conference between Herr Class and the foreign secretary took place; the interview in September, mentioned by Herr von Kiderlen-Wächter in the Reichstag never took place. After July first there was no further conference between *Rechtsanwalt* Class and the Foreign Office.

About the statements of fact, explained by the foreign minister, the business managing committee has nothing to say.

Besides the Moroccan question, the political situation in general received a great deal of attention on the part of the League. A strong strain of pessimism runs through the speeches made at League conventions on the political situa-

[1] *Alldeutsche Blätter*, 1912, p. 57.

tion. The government's foreign policy was never strong enough to suit the Leaguers; Germany's position was never satisfactory. The 1907 elections to the Reichstag gave the League some encouragement and it worked hard to help elect a truly nationalistic body and was pleased with the returns, though the actual work of the newly elected Reichstag pleased it, for the most part, as little as usual. Then, too, there was much dissatisfaction shown with the Kaiser and his policies and acts. It was felt that he did not abide by the constitution of the realm and leave things in the hands of his imperial chancellor but that he endeavored to be his own chancellor. This feeling came to a crisis in 1908 with the *"Daily Telegraph"* incident. The League called a special convention to discuss the events of the so-called " black week " [1] and unequivocally condemned the "personal régime" of the Kaiser. On the other hand, it expressed its faith in *Kaisertum* and its conviction that this institution must be preserved. And the convention, in the final analysis, placed the blame for the humiliation of Germany's Kaiser and her chancellor on the German people themselves, for it felt that had there been an enlightened, intelligent public opinion, the events of the " black week " could not have taken place.

The Pan-German League took a thoroughly alarmist view of the international situation, and the anti-German feeling in England, France and Belgium was stressed in many articles

[1] The publication of an alleged interview with the Kaiser by the London *Daily Telegraph* on October 28, 1908, caused a great sensation. The Kaiser was reported to have said that he was England's only friend in Germany during the Boer War and vague references were made to a plan of campaign against the Boers which he had had drawn up by his generals and despatched to Queen Victoria. References to France, Russia and Japan were intermingled with his professions of friendship for England which were not likely to please those countries. The publication of the interview caused great consternation in Germany and the week following October 28, 1908, is often called "black week" there. *Cf.* Dawson, *The German Empire,* vol. ii., pp. 346 *et seq.*

in the *Alldeutsche Blätter* and in speeches at executive
council meetings and League conventions. The Balkan
wars added to the anxiety, and the picture of Germany's
chief ally, Austria-Hungary, menaced by an encroaching
Slaventum while Germany herself was isolated and sur-
rounded by enemies, was a clear indication to the League of
an approaching struggle for existence for *das Deutschtum*.
Therefore it demanded more armaments, land and sea, and
set itself ever more diligently to the task of creating a patriotic and nationalistic German public opinion. The League
became more and more worried about the international
situation and more and more convinced of the great and
growing danger to Germany of the condition of the world.
It saw enemies and hatred of Germany on all sides; it fore-
saw war in the very near future. On April 19, 1914, the
executive council of the League passed the following resolution summarizing its fears:

The executive council of the Pan-German League announces
that the international situation has not taken the course it was
expected to take at the end of the Balkan wars. On the contrary, because of the extraordinary military preparations of
France and Russia and the anti-German feeling which obtains
among all classes of the people in both these neighboring states
as well as the unfriendly acts of their governments, the situation has become much worse.

The executive council concludes from all this that France
and Russia are preparing a decisive war against the German
Empire and Austria-Hungary and that both plan to start fighting as soon as they consider that the moment is favorable.
Furthermore, the executive council is convinced that this war
will be decisive in determining the far future of the German
people if not its entire fate, and that the destiny of the other
Germanic peoples of Europe is bound up with ours in the closest
possible way. Therefore the Pan-German League feels that it
is its duty to warn our people to face the great hour with vigil-

ance and determination. It must prepare for it by straining every possible fibre and by subordinating all domestic quarrels and finally by willingly making every necessary sacrifice to strengthen our armaments.

The executive council believes that it is the most pressing task of the government to close up entirely any and all holes in our military preparations. It should work particularly for the prompt and complete accomplishment of universal military service. Reassured by its understanding of our public affairs, the government knows that the German people will not hesitate to do its full patriotic duty and make all sacrifices for the fatherland when it understands the true seriousness of the situation.

Finally, the Pan-German League calls the attention of all the related Germanic peoples to the gravity of affairs for all of them. It reminds them of the responsibilities that must come with the will to independence and the feeling of common racial kinship.

Kurt Eisner has said (in *Treibende Kräfte*) that no members of the Pan-German League could have been surprised when the Great War broke out in August, 1914. The League had long been expecting it and calling upon its members to prepare for the struggle. But that the League was doing more than reading the signs of the times when it passed its resolution on April 19, 1914, seems highly improbable. Its connections with the government were not of the sort that would have given it any advance information from that quarter. Naturally suspicious of all non-Germans, and possessed of a terrifically bellicose spirit itself, perhaps the wish of the League was father to its thought. The Leaguers were alarmists of the first water and for years they had been predicting the imminence of a great conflict. Their prediction in 1914 was possibly a bit more emphatic than earlier predictions, and, unlike the others, it happened to be true! Of responsibility for the coming of the Great

War, the Pan-German League can not be held entirely guilt-less, for during a score of years prior to 1914 it had been adding to the spirit of intense hatred and selfish nationalism in Germany and throughout the world. The feeling of the superiority of the German people over all the peoples of the world—a feeling which was at the basis of the League's *Weltanschauung* made it possible for it to see only one side of the tapestry of world affairs. The result was an intolerant and overbearing spirit of nationalism, leading on inevitably to rampant imperialism and war.

CHAPTER IX

The Pan-German League in Germany

The position held by the Pan-German League in Germany before the war can be determined from several sources. Foremost of these is the reaction of the German press to the League and its work. It has been obviously impossible for purposes of the present study to comb the great mass of German periodicals and newspapers for every reference to the League. However, using Dietrich's *Bibliographie der deutschen Zeitschriften-Literatur* which includes a few newspapers [1] also, in its earlier lists, and which for the period after 1908, has a special newspaper supplement based on all the main German newspapers, one can get a fairly serviceable index to the situation.

In periodical literature, except for two or three very minor write-ups, the League is discussed only in its own organ, the *Alldeutsche Blätter*. There was an article in September, 1900, in a Vienna weekly, *Die Zeit,* [2] describing the League and its work quite sympathetically and in some detail. In 1912, an article appeared in the *Burschenschaftliche Blätter,* [3] reporting a League convention which the writer had attended. In a review of the *Pan-Germanic Doctrine,* an English work by Austin Harrison which ap-

---

[1] The *Berliner Tageblatt, Deutsche Tageszeitung, Deutsche Zeitung, Hamburger Correspondent, Hamburger Nachrichten, Leipziger Zeitung* comprised this list.

[2] *Die Zeit*, Sept. 22, 1900, no. 312, p. 178.

[3] *Burschenschaftliche Blätter*, Oct. 1, 1912, pp. 3 *et seq.*

peared anonymously in 1904, the *Preussische Jahrbücher* [1]
expressed itself briefly concerning the League and its work.
In the *Politische Korrespondenz* of the *Preussische Jahrbücher* [2] in 1913, Hans Delbrück wrote on *Die Alldeutschen*
and called them a greater menace to the Empire both in
foreign and in domestic affairs, than the Social Democrats.
He declared that national idealism in Germany was about to
be overwhelmed by national fanaticism. The article is
about the only one of importance which has been discovered
to deal with the League. This is not to say that authors
who wrote for the *Alldeutsche Blätter* did not write for
other publications as well. Lutz Korodi had several
tirades against the Magyars in the *Preussische Jahrbücher,*
though Dietrich's *Bibliographie* does not mention that he
writes for other publications. Many other names well
known in League circles are to be found listed as authors of
articles and books on various subjects. For instance, Dr.
Paul Samassa wrote some things for *Kyffhäuser* and
Daheim (minor German periodicals) on the *Volkstum* and
on foreigners and he is the author of several books dealing
with African affairs and conditions in Austria-Hungary.
For a time, he edited a weekly publication in Vienna called
Deutsch-Oesterreich. Fritz Bley, whose profession was
that of " writer " *(Schriftsteller),* contributed to the
Deutsche Wochenblatt, to *Export,* to *Der Kynast,* to *Grenzboten* and other periodicals, articles dealing with colonial
questions, the Polish danger, politics, and international relations. His books are a mixture of collections of folk
songs and patriotic songs, tales, a novel and a few political
pamphlets, two of which were published in the League's
Kampf um das Deutschtum series. [3]   Karl Pröll wrote for

[1] Vol. 117, pp. 359 *et seq.*

[2] *Preussische Jahrbücher,* vol. 154, pp. 573 *et seq.*

[3] See *infra,* p. 472.

the *Deutsches Wochenblatt,* the *Grenzboten,* the *Deutsches Protestantenblatt, Gegenwart, Historisch-politische Blätter für das katholische Deutschland,* on German-Austria and subjects closely connected with that general heading. Dr. Hasse himself contributed a few things to the *Archiv für soziale Gesetzgebung und Statistik,* to *Die Gesellschaft* and to *Deutsche Erbe.* His articles dealt with emigration, the Social Democrats, and *das Deutschtum.* But aside from the three volumes of his *Deutsche Politik,* Hasse's published books are a few statistical studies on the care of orphans in Leipzig and kindred works.

Of writers interested in the Pan-German League, Paul Dehn and Albrecht Wirth seem to have been the most prolific outside the pages of the *Alldeutsche Blätter.* Dehn wrote on railways, commerce, colonies, travels to all parts of the globe in the *Deutsche Monatsschrift für das gesamte Leben der Gegenwart, Die Gesellschaft, Illustrierte Zeitung* and *Marine Rundschau.* His articles in the *Alldeutsche Blätter* were numerous, and the list of his published books occupies some three pages in the catalog of the *Preussische Staatsbibliothek* in Berlin. They deal with such subjects as German commercial policies, Germany and the Orient, the tobacco monopoly, protection of workers, Nuremberg, transportation problems, the Jews, etc. etc., all written from the extreme nationalist viewpoint. Dr. Albrecht Wirth was also a great traveler and contributed articles on his travels to the *Preussische Jahrbücher, Der Kynast, Die Kunsthalle, Neue deutsche Rundschau,* and *Protestant.* The list of his books too, fills more than three pages of the *Staatsbibliothek* catalog. They describe the history of South Africa, Siberia, Formosa, the development of Asia, Russia, the yellow and Slavic perils, world history of the present, world politics, German foreign affairs, *Volkstum* and world power in history. These are only a few of the subjects which occupied Dr. Wirth's attention.

But with the League proper and its affairs, these writers did not concern themselves. Their writings may be classed, it seems, under the general head of chauvinism; their counterparts appear in all countries.

The situation in the daily press is much the same. The complete list of references to the *Alldeutscher Verband,* taken from Dietrichs,[1] consists of some ten Berlin papers with from one to three notices in each, and some twelve other papers throughout Germany. Upon closer examination, a good many of the items have proven to be reports of League conventions or of meetings of the executive council; and the reports vary so little in context that they have obviously emanated from the League itself. In order to deal more in detail with this subject, we shall divide the newspapers covered into two classes—the liberal and the conservative. The latter is perhaps a polite term for the nationalist press, the right wing of which is loosely termed the " Pan-German press ".

Taking the so-called " liberal " press, we find that the *Frankfurter Zeitung* (Frankfurt-am-Main) notices the League just twice. The first time it devotes a leading article to the Bernstorff affair[2] and soundly berates the League for its policies in general and for making such a fuss about the ambassador's remarks in particular. It quotes the League's open letter to Count Bernstorff and devotes some space to the incident.[3] It may be said in passing, that this particular incident seems to have aroused more interest in the German press than any other thing in connection with the League. The second time that the *Frankfurter Zeitung* gave some space to the League was in connection with a League convention in Karlsruhe.[4] This was no cut and

---

[1] As previously noted, this applies to all important newspapers since 1908.

[2] See *supra,* pp. 151 *et seq.*

[3] *Frankfurter Zeitung,* 3rd morning edition, Sunday, Dec. 5, 1909.

[4] *Ibid.,* second morning edition, Tuesday, April 25, 1911.

dried press-release from the League headquarters but a very humorous account of how the Pan-Germans assembled around a green table in Karlsruhe, and solved all problems, both foreign and domestic, confronting the Empire. It was an article calculated to make the hair on many a cropped Pan-German head rise in righteous wrath. It ended, " The Pan-German League will remain important only to itself and it is well not to take its decrees too seriously for the percentage of German people supporting it is very small."

The *Vossische Zeitung* (Berlin) took occasion to counsel moderation and self-control to the so-called "Pan-Germans". In speaking of a speech made in England by Lord Haldane in which the then British secretary of state for war had said that the Germans and the English should try to look for the best traits in each other instead of the worst, this scholarly, liberal paper remarked that such sensible advice applied especially to " our Pan-Germans ".[1] Two years later,[2] the *Vossische Zeitung* condemned the war-lust of the Pan-Germans and their unreasoning blind desire for armament and more armament. The article declared that this held true of all the " nationalistic associations which they had become accustomed to lump together under the appellation of Pan-German ". However, the work of the League itself in aiding German emigrants and calling governmental attention to them was praised, and for that reason the *Vossische Zeitung* felt that the League was even more to be condemned for its foolish attitude on other matters. The article does not seem to be of particular significance. The *Vossische Zeitung* was evidently not much interested in the Pan-German League.

The *Berliner Neueste Nachrichten*, which the League considered an arch enemy, deigned only once, as far as

[1] *Vossische Zeitung*, evening edition, Aug. 4, 1911.

[2] *Ibid.*, morning edition, Dec. 27, 1913.

could be discovered, to mention the organization. Then it printed the open letter of the League to Count Bernstorff but did not comment upon it.[1]

In the *Kölnische Zeitung* [2] (Cologne) there is an account of a League convention held in Karlsruhe which is almost purely a factual report. That is the single time that the League seems to have managed to get into the columns of this well known paper.

The *Kölnische Volkszeitung*, the most important Catholic paper in the Rhineland, took a bit more notice of the League than the other so-called liberal papers. The Bernstorff episode inspired a long article in its Sunday supplement [3] in which it not only rapped the League but took the government to task for not stating its position as regards the Pan-Germans. It was further stated that the Pan-Germans were a great danger to the peace of Europe, though that bothered the Pan-Germans not at all, for they "believed that the whole world trembled with fear when even the click of a Pan-German beer-stein cover was heard"! A little later the *Volkszeitung* [4] took occasion to refer again to Bernstorff's American speech and said that the ambassador had quite won the hearts of the Americans as an opponent of the Pan-German League. The Americans thought the League important in the fatherland. "However", said the article, "these strong-lunged people don't count for much here at home. They have as good as no following in the Reichstag, and the adage, 'much noise and little wool' applies here."

The next time that the League's actions were considered

---

[1] *Berliner Neuste Nachrichten*, evening edition, Dec. 4, 1909.

[2] *Kölnische Zeitung*, evening edition, September 12, 1910.

[3] *Kölnische Volkszeitung*, second supplement to Sunday edition, Dec. 19, 1909.

[4] *Ibid.*, second supplement to Sunday edition, Jan. 8, 1910.

worthy of note by the *Volkszeitung* was on the occasion of
a visit of three hundred Czechs to Berlin.[1]   The League
raised a great hue and cry and passed a resolution asking
the Minister of the Interior to prohibit for all time the celebration of any Czechish or Slavic holiday in the capital of
the German Empire.   A League committee visited the Berlin *Polizei Präsidium* but the police president himself could
do nothing for them.   This was truly a *reductio ad absurdum* of the League's policies, and the *Volkszeitung* lost no
time in taking the Leaguers to task for their foolishness.
For, as the paper pointed out, the Austrian Germans liked
best of all to make holiday excursions into the Czech por-
tions of Bohemia in order to further the interests of
Deutschtum.   Nor did the Berliners really care who came
to their city so long as they made money by it.   Moreover
the Slavs read all the foolish things that the Pan-Germans
said and remembered them.   In fact this incident did make
quite a sensation in Russia where the papers cried out that
no one but the Germans treated foreigners in that fashion.
These three hundred harmless sight-seeing strangers who
came to try the Berlin beer and perhaps even to visit the
museum aroused as much commotion among the Leaguers
as if three French army corps had tried to visit Berlin.[2]

The *Kölnische Volkszeitung* seems to have had a fairly
clear idea of opinion outside Germany concerning the
League.   In reporting [3] the 1913 convention, this paper
speaks of the fact that in England and America, in China
and Australia, the League was considered the secret leader
of German politics.   It pointed out the absurdity of such
a notion and how the main speeches at the convention criti-

[1] *Ibid.*, August 16 and 17, 1911.

[2] One cannot fail to be reminded by this incident of the American
Defense Society's attempt (Dec., 1922) to have the Moscow Art Theatre
excluded from the United States.

[3] *Kölnische Volkszeitung*, noon edition, Sept. 10, 1913.

cized the government unmercifully, but foreign opinion worried the *Volkszeitung.* Later [1] it published another article entirely on the Pan-German danger to the Empire in which the " union of all Germans in central Europe " is carried to its logical conclusion, and Denmark, the Netherlands, German Switzerland, and Austria are annexed to the Empire, but French Switzerland goes to France and the Slavic peoples of the Dual Monarchy to their Slavic brothers. Obviously international difficulties arise and again it is the *reductio ad absurdum* of League aims.

This completes the survey of the more liberal German press. Meagre as it is, it shows that though the liberally-minded laughed at this insignificant group of fanatics, yet they were afraid of the very noise; for they realized the effect which this irresponsible, vociferous minority could and did have outside Germany.

Let us turn now to the nationalistic press, often spoken of as the " Pan-German press ". This appellation does not seem entirely justified, for these papers are merely part of the *bloc national* of the German press and not primarily Pan-German in the sense of the *Alldeutsche Blätter.*

The *Tägliche Rundschau* (Berlin), edited by Heinrich Rippler, a member of the executive council of the Pan--German League,[2] has as its heading the following: " An independent newspaper for national politics, designed for the education of all classes." It published full reports of the League's conventions and executive committee meetings, and was naturally well-disposed towards the League.[3] In fact

[1] *Kölnische Volkszeitung,* second Sunday supplement, Oct. 26, 1913.

[2] Rippler was elected to the business managing committee in 1912. *Alldeutsche Blätter,* 1912, p. 139.

[3] *Tägliche Rundschau,* evening edition, second supplement, September 11, 1911 a four column account). *Ibid.,* evening edition, main section, September 9, 1912 (six columns). *Ibid.,* evening edition, main section, December 2, 1912 (two columns).

the report of the 1913 convention was so full that it had to
be run over two days. Obviously Herr Rippler, who was
present, did his full reportorial duty by the League and by
his paper.[1]

However, these were merely factual reports, and of editorial comment or articles on the League we find none at all.
The anti-Leaguers had much more comment to make than
the pro-Leaguers.

The *Deutsche Zeitung* (Berlin) an "independent daily
for national politics", whose editor, Friedrich Lange, was
well-known for his super-nationalist ideals, has only a
couple of references to the League.   Once it reports a meeting of the executive council,[2] and once in an editorial under
the headline, *Die Alldeutschen schreien immer*,[3] the *Deutsche
Zeitung* upholds the aim of the League to agitate stridently
and continually for a vigorous foreign policy.   The writer
also takes occasion to say a few unkind words about his con-
temporaries, the *Berliner Tageblatt*, the *Frankfurter Zeitung*, and the *Kölnische Zeitung*.[4]

Die Post, another Berlin paper with a notorious "Pan-
German" reputation, has two small notices of League activities—a convention and an executive council meeting.[5]
The *Deutsche Tageszeitung* (Berlin) the motto of which
was: "For Emperor and right! For German Customs! For
German Work in Town and Country!", carried a signed
article of Count zu Reventlow with an editorial note to the
effect that the editor did not himself belong to the League

[1] *Tägliche Rundschau*, evening edition, first supplement, Sept. 18, 1913
(six and a half columns). *Ibid.*, morning edition, second supplement,
Sept. 9, 1913 (five columns).

[2] *Deutsche Zeitung*, April 22, 1913.

[3] "The Pan-Germans are always shrieking."

[4] *Deutsche Zeitung*, Sept. 26, 1912.

[5] *Die Post*, Sept. 7, 1912, Dec. 9, 1913.

but had gladly given space to Reventlow's article. Aside from this, the *Tageszeitung* gives short accounts of a League convention and of two executive council meetings. In this connection it is of interest to note that on Page 1, Column 1 of the same edition in which one council meeting was reported on the last page of the second supplement, there is a lengthy account of an international socialist congress in Frankfurt-am-Main![1]

Reventlow's article deals with the much discussed Bernstorff speech. The *Norddeutsche Allgemeine Zeitung*[2] (Berlin, semi-official before the war) had stated in the only item we have seen in its columns dealing with the Pan-German League, that the government entertained no prejudices against the League. Nor did the imperial chancellor desire to hinder the patriotic endeavors of the Pan-Germans. On the other hand, he did not wish to identify himself in any way with those endeavors. Further, it was felt that the ambassador's speech called for no rebuke from the government. Count Reventlow, in his article in the *Tageszeitung*,[3] storms at great length about the misunderstood aims of the Pan-German League. He protests that both the ambassador and the government as shown by this item in the *Norddeutsche Allgemeine Zeitung,* were unfamiliar with these ideals and he offers the following explanation:

The foreign anti-German press invents plans and opinions which the Pan-Germans are supposed to hold. The aim of this is simply to stir up distrust of the German Empire, and to strengthen such feelings where they exist already. For this reason, the ridiculous schemes about the Pan-Germans wanting

---

[1] *Deutsche Tageszeitung*, Sept. 10, 1910, Sept. 12, 1910, Sept. 8, 1913.

[2] *Norddeutsche Allgemeine Zeitung*, Dec. 1, 1909.

[3] *Deutsche Tageszeitung*, morning edition, Dec. 3, 1909.

to annex Holland, Belgium and Switzerland have been broad-
casted. . . .

and he goes on to blame England for the American distrust
of Germany, explaining finally that what the League is working for is nothing but that Germans shall uphold *das
Deutschtum* outside Germany—nor does he explain what is
meant by this. The article is a splendid example of the
fruits of mutual international distrust. It makes an already
muddled matter even more muddled and explains neither to
the ambassador nor to the government exactly what it was
the League did want.

Der Tag (Berlin), another paper with more or less of a
Pan-German reputation, but whose motto was " serving no
party; a free organ for all parties ", has only two articles
dealing with the League and both of those have reference
to the Bernstorff incident. Since both articles are based for
the most part on the open letter which the League sent to
Count Bernstorff, it seems advisable to give a summary of
the letter before taking up the articles themselves.

The first assertion which the League makes in this letter
is to the effect that there are in Germany no such " Pan-
Germanists " as Count Bernstorff refers to. Therefore it
considers it to have been his duty as an ambassador to correct the statement made in Professor Archibald C. Coolidge's
book and show the Americans that these mythical " Pan-
Germanists " exist only in foreign anti-German jingo
papers. In the second place, the Leaguers were very much
hurt that they should have been characterized as a " pernicious and very undesirable element ", and that their aims
should have been dubbed " silly ". They ask the ambassador whether agitation for a strong navy, for vigorous colonial policy, for Germanization of the border provinces, is
silly or pernicious. And they point out that instead of say-

ing things of that sort about his fellow-countrymen, the English ambassador to the United States (Lord Bryce) left a meeting at which the British government in India was criticized by a speaker. The letter ends with a recommendation to the ambassador to acquaint himself more thoroughly with German nationalist movements, and is signed by a large committee for the executive and business managing committees of the League.[1]

To return to the articles in *Der Tag*.—The first [2] of these is written by one Günther Thomas who endeavors to soothe the Pan-German League by proving that Bernstorff did not refer to the League but to irresponsible writers and journalists who excite foreign public opinion against Germany. He says that due to the translation of the speech into German, its real meaning was not made clear in Germany. It is, as usual, the translation of *Alldeutsch* by " Pan-German " that causes the trouble. The author tries further to heal the wound made by dubbing Pan-German aims " silly plans ", by calling the League's attention to the fact that the ambassador had said that foreigners attached too much importance to these plans—which the League itself had said that Bernstorff had no clear idea of. The article is not particularly important.

The second article [3] in *Der Tag* is by Count Reventlow who was mightily exercised over the whole Bernstorff affair. He refuses to be comforted by Thomas and says that if Bernstorff did not refer to the Leaguers, he should have named the " Pan-Germanists " he did mean. He proves to his own satisfaction that the ambassador did call the Pan-German Leaguers an " undesirable element of the German

---

[1] *Alldeutsche Blätter*, 1909, pp. 413 *et seq.*

[2] *Der Tag*, illustrated section, Dec. 10, 1909.

[3] *Ibid.*, illustrated section, Dec. 18, 1909.

people ". Reventlow makes the further point that the ambassador did not know what he was talking about and that it was his duty to inform himself before making rash statements about his countrymen, and he scoffs at the American idea of the Pan-German aims—that they wish to annex Brazil the day after tomorrow. These ideas he says are manufactured in England. The whole Bernstorff affair must strike one as so puerile that if viewed in a detached manner it can not but add to the gaiety of nations.

The *Reichsbote* (Berlin), another nationalist paper, has only three items on the League in its columns. One is a full report of a League convention,[1] and one an account of a meeting of the executive council.[2] The third is an article on five recommendations which the Pan-German League made to business men.[3] These five were:

1. Employ German workmen and clerks.
2. As far as possible, have German business abroad represented by Germans.
3. Carry on foreign correspondence as far as possible in the German language.
4. German products sold outside Germany should have German names.
5. German business men should deal as far as possible only in German goods.

The *Reichsbote* agrees with the League and enlarges on each of the above points, stressing the fact that these recommendations can be employed very advantageously to combat the growing Slavic infiltration throughout Germany which this paper, as well as the League, considers a great menace to the Empire. The article ends by entreating German busi-

[1] *Reichsbote*, Sept. 7, 1909.
[2] *Ibid.*, Dec. 10, 1913.
[3] *Ibid.*, Aug. 9, 1911.

ness men to remember the words of the Great Elector— *Bedenke dass du ein Deutscher bist.*[1]

The *Staatsbürger Zeitung* (Berlin), a " paper for national politics with a daily entertainment supplement ", was a particularly anti-Semitic daily. Naturally, it had common interests with the Pan-German League. However, even in this paper, we find only two items concerning the League, one a factual write-up of a League convention,[2] the other a rather full report of a meeting of the Berlin local branch.[3]

The papers outside of Berlin gave about the same sort of treatment to the League as did the Berlin papers.[4] The *Leipziger Neueste Nachrichten* has the largest number of items concerning the League of any paper consulted. It is very friendly in its reports, which number nine in all. Five of these are the usual factual accounts of League conventions and council meetings.[5] The others deal more at length with League affairs. There is the usual Bernstorff article, quoting the League's letter to the ambassador in full and praising it as expressing exactly the sentiments of the *Leipziger Neueste Nachrichten* on the incident. The other articles deal with a League convention at which Liebermann von Sonnenberg, an excitable patriot, member of the Reichstag *(Deutsch Soziale Partei),* lost his temper and insulted the German press.[6] The whole affair shows up the

---

[1] It will be recalled that this is the motto of the Pan-German League: Bear in mind that you are a German.

[2] *Staatsburger Zeitung,* Sept. 10, 1912.

[3] *Ibid.,* March 3, 1912.

[4] We were not able to secure the following papers, which contained the number of items listed: *Strassburger Post* (three items), *Grazer Tageblatt* (two items), *Schwäbische Merken* (one item), *Germania* (one item), *Posener Neueste Nachrichten* (one item), *Leipziger Tageblatt* (two items).

[5] *Leipziger Neueste Nachrichten,* Nov. 23, 1908, Sept. 5, 1909, April 4, 1910, Dec. 5, 1910, April 25, 1911.

[6] *Ibid.,* Sept. 12, 1910, Sept. 14, 1910, Sept. 16, 1910.

general petty character of the League rather well. It seems that a Bordeaux (France) paper had commented on the League convention and especially on the fact that the members assembled in Karlsruhe, where the meeting was taking place, were planning an excursion to the battlefield of Weissenburg. This piqued the French paper and it remarked sarcastically that it would be more appropriate for the Pan-Germans to celebrate the Weissenburg victory over their beer and sausages than over the graves of French heroes. Liebermann von Sonnenberg arose in wrath and burst out that " the newspaper writers in France were just as mean as those in Germany ". The League's president, Herr Class, tried to smooth things over and Liebermann von Sonnenberg finally retracted, but Count Reventlow, speaking next, repeated what Liebermann von Sonnenberg had said and the newspaper correspondents present threatened to boycott the meeting. Class pacified them by telling them that he would not have given Reventlow the floor had he known what he would say, and later read a long official apology.

The *Leipziger Neueste Nachrichten* took this entirely infantile episode quite to heart and lectured both Reventlow and Liebermann soundly on the corruption of the French press and the dignity, worth and respectability of the German press. It pointed out that as members of the Reichstag,[1] both of these gentlemen were extremely dependent on the press and threatened to boycott the entire League as a result of the insult. The president of the Leipzig local branch, Dr. Felix Hänsch, wrote the *Neueste Nachrichten* a very complimentary and soothing letter of apology and the whole affair blew over.

The *Hamburger Nachrichten*, Bismarck's organ, has a few items dealing with the League. It reports quite fully

---

[1] As a matter of fact, Count Ernst zu Reventlow did not then belong to the Reichstag.

and in a friendly spirit but without comment,[1] two council meetings and has a long article dealing with a resolution passed at a League convention.[2]   This resolution concerned itself with the Guelphs in Brunswick and advised the incorporation of this duchy as a *Reichsland* directly under the German emperor.   The *Hamburger Nachrichten* expresses itself as being very anti-Guelph, but it does not desire the duchy to lose its identity, for it was Bismarck's view that the individual states comprising the German Empire, by their very individuality, are a source of great strength. This seems rather a joke on the Pan-German League, which never lost a chance to say it was carrying out Bismarck's policies!   At the League convention it had been stated that Bismarck would without doubt have voted for a *Reichsland,* but the *Hamburger Nachrichten* says that it very strongly doubts this, for in its eight years' association with the great statesman, he was never heard to give utterance to such a view.   Bismarck's organ does not seem very ardent in its support of his most vociferous worshipers.

The *Rheinisch-Westfälische Zeitung* (Dortmund), one of the best known Rhineland papers and of a strongly nationalist bias, has some three or four items dealing with the League.[3]   It reports two League conventions rather fully but without comment, and has one short article [4] on the Bernstorff affair in which it worries much more about a rumor of better Anglo-German relations as a result of the ambassador's speech, than about his remarks concerning the Pan-Germans.   In fact the latter are scarcely mentioned.

[1] *Hamburger Nachrichten*, morning edition, April 22, 1913, morning edition, Dec. 9, 1913.

[2] *Ibid.*, evening edition, Sept. 7, 1909.

[3] *Rheinisch-Westfälische Zeitung*, Sept. 8, 1912, Sept. 9, 1912, Sept. 8, 1913.

[4] *Ibid.*, Dec. 27, 1909.

The *Hannöverische Courier* (Hanover) has accounts, short and to the point, of three League conventions.[1] It did not comment even when the League dealt with the Guelph question, though naturally that was of primary importance to Hanover.

This completes the survey of the German press and periodical literature. It makes no claim to being in any way definitive, but it would seem sufficient to justify an opinion that the Pan-German League appeared remarkably little in the press outside of its own organ, the *Alldeutsche Blätter*. On the whole, the reaction of the press to the League and its work was a rather negative one; for the most part it ignored it.

Another index to the League's standing in Germany is to be found in the Reichstag. This question has already been dealt with at length in an earlier chapter,[2] but further inferences may be drawn in direct relation to the League's position at home in the fatherland. First of all it has been shown that the members of the Reichstag, who were also members of the Pan-German League, were good party men first, for the most part, and good Leaguers second. Dr. Hasse is the most outstanding exception to this rule, and he sat in the Reichstag only five years of the twenty covered by this study. Thus the appearances in the Reichstag of Leaguers in the rôle of Pan-Germans were relatively few. Almost always the League was to be found on the defensive. It was accused by the Foreign Office of stirring up trouble; it was attacked by the Center and Left and made fun of on all occasions. Its members—particularly Hasse—assailed the government's foreign policy with such vigor that the chancellor was forced now and then to defend himself and his policies in no uncertain fashion. But these explosions

[1] *Hannöverische Courier*, Sept. 12, 1911, Dec. 3, 1912, Sept. 9, 1913.
[2] See *supra*, pp. 132 *et seq.*

took place for the most part during Hasse's term as a member of the Reichstag, and he did not neglect to place the League's platform and aims before that body on every conceivable occasion. Undoubtedly he bored the members terribly, and the shouts of laughter which often greeted him or the mention of his name are a significant indication of the seriousness with which the Reichstag took the League and its president.

In view of the mighty reputation acquired by the " Pan-Germans " during the War, and the natural desire on the part of most Germans to lay the ghost of that " peril ", the current opinions of scattered Germans as to the position and importance of the Pan-German League in Germany, can not be relied upon too strongly, though they are none the less significant. The writer has talked the matter over with many Germans, writers, business men, college professors, students, and always the statement is made that the influence of the Pan-German League before the War has been tremendously overestimated. Many say that they had never heard of the League before the War; others that it was an association of harmless, shrieking fanatics; still others that its members were " *streng begeistert* " [1] patriots. But one and all maintain that the influence of the association within Germany itself was negligible.

Various German statesmen and politicians in recently published memoirs and apologia have expressed opinions concerning Pan-Germanism and its importance. These, too, must be taken for what they are worth and considered in relation to the past positions of the authors. Viewed in that light, they are interesting, however.

Prince von Bülow, ex-imperial chancellor, says in his *Imperial Germany*: [2]

[1] Ultra-enthusiastic; there is no adequate translation for this expression.
[2] London, New York, Toronto, Melbourne, 1914, pp. 107 *et seq.*

The old joke that two Germans can not meet without starting a club has a serious significance. The German feels at home in his clubs and societies, and if such an association exists for greater purposes of an industrial or a political kind, then its members, and especially its leaders, soon see in it the Archimedian point whence they would like to unhinge the whole political world. The late member of the Reichstag, von Kardorff, said to me not long before his death: " Look, what maniacs we are about associations. The association itself becomes our be-all and end-all. The *Alliance Française* collected millions to establish French schools abroad, but it never dreamt of shaping the policy of the government. Our Pan-German League has done much to arouse national feeling, but on the other hand, it considers itself the supreme court of appeal in questions of foreign policy. The Navy League has done great service in popularizing the idea of a navy, but it has not always resisted the temptation to prescribe to the government and the Reichstag what course to pursue in naval policy. The *Bund der Landwirte* founded at a time of great stress in the agricultural world, has benefitted the farmers as a whole very greatly, but has now reached such a point that it wants to treat everything in its own way, and runs a great risk of over-shooting the mark. We get so wrapped up in the idea of our association that we can see nothing beyond it."

The homely side of the Pan-German League and its appeal to the sociability of the German nature must not be lost sight of as an important factor in its existence. In this connection, the following opinion expressed by the ex-secretary of state for foreign affairs, von Jagow, in a footnote in his apologia, is interesting as a characterization of the League's position in Germany:

Before the War, the so-called *Alldeutschtum* was felt to be an uncomfortable factor, hindering political action, but it had no authoritative influence upon the decision of the government. Perhaps there was now and then too much forebearance with it because occasionally it served to furnish fresh relays in domestic affairs, as for example in the navy question. But in no way could it be considered as an expression of the real opinion of the people; it was in part merely an echo from beer-hall benches, isolated editorial rooms and club meetings which found support among only a fraction of the people.[1]

On the other hand, Karl Kautsky, the eminent Social Democratic author, who was called upon after the German Revolution to prepare the Foreign Office documents for publication, says in his *Wie der Weltkrieg entstand:*[2]

The Pan-German section in particular exceeded all bounds in the provocations it uttered. These were of serious significance, for the Pan-Germans were the leading element in those circles of society which formed the ruling class in Germany and from which its government sprang.

But it must not be forgotten that Kautsky is a Social Democrat first and foremost, and desirous of putting the entire blame for the War on the so-called " ruling class ".

The late Dr. Karl Helfferich, formerly minister of finance, at one time managing director of the *Deutsche Bank,* and who played a great part in the development of the Bagdad Railway, narrates the following incident as the only comment in his *Vorgeschichte des Weltkrieges*[3] on the League or on Pan-Germanism. Incidentally it throws an interesting side-light on the supposed connection between von Kiderlen-Wächter and the Pan-German League. Dr. Helfferich says:

[1] G. von Jagow, *Ursachen und Ausbruch des Weltkrieges* (Berlin, 1919) footnote, pp. 31 *et seq.*

[2] Kautsky, Karl, *Wie der Weltkrieg entstand; dargestellt nach dem Aktenmaterial des deutschen auswärtigen Amts* (Berlin, 1919). English translation under the title of *The Guilt of William Hohenzollern* (London), p. 28.

[3] (Berlin, 1919), pp. 82 *et seq.*

After Kiderlen, who had been away from Berlin on July first, the day when the " Panther " appeared before Agadir, had returned, I visited him at the Foreign Office.   In the ante-room I met a well-known Pan-German writer who told me that he had come to see Kiderlen to congratulate him on the guarantee of Germany's share in Morocco.   When Kiderlen received me after having given the gentleman a few moments of his time, I asked the Secretary about his previous interview.   Kiderlen dashed his hand across his forehead and said, with a smile: " I told him in plain language that we did not want anything in Morocco; but my words were in vain; the — fool simply would not believe me."

Admiral von Tirpitz, long chief of the German Navy League and secretary of state for the navy, makes no mention of the Pan-German League or Pan-Germanism as such in his memoirs.   But his own philosophy found much in common with that of the League and he may safely be classed as a " Pan-German ".   His *idée fixe* was of course the building of a huge German navy and his reason for the necessity of such a policy was strictly " Pan-German ".[1]

The ex-chancellor, von Bethmann Hollweg, expresses the following opinion in his *Betrachtungen zum Weltkrieg:*[2]

As untrue as were the ideas which were spread broadcast during the War to the effect that German ideas found their expression in the *Pan-Germanentum* (*Alldeutschtum*), nevertheless, by 1909, the fact could not be mistaken that the Pan-German movement had begun to make some headway in the Conservative and National Liberal parties.   This did not react upon the policy of the government.   In the very beginning of my chancellorship I had occasion sharply to reject the advances of a Pan-German society.   However, in the Morocco crisis

[1] von Tirpitz, *My Memoirs*, English translation in two volumes (New York, 1919) vol. i, pp. 106 *et seq.*; pp. 198, 237 for example.

[2] (Berlin, 1919), pp. 22 *et seq.*

of 1911, and in the attempts to arrive at an understanding with England, I had ample opportunity to ascertain in what degree our foreign policy was made more difficult by the fact that parties possessing strong support in the Prussian state system, in the army and navy as well as in the ranks of big business, should incline towards tendencies which touched upon Pan-German ideas.

Finally, there is Dr. Otto Hammann, for years director of the press section of the *Wilhelmstrasse*. He characterizes the work of the Pan-Germans in general, as follows:[1]

The activity of the Pan-Germans with its sytematic madness was confined to an upper nationalistic stratum of people, with all the utter deficiency of half-education in political affairs and did not reach deep down into the people as a whole. In this class, the superman of Nietzschian philosophy was embodied in its grossest form—a German Michel who imagined himself to be the true heir of Bismarck even though he lacked the best qualities of his hero—the fine feeling for what was possible in the field of *Realpolitik*. . . . (They) exerted some influence upon domestic affairs, but none upon foreign policy.

What then must be our conclusions as to the position of the Pan-German League in Germany?

From the reaction of the press to the League, it is no wonder that many well-informed Germans confess never to have heard of the League before the War. Members of the League were to be found in the Reichstag, but apart from Dr. Hasse, they were men of sound party principles who did not allow their membership in the League to interfere with strict party discipline. And the aims and ideals of the League as expounded and made the basis of a general view of life by Dr. Hasse, were the cause of much

[1] Hammann, Otto, *Der misverstandne Bismarck* (Berlin, 1921), pp. 72, 188 *et seq.*

mirth on the part of many members of that august body. The League was laughed at the while it was recognized as containing the seeds of grave danger to Germany. Finally, the opinions of various prominent Germans do not attach much importance to the organization or its work. It is recognized as a factor in the rising tide of German nationalism but as a relatively minor one.

CHAPTER X

Non-German Opinion of the Pan-German League; Conclusions

In the preceding chapter the position of the League within Germany has been reviewed with reference to the reaction of the press to the League, its position in the Reichstag and the opinions of leading German statesmen concerning its activities. Non-German opinion of the League, however, is so hopelessly intermixed with opinion of Pan-Germanism, Pan-Teutonism and German chauvinism in general, that it is almost impossible to isolate it.

Perhaps the best known non-German writers on the subject of " Pan-Germanism " — for it must be given its best known title outside Germany—are Roland G. Usher (*Pan-Germanism*, London, 1914) and André Chéradame (*Le plan Pangermaniste démasqué,* Paris, 1916; *The United States and Pan-Germania,* New York, 1918). There is, too, a great mass of war literature on the subject, pamphlets, books and articles, but the works of Usher and Chéradame are representative.

Written in a facile style, Professor Usher's *Pan-Germanism* flows on in glittering generalities and is quite innocent of bibliography and as a rule of references and footnotes. The broad, sweeping strokes of his pen paint a lurid picture of the vast scheme of Pan-Germanism, a sort of mysterious cult, which " aims at obtaining for Germany and her allies control of the world and at insuring their retention of that control for at least a generation." [1]

[1] Usher, R. G., *Pan-Germanism* (London, 1914), p. 101.

The authorship of the great scheme which we call Pan-Germanism is least of all a matter of certainty. There seems to be little doubt that it was the product of German thought and of German interests, but no student of current affairs can believe for a moment that important aspects of it were not the result of the views and interests of Austria and Italy. Bismarck was the first statesman to see all its possibilities, though we are as yet unable to be certain how much of what is now called Pan-Germanism he is actually responsible for. Von Bieberstein, von Tirpitz, and above all the present emperor, are responsible for much, and certainly deserve the credit (or discredit) of bringing the scheme to its present state of perfection. The date of its origin [1] is an even more perplexing question, and could be more definitely settled if we were sure that events of the past generation were all steps in the development or furtherance of the same scheme and not of two or three schemes, out of which the exigencies of times and occasions gradually developed the present Pan-Germanism. The historian, who wishes to be cautious, is inclined to take the latter view and to conclude that Pan-Germanism is an outgrowth of the various policies advocated by German statesmen after the formation of the present empire.[2]

Of the work, aims or importance of the Pan-German League, Professor Usher makes no mention. His book is as vague and general as "Pan-Germanism".

Monsieur Chéradame is more definite. He says: [3]

Again, William II encouraged the creation of the *Alldeutscher Verband*. This association or Pan-German Union, counts

---

[1] " Cecil Battine, in the *Fortnightly Review*, XCI, New Series, 1056, 1057, places the beginning of Pan-Germanism between 1893 and 1895. Article 4 of the constitution of 1871 indicates that colonies were foreseen at the very beginning."

[2] Usher, *op. cit.*, pp. 117 *et seq.*

[3] Chéradame, André, *The Pan-German Plot Unmasked* (New York, 1917), pp. 7 *et seq.*

among its members a large number of important and influential persons, and at the door of this society must be laid the most overwhelming responsibility for the outbreak of the war. Founded in 1894, it has organized thousands of lectures besides scattering broadcast millions of pamphlets to spread Pan-German notions and to get masses of the people to favor schemes of aggrandizement. It was due to the *Alldeutscher Verband* that all the Germans living outside the Empire were formed into a systematic organization for the present war; this being specially the case in Austria and in the United States. . . . For twenty-five years, and by order of the Kaiser, a violent Pan-German propaganda had been carried on throughout the Empire.

Monsieur Chéradame's work is as bare of references and bibliographies as is that of Professor Usher, but he assures the reader that he has made the study of Pan-Germanism his life-work. Anything appearing on a printed page at once acquires a certain amount of authoritativeness and the casual reader does not question a statement to the effect that William II encouraged the creation of the Pan-German League, or that millions of pamphlets were spread broadcast by that organization, even though the author cites no authority for his statements. It is probably due to the books of Monsieur Chéradame more than to any other single factor that the belief is current that " from Hamburg to the Persian Gulf the net is spread," as the late President Wilson expressed it in his Flag Day Address, June fifteenth, 1917. That in a nutshell is the popular non-German conception of Pan-Germanism and of the work of the Pan-German League.

How, then, is one to reconcile the divergent points of view as expressed in non-German and German opinion of Pan-Germanism? The truth probably lies somewhere between the two extremes.

The Pan-German League was a manifestation of the

virus of selfish super-nationalism which infected all the great nations of the world. " Pan-German " has become a loose term covering German imperialism, militarism, nationalism —in a word, the German brand of widespread chauvinism.

The nineteenth and early twentieth centuries witnessed a tremendous growth of industry in the world and an unparalleled expansion of trade. During the same period, the spirit of nationalism became a major force in the ideas of mankind. The rise of cheap chauvinistic journalism contributed to spreading and intensifying nationalism, and the popularization of education, particularly state-directed education, added to the potency of the printing press by supplying hundreds of thousands of readers where there were only hundreds before. Nor did this education fail to add to the growth of the new nationalism by emphasizing the glorious past deeds of mother country or fatherland. The rise of " national history " accompanied it, and the historian who dares to insinuate that the history of his country may have inglorious periods must take care. History has become, in many cases, a splendid medium for proving that a nation, like the divine-right kings of old who received their power from God, can do no wrong. My country, right or wrong, my country— but when has my country ever been wrong? Instead of stressing the likenesses of all mankind, the selfish spirit of nationalism has pointed out the differences and peculiarities of other peoples. This has led to intolerance of other states and peoples and to unwarrantable pride in the accomplishments of one's own nation.

As trade and industry have developed, a great scramble has ensued for markets, raw materials, colonies, and trade-routes, and the spirit of nationalism has transformed competition for these desiderata from an individual matter between rival firms into competition between nations. Instead of two companies struggling for the control of oil in Asia

Minor, for instance, whole nations have been urged to go to war in support of the "interests" of individual citizens. The jingo press of the rival nations pictures the affair as a matter involving " prestige " and " national honor "; sensitive nationalism is wounded and must be appeased by the sword.

The Pan-German League was an example *par excellence* of an organization founded to agitate for extreme nationalism. The industrial development of Germany had taken place later than that of other powers; she had achieved national unification later, and as a result, her expansion into a colonial power was retarded. When she set out to found a colonial empire, others had been before her and many of the choice backward regions of the globe were already appropriated. In 1884 the colonial interests in Germany had forced the government to undertake a colonial policy officially, but it was felt to be an uphill task. It was out of the movement for colonial expansion that the Pan-German League was born. The League was interested in stimulating that spirit of nationalism in the German people which would back any German anywhere and be super-sensitive to any suspected tarnish on the clear surface of the national honor. Other patriotic societies worked for specific things; acquisition of colonies, enlargement of the navy, national security, German schools abroad. The League advocated all these, agitated for all of them, but strove in particular to inspire in the German people a spirit of nationalism which should always be ready to burst into flame. Because it felt that the only way in which Germany's position as a world power could be advanced and assured was through the support of an intensely nationalist-minded public opinion, the Pan-German League worked primarily to create such an opinion. To it, the questionable premise that the interests of the few should be protected even by the death of the many, was an axiom of faith. And it was an intolerant and frankly selfish nationalism, based philosophically on belief in the inherent superiority of the German race.

The Pan-German League had two major fields of interest, both of which lent themselves to exaggerated descriptions outside Germany. The League was concerned with the state of *Deutschtum* in the world and with the foreign policy of the German Empire. Its demands and opinions in these related fields were of the sort to conflict with the patriotism and interests of other nations and peoples, and as a result an opinion has grown up outside Germany attaching an importance and significance to the ideas and work of the Pan-German League which its standing at home would hardly warrant. It has lent itself admirably as a basis for anti-German propaganda elsewhere, just as the words of inspired patriots outside of Germany were used to advantage in Germany to show the perilous position and isolation of the German Empire. The League itself was cognizant of this fact and Count Reventlow, in his speech on *The Pan-German League and Practical Policy*,[1] says:

One needs only to have followed the foreign press for several years to know that all those truly fantastic plans which are ascribed to the Pan-German League have been invented in foreign countries. . . . It is obvious that inventions of this sort can be very useful for the creation of sentiment in foreign countries. If one asks why it is that just the Pan-German League is used in foreign countries for such tales, the simple answer is that in the first place it is the name which is seized upon and exploited in the manner of the Pan-Slavs and the Pan-Americans. But the chief reason is, that the Pan-German League stands politically on a non-partisan basis and that it makes no secret of its conviction that it is right as well as necessary for the German Empire to conduct a vigorous national

[1] Class, *Zwanzig Jahre alldeutscher Arbeit und Kämpfe*, pp. 458 *et seq.*

policy in foreign affairs. Of course we can not now go into all those stories and we may only state briefly *that the Pan-German League has no intention of annexing to the German Empire Belgium and the Netherlands, of annexing Switzerland or Denmark, German Austria or Brazil,*[1] moreover, it has for the time being postponed its plans for an " invasion " of the moon. If, on the other hand, it strives to preserve and strengthen *das Deutschtum* in foreign countries, then it does nothing different from what other associations, related to it, do, against which a charge is never made, and its purpose is in reality not different from that of the German imperial government, when the latter supports German schools in foreign countries, maintains consuls, etc. there, and also increases them according to the growth of the German interests in these very same countries. The latter is, mind you, something which the imperial government does and must do, like the government of any other power, but it is at the same time a point in which the activity, and we may say the interest also, of the German government leaves much to be desired.[2]

Doubtless the League has contributed to keep alive the spirit of *das Deutschtum* in foreign parts. In the Baltic states, in Austria, in Hungary, among the Boers in South Africa, in Brazil and elsewhere in the New World, its local branches were gathering places for Germans far from the fatherland or oppressed by foreign governments. It has been alleged that the German government did not scruple to make use of the League where its purposes suited its own. Perhaps it did; absolutely no documentary evidence is available to prove it; in fact the times when the League approved of governmental policy on any issue in any place in the world were so few and far between that the burden of proof seems to be against rather than for such an assertion. The League was much more of an embarrassment to the government than an aid.

[1] The italics are Count Reventlow's.

[2] Translated by Rüdiger Bilden.

Especially was this true in its criticisms of German foreign policy. The notorious reputation of the " Pan-Germans " outside Germany was a constant handicap to the German government. The League's feeling about hindering the government rather than helping it is well described by Prince Bülow in the following incident, for though the member of the Reichstag is not named, his position was that taken by the League:

> Once, during the Boer War, (says Prince Bülow),[1] standing in the lobby of the Reichstag, I remonstrated with one of the members on account of his attacks on England, which did not exactly tend to make our difficult position any easier. The worthy man replied in a tone of conviction: " It is my right and my duty, as a member of the Reichstag, to express the feelings of the German nation. You, as Minister, will, I hope, take care that my feelings do no mischief abroad." I do not think that such a remark, the naïveté of which disarmed me, would have been possible in any other country.

The League embodied a real attempt at popular control in foreign affairs. It believed firmly in the efficacy of a strong, nationally-minded public opinion supporting the government, and more than that, initiating national policies through force of popular demand. To achieve that, an educated and politically-minded electorate was necessary, and this was what the League endeavored to secure. For it was difficult for this nationally-minded public opinion which the League considered itself to represent, to support the government when the policies which the latter advocated were contrary to the aims of the League. Therefore the League found itself almost always in the position of criticizing the government. Its criticism was directed toward the establishment of a consistently " national ", aggressive foreign policy and a cessa-

[1] *Imperial Germany*, pp. 123 *et seq.*

tion of the zigzag course which the German government was pursuing. Curiously enough, this zigzag course has been characterized by German diplomats of the decade before the war, as one of the chief reasons for the so-called isolation of Germany. The policy of the *Wilhelmstrasse* was so unreliable that Germany could not be counted upon as an ally. The attempts at the formation of an Anglo-German alliance, so well described by Baron von Eckardstein, the first secretary of the German Embassy in London, in his memoirs, bear this out very fully.[1] And a factor which contributed largely to the failure of the policy of Anglo-German friendship was the continued Anglophobe agitation in Germany. Von Eckardstein says:[2]

London life was very pleasant and easy under the old Queen. It was the good old days, not only for England, but for all Europe. And, apart from excitement caused by the Kaiser, Anglo-German relations were very tolerably good. There was not the least ill-feeling against Germany, either in public or in the government. On the other hand, there was in the German Empire, from 1890 onwards, an absurd and quite artificial agitation against England and everything English, which in the end was to bring our credulous German Michael into an antagonism with England that was as unnatural as mischievous.

The Pan-German League was a ringleader in the anti-English agitation in Germany. However, the sole blame for German Anglophobia can not be forced on the League, for its height was reached during the Boer war and the League was not alone in its support of the Boers. Nevertheless a large share must be attributed to the League as well

[1] Hermann, Freiherr von Eckardstein, *Lebenserinnerungen und politische Denkwürdigkeiten,* in three volumes (Leipzig, 1919).

[2] *Ibid.*, vol. i, pp. 178 *et seq.*, translated by Professor George Young. *Ten Years at the Court of St. James* (1895-1905), (New York, 1922), p. 44. The translation of the original work has been compared with the original in all cases.

as to the other chauvinist societies which are generally dubbed " Pan-German ". When relations between England and Germany came almost to a break over the capture of some German mail-boats by the British, von Eckardstein says that the only person to gain anything from the affair was Admiral von Tirpitz, the protagonist of great naval expansion and director of the German Navy League.[1] So great was the abuse of England by the Navy League that King Edward VII said to Eckardstein, in 1901 : " The abuse and threats that the German Navy League and its organs are perpetually pouring on us are not exactly calculated to get rid of our distrust." [2] It was at this time that the most delicate negotiations for an Anglo-German alliance were going on.

von Eckardstein continues : [3]

The greater part of the German press still raged furiously against England. The abuse of the British authorities and of the British army became more and more offensive, until at last even the protagonist of the German alliance, Chamberlain, was compelled to make a very sharp reply in defence of the army. In this Edinburgh speech of October 25, 1901, his resentment against these unfair attacks carried him perhaps too far in leading him to make counterattacks on other armies, and among others on the behavior of the Germans in 1870. These observations were at once seized on indignantly by many German papers and for months the abuse of England went on, and was of course answered in the same tone by the British press. Indignation at Chamberlain's remarks also found expression in the Reichstag, and Count Bülow so far gave way to the Anglophobes as to criticize Mr. Chamberlain in the very strongest terms, whereupon Mr. Balfour retorted in equally strong language.

[1] von Eckardstein, *op. cit.* (German edition), vol. ii, pp. 159 *et seq.*

[2] *Ibid.* (English translation), p. 217.

[3] *Ibid.* (English translation), pp. 227 *et seq.*

On February 8, 1902, von Eckardstein reports that he attended a large official dinner at which Joseph Chamberlain and Paul Cambon, the French ambassador to the Court of St. James, had a long conversation during which Eckardstein overheard the words " Morocco " and " Egypt ". As soon as Chamberlain and Cambon had finished their talk, Eckardstein engaged Chamberlain in conversation, and the latter complained bitterly of the bad behavior of the German press toward England and himself. He also referred to von Bülow's speech in the Reichstag and said: " It is not the first time that Count Bülow has thrown me over in the Reichstag " (referring to Bülow's public repudiation of the offer of alliance made in Chamberlain's Leicester speech of November 30, 1899 — Eckardstein). " Now I have had enough of such treatment and there can be no more question of an association between Great Britain and Germany."

After the end of the Boer War in 1902, the Boer generals, Botha, Delarey and DeWet, went to London to try to obtain alleviation of the peace conditions. " From London," says Eckardstein, " they went on to Amsterdam and thence to Berlin. In an appeal addressed to the civilized world, asking for relief for distressed Boers, they had greatly irritated the political circles and public opinion of England. But the Berlin Boer Relief Association proceeded to get up a press campaign for their reception by the Kaiser; the German Anglophobes generally did their best to convert the visit of the Boer generals to Berlin into a great anti-English demonstration." [1]

The Pan-German League tendered the generals a large banquet in Berlin and was almost savage in its abuse of the Kaiser for refusing to receive them. As a matter of fact, Eckardstein reports that it was only with the greatest diffi-

---

[1] Eckardstein (English translation), pp. 235 *et seq.*

culty that the Kaiser was restrained from a meeting with the generals, which would have been most embarrassing to England. This narrowly averted affront aggravated the displeasure felt by Downing Street toward the *Wilhelmstrasse;* and added to all this was a distrust of German policy because of its wavering, zigzag course. "They (the German government) didn't know what they wanted," said Chamberlain to Eckardstein in September, 1902, " and therefore they couldn't be trusted." [1]   Ironically, it was the consequences of this very uncertain and zigzag policy of the German government that the Pan-German League itself feared most.

The indirect influence of the League was probably larger than its direct importance. It characterized itself as a pioneer, a ground-breaker for the other nationalist societies in Germany, dealing with more specific issues. The catch phrase " Pan-German " has been used to cover the agitation of all the German patriotic societies, the Navy League, the National Security League, the societies to care for Germans outside of Germany, schools, language, colonies—all the innumerable German nationalist organizations.[2]   Smaller than its sister associations and, because of its indefinite constitution, unlimited in its field of action, the work of the League represented a rather thin veneer on the nationalist movement in Germany. Because of the vigor with which the League's agitation was conducted, the name *Alldeutsch* came to be applied to the entire German chauvinist movement, and thus we seem to have the phenomenon of the tail wagging the dog. It was not strong enough, however, before the war to do more than lend its name to the dog and infect his subconscious mind.

[1] *Ibid.,* p. 239.

[2] See appendix number 2 for list of such organizations compiled by the Pan-German League.

What was the organization that gave forth such high-sounding aims; who were its members; how numerous were they; what was its financial status? It is questions of this sort that the present study has attempted to answer and the results of our research have brought out the following facts:

The number of members of the League was relatively small, and when measured by the talk about " Pan-Germanism ", " Pan-German plots ", " Pan-German schemes ", etc., seems almost laughably insignificant. Because of the fact that the members belonged to the more or less educated classes, their organization had an importance somewhat out of proportion to the actual size of its membership. Even in the rising tide of German nationalism, however, these pioneers were sneered at by most of their own compatriots as a small and uninfluential group of fanatics.

The survey of the financial history of the Pan-German League has served to show that the League was at no time in possession of any very large sums of money. Neither the actual running expenses nor the *Wehrschatz* were large enough to allow the League much freedom of action. Taken as lump sums they may seem fairly large, but considered as they must be over a term of years, they are relatively trifling. On the other hand, the League was able to raise a good deal of money for specific causes and in aid of individuals, all of which, no doubt, gave it a good deal of advertising. But it costs a great deal of money to spread propaganda broadcast and support movements of any sort, and obviously the League did not possess any really large resources. Nor can any connection be found before the war between the League and big business. Rather, the financial survey bears out the conclusions reached concerning the membership of the League and the walks of life represented. The distinctly human touches concerning the various uses to which League money was put and some of the rather naïve contributions of Dr. Hasse especially, add a homely flavor to the Legaue's work. One can not but think of the organization as a small intensely sincere band of evangelists, bent on reforming the world according to their own doctrines, and in their own way, and willing to make some financial sacrifice to spread their gospel. The fact that these doctrines though preached by a relatively small number of persons, were thought of by people outside Germany as representative of the views of a large section of the German people, made them dangerous. —not intrinsically but in their ultimate effect. Thus the Leaguers, sincere as they were, were playing with fire.

The survey of the whereabouts of the material concerning the Pan-German League or issued by it shows that the statements about the " masses of Pan-German propaganda " and the " millions of pamphlets scattered broadcast by the League " are mere fairy tales. The number of subscribers to the *Alldeutsche Blätter* and the figures showing the amount of mail which passed through the main office in Berlin go to bear this out, and one cannot but marvel that such a small organization could have acquired such a mighty reputation.

And finally, that the great " Pan-German plan ", by which it was plotted that the meshes of German influence should be spread from Hamburg to the Persian Gulf, was initiated or received support from the Pan-German League is totally unsupported by any evidence.[1] Though the Pan-German League was interested in the Bagdad Railway as it was in all German expansionist schemes, it was much more inter-

---

[1] Dr. von Gwinner of the *Deutsche Bank,* made the statment to Professor E. M. Earle, the author of *Turkey, the Great Powers and of the Bagdad Railway* (New York, 1923), that any interest which was shown by German chauvinists in the Bagdad Railway greatly incensed the backers of the *Bahn.*

ested in German African affairs and especially in Morocco, and expended its energies in agitation in that field.

The Kaiser had no connection with the League, and except as a symbol of the monarchic principle in which it firmly believed, the League had no regard for the Kaiser. Nor did the League have any connection with the German government. No documentary proof has come to light that the government ever made use of the League, except as it used any political agency which supported its policies. And the governmental policies which met with the approval of the League and were supported by it were the exception, not the rule. There was no such thing as a great " Pan-German plot ".

The distinguished Russian diplomat, Baron Rosen, says in his memoirs : [1]

Of infinitely wider scope and immeasurably greater importance was Pan-Slavism's counterpart—Pan-Germanism—not only as a political doctrine professed by a limited circle of militant intellectuals and professional militarists, but as a deep-seated race consciousness permeating the whole nation. Strangely enough, this extravagantly exaggerated race feeling was vouchsafed a semblance of justification in the writings of two foreigners, one French and the other English, who both proclaimed the superiority of the Germanic race over all others: The Comte de Gobineau, in his *Essai sur l'inégalité des races humaines* (1853-55) . . . . and Mr. Houston Stewart Chamberlain, in his remarkable book (*Die Grundlagen des neunzehnten Jahrhunderts*) . . . . (The latter) may have contributed to the development of that particular disease of " swelled head " with which the German people have been afflicted ever since the victories achieved in the Franco-Prussian War which has brought down upon it the dislike and ill-will of all nations, and which has tempted its leaders to risk the adventure of a

[1] Baron Rosen, *Forty Years of Diplomacy* (New York, 1922), vol. ii, pp. 156 *et seq.*

general European war destined to end in Germany's downfall and ruin.

There is no doubt but that Baron Rosen's characterization is fairly typical of a large part of non-German opinion of Germany throughout the world. Certainly the ideas which are described were part of the League's philosophy. But it is implied that only the Germans felt such a deep-seated consciousness of race; the world forgets that other races too have felt a consciousness of superiority over their brothers and that almost every country has its prophets who proclaim that theirs is the chosen and superior people. Our task has been to study the German manifestation of the phenomenon, which assumed there a particularly virulent form.

Almost every country has its Navy League, Security League, Agrarian League, under one name or another, and each society works for the aggrandisement of its own nation, attempting as far as possible to influence its government. Each in its way adds fuel to the flame of intense nationalism at home and selfish intolerance of other people abroad. Somewhere a conflict of interests is bound to occur and war has been the inevitable consequence.

It does not seem quite fair to characterize German chauvinism as a whole as "Pan-Germanism" and consider it as something peculiar to Germany alone. However, the Pan-German League itself was doubtless one of the most strident jingo societies in the world and its noise was quite incommensurate with its size. It is notorious for its views on foreign policy and here it might be compared with jingo societies in other lands. But it is also notorious for its strictly " Pan-German " doctrines, the so-called union of all the Germans in the world. In the latter field, it differs a bit from kindred hundred-per-cent organizations in other countries and shows the philosophical trend that is supposed to be typical of the German mind. Even in this field, however, the size and resources of the League must be taken into consideration. But the influence of the League on German chauvinism as a whole was distinctly bad and tended to introduce an aggressively egotistical note that has acquired for German chauvinism such an unpleasant reputation.

On the whole, the Pan-German League is an excellent example of the type of nationalist association which has done much to develop the spirit of intolerant nationalism in the world today. It is this spirit which makes infinitely more dangerous the " international anarchy " of our day.

BIBLIOGRAPHY [1]

I. Publications of the Pan-German League and documents issued or distributed under its auspices.

Flugschriften des alldeutschen Verbandes.[2]

(1) Heyck, Edward, *Die geschichtliche Berechtigung des deutschen Nationalbewusstseins.* Munich, 1897, 20p. N. A short, historical survey of the development of German nationalism; reprint of a speech made at the League convention in Berlin, 1896.

(2) *Alldeutscher Verband* (editor), *Deutschlands Ansprüche an das Türkische Erbe.* Munich, 1896, 16p., C. See *supra*, p. 170 of the text for description.

(3) Prade, Heinrich, *Die Behandlung der nationalen Minderheiten und die Lage des Deutschtums in Böhmen.* Munich, 1896, 16p. M., C. Reprint of a speech made in the Austrian *Abgeordnetenhaus,* October 5, 1896, asking for specially favorable treatment of Germans in the Dual Monarchy and protection against aggression of Austro-Hungarian racial minorities.

(4) *Genügt Deutschlands Wehrkraft zur See? Ein Mahnruf.* Munich, 1897, 24p., M., C. A plea for the increase of the German navy to protect the German coast and adequately guard her colonies, overseas commerce and interests.

(5) Hasse, Ernst, *Deutsche Weltpolitik.* Munich, 1897, 16p., C. Reprint of a speech made by Dr. Hasse at Barmen. It is a strong plea for Germany to engage in *Weltpolitik* and for the flag to follow the trader.

(6) Weyer, Bruno, *Deutschlands Seegefahren. Der Verfall der deutschen Flotte und ihr geplanter Wiederaufbau.* Munich, 1898, 60p., M., C. A short survey of German naval history and a plea for the immediate strengthening of the German navy with invidious comparisons between the naval strength of Germany and of other powers.

---

[1] The following abbreviations have been used in designating the places where various publications may be found: B. *Preussische Staatsbibliothek,* Berlin, Germany; C. Columbia University Library, New York City; M. *Mainz Stadtbibliothek,* Mainz, Germany; N. New York Public Library.

[2] The numbers have been used by the Pan-German League in designating its pamphlets.

(7) Werner, Reinhold, *Die deutsche Flotte*. Munich, 1898, 20p., C. Reprint of a lecture delivered by Rear Admiral Werner before many of the local branches of the Pan-German League, exhorting the members to work for the enlargement of the German navy.

(8) Grell Hugo, *Der alldeutsche Verband, seine Geschichte, seine Bestrebungen und Erfolge*. Munich, 1898, 25p., M., N. A description of the early history and aims of the Pan-German League.

(9) Bassenge, Dr. Edmund, *Deutschlands Weltstellung und die nächsten Aufgaben deutscher Politik*. Munich, 1899, 15p., C. Reprint of a lecture delivered before the Dresden local branch of the League. The speaker iterated the League's aims and stressed Germany's need of sea-power and colonies.

(10) Lehr, Adolf, *Warum die deutsche Flotte vergrössert werden muss*. Munich, 1899, 16p., M., C. Reprint of a speech made at the League's convention in Hamburg.

(11) Reismann-Grone, *Die slawische Gefahr in der Ostmark*. Munich, 1899, 16p., M., N. Reprint of a speech made at a League convention in Hamburg. It deals with the immigration of Poles into eastern Germany and the desirability of eventually stopping all such immigration entirely.

(12) Reismann-Grone, *Die deutschen Reichshäfen und das Zollbündnis mit den Niederlanden*. Munich, 1899, 20p., M., C. Reprint of a speech made at a League convention in Hamburg, urging that Germany eventually effect a custom's union with Holland and Belgium, but that in the meantime as much German commerce as possible be directed to Germany's ports.

(13) Schultheiss, Dr. F. Guntram, *Alldeutschland an der Jahrhundertwende (1800-1900)*, Munich, 1900, 48p., C. Reprint of a speech made at a meeting of the Stuttgart local branch of the League, giving a patriotic survey of German history during the nineteenth century and ending with an explanation of *Alldeutschland* and a hope for its success.

(14) *Kundgebungen, Beschlüsse und Förderungen des alldeutschen Verbandes, 1890-1902*. Munich, 1902, 131p., M., C. A compilation of the resolutions, decrees and demands of the League passed by its executive branches and annual conventions and for the most part reprinted from the *Alldeutsche Blätter*. A list with dates and places of meetings of the executive council, business managing committee and League conventions is appended.

(15) Winterstein, Dr. jur. Franz, *Kleindeutschland, ein Kehrbild*. Munich, 1903, 12p., N. A map in the forepart of this pamphlet showing the menace to Germany of her enemy neighbors and the section of her territory that each has his eye on, epitomizes the content of the whole.

(16) Class, Heinrich, *Die Bilanz des neuen Kurses.* Berlin, 1903, 42p., N., M., C. See *supra,* p. 164 for summary.

(17) Class, Heinrich, *Marokko Verloren?* Munich, 1904, 16p., C. See *supra,* p. 169 of the text for a résumé of this pamphlet.

(18) Pfeil, Dr. Joachim Graf von, *Warum brauchen wir Marokko?* Munich. (Not available).

(19) Zieher, Dr. Julius, *Über Volkserziehung im nationalen Sinn.* Munich, 1904, 23p., C., N. Reprint of a speech made at the League convention in Lübeck.

(20) Von Liebert, E., *Nationale Forderungen und Pflichten.* Munich, 1905, 22p., C., N. General von Liebert bewails the fact that the German people are not possessed of as much national pride and patriotic feeling as other nations. He makes an ardent plea for navy, army and colonies.

(21) Pfeil, Dr. Joachim Graf von, *Deutsch-Südwest Afrika jetzt und später,* Munich, 1905, 16p., C., M. The pamphlet paints a dreary picture of German Southwest Africa and suggests a military and settlement program for its development.

(22) Reismann-Grone and von Liebert, E., *Überseepolitik oder Festlandspolitik?* Munich, 1905, 24p., M., N. Reprint of speeches made at the League convention in Worms.

(23) Kuhlenbeck, Prof. Dr. L., *Rasse und Volkstum,* Munich, 1905, 32p., N. Reprint of a speech made at the League convention in Worms.

(24) Hensing, Karl, *Die Ausländerfrage an den deutschen Hochschulen.* Munich, 1905, 12p., M. Reprint of a speech made at the League convention in Worms.

(25) Geiser, Alfred, *Die russische Revolution und das baltische Deutschtum.* Munich, 1906, 20p., N. Reprint of a speech made at the extraordinary League convention in Leipzig in 1905.

(26) Faure, A., *Das Deutschtum in Süd-Russland und an der Wolga.* Munich. (Not available).

(27) Hötzsch, Otto, *Die dringendste Aufgabe der Polenpolitik.* Munich, 1907, 23p., C. Reprint of a speech made at the League convention in Wiesbaden.

(28) Klingemann, Sup't. C., *Grenzen alldeutscher Arbeit.* Mainz, 1910, 1910 40p., C. An explanation of the aims of the Pan-German League in working for *Deutschtum* on the frontiers of Germany. The pamphlet seems to have been written as a supplement to the appeal for funds for the *Alldeutscher Wehrschatz.* It is less extravagant in its expressions than most League publications.

(29) Class, Heinrich, *Westmarokko deutsch!* (with a map). Munich, 1911, 47p., C. See *supra,* p. 171 of the text.

(30) Regierungsrat Schöhl, *Die Polenfrage in Oberschlesien.* Mainz, 1911, 32p., C. Reprint of a speech made at the League convention in Düsseldorf.

(31) Hänsch, Dr. Felix, *Grundzüge deutscher Siedlungspolitik in den Kolonien.* Mainz, 1912, 47p., C. An elaboration of a speech made before the executive council of the League in Hanover.

(32) Bongartz, *Die Lage der Volkschule im Reichsland Elsass-Lothringen.* Leipzig, 1912, 48p., M. An historical description of the German schools in Alsace-Lorraine and a discussion of the teachers, their training and needs as well as the great part taken by the schools in building up *Deutschtum* in the *Reichsland.*

(33) Trautman, Dr. Moritz, *Die Fremdwörtersucht im geschäftlichen Leben und ihre Bekämpfung.* Mainz, 1912, 16p., C. Reprint of a speech made at the League convention in Erfurt.

Der Kampf um das Deutschtum [1]

(1) Bley, Fritz, *Die Weltstellung des Deutschtums.* Munich, 1897, 48p., N., C. A sort of "outline of history" from the Pan-German point of view, exhorting the German people to work and to take their rightful position in the world.

(2) Schultheiss, Dr. F. Guntram, *Deutschnationales Vereinswesen.* Munich, 1897, 82p., M., N., C. A description of the origin and work of many of the "nationalist" societies in Germany—religious, educational, commercial and whatnot.

(3) Petzel, Christian, *Die preussischen Ostmarken.* Munich, 1898, 72p. with a map. C., M., N. A description of the Prussian Eastern Marches from a Pan-German viewpoint, designed to awaken the German people to action to preserve *Deutschtum* in those parts.

(4) Pastor Jakobson, *Schleswig-Holstein.* Never published.

(5) Peterson, Dr. Julius, *Das Deutschtum in Elsass-Lothringen.* Munich, 1902, 138p. with a map, M., C., N. A scholarly appearing work with well-tabulated table of contents and a bibliography which gives the history of Alsace-Lorraine as viewed through Pan-German eyes.

(6) Türk, Karl, *Böhmen, Mähren und Schlesien,* Munich, 1898, 83p. with a map. M., N. An historical study of *Deutschtum* in the three provinces of Bohemia, Moravia and Silesia.

(7) Nabert, H., *Das Deutschtum in Tirol.* Munich, 1901, 128p., M., N. A detailed study of the subject including its ecclesiastical, educational, economic and geographic aspects.

(8) Wellenhof, Dr. P. Hoffmann, v., *Steiermark, Kärnten, Krain und Küstenland,* Munich, 1899, 104p., M., N. A study of *das Deutschtum* in the provinces of Austria-Hungary enumerated.

(9) Schultheiss, Dr. F. Guntram, *Deutschtum und Magyarisierung in Ungarn und Siebenbürgen.* Munich, 1898, 96p., N. An historical sketch of the Germans and Magyars in Hungary and Transylvania and their interrelations.

(10) Hunziker, Professor Dr. Otto, *Schweiz.* Munich, 1898, 72p., M., N. A history of *Deutschtum* in Switzerland.

[1] Edited by the Pan-German League.

(11) Bley, Fritz, *Die alldeutsche Bewegung und die Niederlande*. Munich, 1897, 72p., M., N. An emotional pamphlet describing the close ties binding the Netherlands and Germany. It is based upon the major premise that the Dutch are "low Germans"—"*Stammes-brüder*" of the Germans.

(12) Löwenthal, F. v., *Russland*. Never published.

(13) Unold, Dr. Johannes, *Das Deutschtum in Chile*. Munich, 1899, 68p., M., N. An historical sketch praising the German settlers in Chile.

(14) Sellin, *Brasilien und die La Plata-Staaten*. Never published.

(15) Wintzer, Dr. Wilhelm, *Die Deutschen in tropischen Amerika (Mexiko, Mittelamerika, Venezuela, Kolumbien, Ekuador, Peru und Bolivien)*. Munich, 1900, 82p., C., N. An historical survey of the German settlements in Mexico, Central America, Venezuela, Colombia, Ecuador, Peru and Bolivia.

(16) Goebel, Dr. Julius, *Das Deutschtum in den Vereinigten Staaten von Nord-Amerika*. Munich, 1904, 88p., N., M., C. Dedicated to "the historian of the American West, President Theodore Roosevelt, as a testimonial of German cooperation in the settlement and development of the United States," this pamphlet gives a brief historical survey of the work of the Germans in the United States. The author pleads for the preservation of the German language and customs in America.

(17) Bley, Fritz, *Südafrika nieder-deutsch*. Munich, 1898, 48p., C., M. A plea for German expansion in South Africa together with their "blood-brothers," the Boers.

(18) Neubaur, Dr., *Asien*. Never published.

(19) Jung, Dr. Emil, *Das Deutschtum in Australien und Ozeanien*. Munich, 1902, 86p., C., M., N. A description of *Deutschtum* in Australia and the South Seas and of that section of the earth as a field for German colonization.

OTHER PUBLICATIONS OF THE PAN-GERMAN LEAGUE

Alldeutsche Blätter, 1894-1918. Published weekly.

Der alldeutsche Verband im Jahre 1901. Berlin, 1901, 64p., M.

Ein Beitrag zur Beleuchtung der Flottenfrage. Reprint from the *Münchener Allgemeine Zeitung*, for the Pan-German League, Munich, 1899, 29p., M.

Beiträge zur Beleuchtung der Flottenfrage. Reprint from the *Münchener Allgemeine Zeitung, Munich, 1900*, 2nd Series. Wagner, Ad., *Von Territorialstaat zur Weltmacht*, 31p. Schulte, Aloys., *Deutschland und das Meer*, 17p. Meyer, George, v., *Flotte und Finanzen*, 8p. Sicherer, Hermann V., *Der neutrale Handel und die Flotte*, 7p. Hasse, Ernst, *Die natürliche Berechtigung Deutschlands zur Seegewalt*, 7p. M.

Beiträge zur Beleuchtung der Flottenfrage. Reprint from the *Münchener Allgemeine Zeitung*, Munich, 1900, 3rd Series. *Die See-Interessen Süddeutschlands*, 14p., M.

Beiträge zur Beleuchtung der Flottenfrage. Reprint from the *Münchener Allgemeine Zeitung,* Munich, 1900. Schäfer, Dietrich, *Was haben wir aus dem Untergang der Hansa zu lernen?* 10p. Francke, Ernst, *Die deutsche Kriegsflotte und die Arbeiter-Interessen,* 8p. Lexis, W., *Die Zukunft Hollands und seiner Kolonien,* 8p. Neumayer, G., *Die Kriegsflotten und die wissenschaftliche Forschung,* 8p. v. Saur, *Militärische Betrachtungen über die Flottenfrage,* 12p., M.

Beiträge zur Beleuchtung der Flottenfrage. Reprnt from the *Münchener Allgemeine Zeitung,* Munich, 1901, 5th Series. Stavenhagen, W., *Neben die englische Flotte,* 9p. Hasse, Ernst, *Der Handel des deutschen Reichs mit seinen Kolonien und mit fremden Kolonien,* 8p. Michael, Wolfgang, *Englands Flottenpolitik unter der Republik und der Untergang Hollands,* 8p. Montgelas, Max, *Die deutsche Flotte als Theil der deutschen Wehrmacht,* 19p. Peez, Alexander v., *Wie verlor Süddeutschland seinen Antheil am Welthandel?* 7p. Brandt, M. von., *Die Entwicklung der Dinge im fernen Osten und die Wahrung der deutschen Interessen,* 6p. *Ein Beitrag zu den Erörterungen über Bayerns See-Interessen,* 5p. *Die See-Interessen Mittelfrankens,* 3p. *Die See-Interessen Schwabens,* 2p., M.

Bonhard, Otto, *Geschichte des alldeutschen Verbandes,* Leipzig, Berlin, 1920. Recommended to the writer by the Pan-German League as its official history.

Bonhard, Philipp, *Denkschrift betrefend die innerpolitische Tätigkeit des alldeutschen Verbandes,* Berlin, 1902, 28p., M. An appeal for non-partisanship in the Pan-German League and the need of unity among the parties of the right against the Social Democrats, the Center and the Liberal party.

Calmbach, Heinrich, *Alldeutscher Katechismus.* Mainz, 1911, 84p., C.

Class, Heinrich, *Zwanzig Jahre alldeutscher Arbeit und Kämpfe.* Leipzig, 1910, 467p., M., C.

Diederichs, August (editor), *Satzungen der Diederichsstiftung des alldeutschen Verbandes (mit Vor- und Zubemerkungen versehen und zum besten eines vaterländischen Zweckes),* Leipzig, 1903, 24p., M.

Fick, A., *Zwanzig Jahre alldeutscher Arbeit.* Zürich, 1911, 8p., M.

Gauverband Berg und Mark des alldeutschen Verbandes (publisher), *Wo liegt das Sedan der Zukunft?* Elberfeld, 1899, 1p., M.

Grosse, Friedrich, *Deutsche Ziele. Vortrag zur Gründung der Ortsgruppe New York des alldeutschen Verbandes, 25 März, 1906,* Gräfenhainschen, 15p., N.

Handbuch des alldeutschen Verbandes. Munich, 1905 (B.) ; 1906 (N.) ; 1908 (N.) ; 1914 (C.) ; 1916 (Bonn, N.) ; 1917 (C.) ; 1918 (C.)

Hasse, Ernst, *Die bisherigen Ergebnisse deutscher Kolonialpolitik,* 1902. Speech made at League convention in Eisenach, May, 1902.

Hauptleitung des alldeutschen Verbandes (editors) *Der alldeutsche Verband. Eine Aufklärungsschrift*, Mainz, 1916, 15p., M.

Jahresbericht der Ortsgruppe Leipzig des alldeutschen Verbandes über das Jahr 1900, Leipzig, 1900, M.

Jahresbericht der Ortsgruppe Lübeck des alldeutschen Verbandes, Lübeck, 1902-1903, M.

Langhans, Paul (editor), *Alldeutscher Atlas*, Gotha, 1900, N.

Mitteilungen des allgemeinen deutschen Verbandes, 1891, 1892, 1893. Issued irregularly during this period, B.

Die nationalpolitischen Forderungen der deutschen opposition-Parteien in oesterreichischen Abgeordnetenhause. Das Linzer Programm. Berlin, 1899. Special supplement to the *Alldeutsche Blätter* of June 4, 1899, M.

Schönerer, Georg, *Rede gehalten in der zur Erinnerung an den denkwürdigen deutschen Volkstag vom 1 Juli 1897 am Sonntag den 10 Juli 1904 zu Eger stattgehalten alldeutschen Versammlung*, Rosenau, 1904, 44p., M.

Was errettet uns aus der Kolonialmüdigkeit? Bericht über die Seitens der Ortgruppe Berlin des alldeutschen Verbandes zu Berlin veranstaltete Versammlung, Berlin, 1904, 28., M.

Zur Flottenfrage—Die Reden der Bevollmächtigten zum Bundesrat gelegentlich der ersten Lesung des Etats im Deutschen Reichstage, Berlin, 1899, 39p., M. Reprint made by the Pan-German League.

SOURCE MATERIAL FOR THE PERIOD 1890–1914

HANDBOOKS, MANUALS, Etc.

Allgemeine deutsche Biographie.

Annual Register.

Dietrich, *Bibliographie der deutschen Zeitschriften-Literatur.*

Encyclopedia Americana, 1920 edition.

Encyclopedia Britannica, 11th edition, 1910-1911.

Der europäische Geschichtskalender.

Kürschners deutscher Reichstag, 1912-1917, Berlin and Leipzig.

Meyers, *Kleiner Handatlas*, Leipzig, 1921.

Meyers, *Konversations Lexikon.*

Murray's *New English Dictionary.*

Schmoller's Jahrbuch.

Statesman's Year Book.

Wer Ist's?

DOCUMENTS AND OFFICIAL RECORDS

Die grosse Politik der europäischen Kabinette, 1871-1914. Edited by Lepsius, Mendelssohn-Bartholdy, Thimme. Commissioned by the German Foreign Office, 6v., Berlin, 1922.

Stenographische Berichte über die Verhandlungen des Deutschen Reichstags.
Stenographische Protokollen des Hauses der Abgeordneten des Reichsraths.

NEWSPAPERS AND PERIODICALS

American Academy of Political and Social Science, *Annals.*
Berliner Neueste Nachrichten.
Berliner Tageblatt.
Burschenschaftliche Blätter.
Deutsche Zeitung.
Deutsche Tageszeitung.
Frankfurter Zeitung.
Hamburger Nachrichten.
Heimdahl, Zeitschrift für reines Deutschtum und All-Deutschtum.
Kölnische Volkszeitung.
Kölnische Zeitung.
Leipziger Neueste Nachrichten.
Die Neue Zeit.
Norddeutsche Allgemeine Zeitung.
Die Post.
Preussische Jahrbücher.
Der Reichsbote.
Rheinisch-Westfälische Zeitung.
Staatsbürger Zeitung.
Der Tag (Berlin).
Tägliche Rundschau.
Vossische Zeitung.
Die Zeit (Vienna).

MEMOIRS AND WORKS BASED ON PERSONAL RECOLLECTIONS OR OFFICIAL DOCUMENTS [1]

von Bethmann Hollweg, Th., *Betrachtungen zum Weltkriege* (part 1.—before the war), Berlin, 1919.
Bismarck, Fürst Otto von, *Erinnerung und Gedanke*, Stuttgart and Berlin, 1919. Vol. 3 of Bismarck, *Gedanken und Erinnerungen*, Stuttgart, 1898-1922.
Bülow, Fürst von, *Deutsche Politik*, Berlin, 1917. (English translation as *Imperial Germany*, London, 1914).
The Disclosures from Germany. I. The Lichnowsky Memorandum. The Reply of Herr von Jagow. II. Memoranda and Letters of Dr. Muchlon, New York, 1918.
v. Eckardstein, *Lebenserinnerungen und Politische Denkwürdigkeiten*, 3v., Leipzig, 1919. (English translation and arrangement by Prof.

[1] Translations have been compared with the original wherever possible.

Geo. Young as *Ten Years at the Court of St. James*, New York, 1922.)

Hammann, Otto, *Der neue Kurs, Erinnerungen*, Berlin, 1918.

Hammann, Otto, *Zur Vorgeschichte des Weltkrieges; Erinnerungen aus den Jahren 1897-1906*, Berlin, 1919.

Helfferich, Karl, *Die Vorgeschichte des Weltkrieges*, Berlin, 1919.

v. Hindenburg, *Out of My Life*. (English translation by F. A. Holt), London, New York, Toronto and Melbourne, 1920.

von Jagow, G., *Ursachen und Ausbruch des Weltkrieges*, Berlin, 1919.

The Kaiser's Letters to the Tsar, edited by N. F. Grant, London, 1920.

Kautsky, Karl, *The Guilt of William Hohenzollern*, London, 1920.

The Memoirs of the Crown Prince of Germany, London, 1922.

Rosen, Baron, *Forty Years of Diplomacy*, New York, 1922, 2v.

von Schoen, *The Memoirs of an Ambassador*. (English translation by Constance Vesey), London, 1922.

von Tirpitz, Alfred, *Erinnerungen*, Leipzig, 1919. (English translation in 2v. New York, 1919.)

Wilhelm II, *The Kaiser's Memoirs*. (English translation by T. R. Ybarra), New York and London, 1922.

Secondary Sources

Andler, Charles, *Collection de Documents sur le Pan Germanisme*, 4v., Paris, 1915, 1916, 1917.

Bornhak, Conrad, *Deutsche Geschichte unter Kaiser Wilhelm II*, Leipzig, 1921.

Busch, Dr. Moritz, *Bismarck. Some Secret Pages of his History*, 2v., New York and London, 1898.

Chamberlain, Houston Stewart, *Die Grundlagen des neunzehnten Jahrhunderts*, Munich, 1901.

Chéradame, André, *The Pan-German Plot Unmasked*, New York, 1917; *The United States and Pan-Germania*, New York, 1918.

Dawson, W. H., *The German Empire 1867-1914*, 2v., London, 1919.

Dewey, John, *German Philosophy and Politics*, New York, 1915.

Dunning, W. A., *A History of Political Theories from Rousseau to Spencer*, New York, 1920.

Earle, Edward Mead, *Turkey, the Great Powers and the Bagdad Railway*, New York, 1923.

Einhart (Heinrich Class), *Deutsche Geschichte*, Leipzig, 1910.

Fuller, Joseph Vincent, *Bismarck's Diplomacy at its Zenith*, Cambridge (Mass.), 1922.

Gauss, Christian, *The German Emperor as shown in his Public Utterances*, New York, 1915.

Gobineau, Count Arthur de, *The Inequality of the Human Races* (translated by Adrian Collins), New York, 1915.

Gooch, G. P., *Nationalism,* London and New York, 1920.

Grundzweig, Armand, *Activism in Belgium.* Manuscript thesis for the
    M. A. degree, Columbia University, 1922.

Guilland, Anton, *Modern Germany and her Historians,* London, 1915.

Hammann, Otto, *Der misverstandne Bismarck. Zwanzig Jahre deutscher
    Weltpolitik,* Berlin, 1921.

[Harrison, Austin], *The Pan-Germanic Doctrine,* London and New York,
    1904.

Hasse, Ernst, *Ein Besuch bei dem Fürsten Bismarck in Friedrichsruh,*
    1894, M.

Hasse, Ernst, *Deutsche Politik,* Munich, 1905-1906, 3v. I. *Das deutsche
    Reich als Nationalstaat.* II. *Die Besiedelung des deutschen Volks-
    boden.* III. *Deutsche Grenzpolitik.*

Hasse, Ernst, *Nachrichten über die Familie Hasse und einige verwandte
    Familien,* Leipzig, 1903, M.

Hayes, Carlton, J. H., *A Brief History of the Great War,* New
    York, 1921.

Hayes, Carlton, J. H., *A Political and Social History of Modern
    Europe,* 2v., New York, 1916.

Hayes, Carlton, J. H., *Sources of the Germanic Invasions,* New York,
    1909.

Hegel, Georg W. F., *Grundlinien der Philosophie des Rechts,* vols. 8-9,
    2nd edition, Berlin, 1840.

Hertslet, Sir Edward, *The Map of Africa by Treaty,* 3v., London, 1909.

Hertslet, Sir Edward, *The Map of Europe by Treaty,* 4v., London, 1891.

Hobohm, Martin, *Vaterlandspolitik,* Berlin, 1918.

Hübbe-Schleiden, Wilhelm, *Deutsche Colonisation,* Hamburg, 1881.

Morley, Viscount John, *Politics and History,* New York, 1914.

Nippold, Dr. Otfried, *Der deutsche Chauvinismus,* Berne, 1917.

Penzler, Johannes, *Fürst Bismarck nach seiner Entlassung,* 7v. in 4,
    Leipzig, 1897.

Reichstagwahl 1898. Hasse als Politiker. Leipzig, 1898.

Reventlow, Graf Ernst zu, *Deutschland's auswärtige Politik, 1888-1914,*
    Berlin, 1916.

Rohrbach, Paul, *Die alldeutsche Gefahr,* Berlin, 1918.

Rohrbach, Paul, *Deutschland unter den Weltvölkern,* Stuttgart, 1921.

Schemann, Ludwig, *Gobineau, eine Biographie,* 2v., Strasburg, 1916.

Stocks, J. L., *Patriotism and the Super-State,* London and New York,
    1920.

Townsend, Mary E., *Origins of Modern German Colonialism, 1871-1885,*
    New York, 1921.

Veblen, Thorstein, *An Inquiry Into the Nature of Peace,* New York
    and London, 1917.

Wenck, Martin, *Alldeutsche Taktik,* Jena, 1917.

APPENDIX I

The Constitution of the Pan-German League

I PURPOSE

1. The Pan-German League strives to quicken the national sentiment of Germans and in particular to awaken and foster the racial and cultural homogeneity (*Zusammengehörigkeit*) of all sections of the German people.

2. These aims imply that the Pan-German League works for:

1. Preservation of the German *Volkstum* in Europe and oversea and its support whenever it is threatened;
2. Settlement of all cultural, educational and school problems in ways that shall aid the German *Volkstum*;
3. The combating of all forces which check the German national development;
4. An active policy of furthering German interests in the entire world, in particular continuance of the German colonial movement to practical results.

3. The League pursues its aims through:

a. Club activities along those lines provided for in its constitution. In countries outside of Germany the members may work under different plans and for special ends, but only with the approval of the League's executive.

b. The publication of a periodical, the *Alldeutsche Blätter*.

II MEMBERSHIP

4. Every German may become a member of the League without regard to his citizenship, if he is in accord with the purposes of the League.

5. Every member must pay one mark to the League treasury when he joins. The annual dues shall be at least two marks.

A minimum payment of 100 marks is required to become a life member.

6. Clubs of Germans may become members of the League as units. The conditions of their joining must be acceptable to the executive committee of the League.

7. Anyone who has done especially meritorious work either in the service of the League or of *Deutschtum,* may be elected to honorary membership.[1]   Honorary members are not required to pay dues.

8. Members receiving the *Alldeutsche Blätter* pay an extra fee.

9. Contributions and dues are payable in the first quarter of each year to the League treasury.

10. Resignation from the League and the stopping of subscriptions to the *Alldeutsche Blätter* must be in writing.   Resignations take effect at the expiration of the year in which they are made.

11. Members who act contrary to the ideals of the League may be forced to resign.

12. Members whose dues are more than a year in arrears lose their right to vote until they have paid up.

III ORGANIZATION

13. The seat of the League is Berlin.

14. The League is formed of local branches of at least ten members.

15. Several local branches may band together in a district organization.

16. In communities where there are no local branches, the executive committee of the League may name agents who are subject to recall.   Appointment and recall must be in writing.

17. The local branches and district organizations elect their own officers and make their own constitutions.

18. The business of the local branches and district organizations is to provide for local needs of *Deutschtum.* In particular, they must see to it that there is discussion as often as

---

[1] Bismarck, Karl Peters and Ernst Hasse received this honor.

possible of questions of the day important to Pan-Germans (*Alldeutsche*), and that resolutions giving the judgment and position of the League on these questions are drawn up. The local branches and agents are authorized to make recommendations to the council and committee of the League. Such recommendations must be taken up at the next executive committee meeting if they have been received by the central office at least ten days before the meeting.

19. The business of the district organizations is also to make easier the recruiting of members by the local branches by means of joint arrangements.

20. The local branches and district organizations must promptly inform the executive committee of the League concerning their constitutions, elections and expressions of opinion. The constitution is valid only after it has been approved by the executive committee of the League.

21. The local branches, district organizations and agents must present a report each March of activities of the preceding year. This report must contain the number of members, the state of the treasury and the activities for the League.

22. The local branches are responsible for the minimum dues for each member being promptly turned into the League's treasury. Contributions of members of long standing are to be halved with the League treasury. The local branch has complete control over the remainder of the cash. In case of the dissolution of a local branch, whatever cash is on hand goes to the League treasury.

23. The agents are responsible for the prompt payment of dues to the League treasury by members in their territory. They must turn in the contributions of life-long members uncurtailed. Where the agent's expenditures for their territories, other than those for the distribution of the *Alldeutsche Blätter*, grow in size, the officers of the League may at their (the agents') proposal, raise the membership dues for that territory to three marks. In so far as the annual contributions of members of the territory exceed two marks they remain at the service of the agent.

IV DIRECTION (*Leitung*)

24. The fiscal year of the League is the calendar year.

25. The League shall be directed by the executive council (*Vorstand*), the business managing committee (*Geschäftsfuhrende Ausschuss*), the executive committee (*Hauptleitung*) and the convention (*Verbandstag*).

26. The executive council consists of:

The honorary members.

The members of the executive committee.

The members of the business managing committee.

The presidents of all the district organizations.

The presidents of all local branches.

The local agents.

Members at large elected as per paragraph 27.

Representatives of the local branches as per paragraph 28.

Members who resign from the executive committee or the business managing committee remain members of the executive council for the following three years.

27. The executive council elects its permanent members up to the number of one hundred.

The term of office of those elected begins with the acceptance of the election and continues for three full fiscal years, the actual work starting with the beginning of the fiscal year following the election. Outgoing members are eligible for reelection.

28. Local branches having more than one hundred members, have the right to elect one representative on the executive council for each one hundred members. The number of members shall be determined from the number of dues paid into the central treasury before the date fixed by the constitution. The responsibility for electing their representatives either through general meetings of their membership or through their own executive committees devolves upon the individual local branches. The representatives require written power of attorney. This is valid for only one main meeting.[1]

---

[1] In a meeting of the executive committee one person may not exercise the right of casting several votes, but may cast only his own vote. (Ruling made by business managing committee, Feb. 8, 1908, Berlin).

29. The executive council annually elects twenty of its members to the business managing committee for the following fiscal year. The members of the executive committee and specially elected representatives further comprise this business managing committee. The committee can elect to itself:

a. The directing officers of the League for their entire term of office (*Tätigkeit*).

b. Several members of the executive committee for special subcommittees.

30. The executive council elects the executive committee from its own members every three years; not less than three nor more than six members shall comprise the committee; among these are a president and a vice-president. Their term of office begins with the acceptance of the election and continues to a new election.

31. The president represents the League legally and otherwise. He calls the business managing committee together in the name of the executive committee and arranges meetings of the council and the League conventions. He directs their procedure and carries out their decisions. He superintends the activities of all the League's officers and gives them their instructions, and the under officials are employed and dismissed by him.

32. The executive committee has its seat in Berlin or one of the suburbs.

It supports the president in the management of the League and prepares work for the committees, for the council and for the League's convention and decides on the agenda.

It chooses and dismisses the local agents of the League.

All reports, opinions, and proposals of the local branches, district organizations and local agents must be sent to the executive committee.

33. The business managing committee directs all the affairs of the League.

It oversees the activities of the executive committee including the president.

It chooses and dismisses the following officials of the League:

    a. The editor of the *Alldeutsche Blätter.*

    b. The business manager or managers.

    c. The clerical force.

It passes upon complaints of the League's officers about the instructions of the president.

It attends to reports, expressions of opinion and requests from the local branches and district organizations about the admissibility of their constitutions.

It governs the affairs of groups of members not Germans and decides upon the conditions for clubs of entrance into the League.

34. It is the duty of the business managing committee to urge the local branches and district organizations to the discussion of important problems and give them any support they may need.

Under pressing circumstances, the president may undertake this task.

35. Meetings of this committee are to be called when the situation warrants such action or when five of its members ask the executive committee to call such a meeting.

36. The council decides the policy of the League in all fundamental questions.

It receives the report of business on hand from the business managing committee and divides the discharging of the work between this committee and the executive committee.

It decides difficulties over refusals to do certain things and concerning exclusion of members by the local branches or the business managing committee.

Exclusion from a local branch is followed by exclusion from the League if the council confirms the decision.

Decisions are made by a simple plurality of those voting.

37. The council makes decisions by a two-thirds vote on questions concerning

    a. The bestowal of honorary membership.

    b. Change in the constitution.

c. Dissolution of local branches and district organizations whose activities are counter to the aims of the League or endanger its existence.

38. Suggestions concerning the policies of the council upon which a vote is to be taken must be sent in in writing at least ten days before the matter comes up for consideration.

Communications that are not received in time will be reconsidered only if they are sent in again.

39. The council must meet twice a year. It must be called together within four weeks, if the business managing committee requests it or if ten local branches or twenty members of the council ask for a meeting for a special purpose.

Members are notified of the meetings of the council three weeks in advance, in writing, and the agenda is announced at the same time.

40. League conventions [1] receive a report of the council concerning the business managing committee. This has to do with those matters which cannot be dissociated from the great goals of the League. Decisions are made by a simple plurality vote.

41. Upon motion of the council, the League convention may vote the dissolution of the League by a two-thirds vote. It must be decided at once how the property of the League is to be disposed of.

42. All members may vote who can identify themselves before the meeting by a membership card or a receipt for their last year's dues.

43. A League convention must meet every three years. Simultaneously with a regular convention, a meeting of the executive council must be held. The constitutional elections are on the agenda of this meeting.

44. An extraordinary convention of the League may be called either by the business managing committee or by the executive council.

45. League conventions may be called by announcements in

---

[1] *Verbandstage.*

three issues of the *Alldeutsche Blätter*. The first announcement must be made at least three months in advance.

The agenda is to be announced at the same time. Suggestions concerning matters not on the agenda must be sent in writing to the executive committee by at most a month after the first announcement has been made of the convention. Such suggestions will be acted upon only if they are endorsed by ten local branches or twenty members of the council. Suggestions not sufficiently supported or coming too late may be acted upon if the council decides to do so.

V. FINANCIAL ADMINISTRATION

46. The entire administration of the finances of the League, including the publication of the *Alldeutsche Blätter* and any money donated or entrusted to the League shall be charged to the financial administration of the Pan-German League, as a corporation with limited liability.[1]

47. To that end property may be made over to the financial administration of the League. Decisions under these circumstances concerning the expenditure of moneys thus administered, must be made by the executive committee.

48. The business managing committee watches over the administration of the corporation. It is responsible to the League and by the constitution is guaranteed the predominant interest in the corporation in the disposition of the League's funds.

49. The claims of the League on its members and local branches for dues payable and initiation fees are to be given over to the corporation. All constitutional payments made into the League treasury are directly payable to the Financial Administration of the Pan-German League, Limited, in Mainz.

---

[1] *Vermögens Verwaltung des alldeutschen Verbandes Gesellschaft mit beschränkter Haftung.*

APPENDIX II

The following list of German associations and societies is published in the *Handbuch* for 1914—(pp. 56 *et seq.*):

1. *Deutsche Kolonialgesellschaft.*
2. *Zentralverein für Handelsgeographie und Förderung deutscher Interessen im Auslande.*
3. *Frauenbund der deutschen Kolonialgesellschaft.*
4. *Verein für Deutschtum im Auslande . (Allgemeiner deutscher Schulverein).*
5. *Allgemeiner deutscher Sprachverein.*
6. *Deutscher Flottenverein.*
7. *Hauptverband deutscher Flottenvereine im Auslande.*
8. *Flottenbund deutscher Frauen.*
9. *Deutscher Ostmarken-Verein* (H. K. T. So called from the initials of the three founders of the society: Hansemann, Kennemann and von Tiedemann.)
10. *Deutsche Kleinsiedlungsgenossenschaft.*
11. *Deutscher Stipendienverein in Ostrowo.*
12. *Reichsverband gegen die Sozial Democratie.*
13. *Deutschbund.*
14. *Deutscher Wehrverein.*
15. *Deutscher Bismarckbund.*
16. *Deutsche Vereinigung.*
17. *Verband nationaler Jugendbünde.*
18. *Deutschnationaler Handlungsgehilfen Verband.*
19. *Gesellschaft für deutsche Erziehung.*
20. *Zentral-Ausschuss zur Förderung der Volks-und Jugendspiele in Deutschland.*
21. *Verein zur gemeinnützigen Verbreitung von Volksschriften.*
22. *Vaterländischer Schriftenverband.*
23. *Evangelischer Bund.*
24. *Fürsorgeverein für die deutsche Rückwanderer.*
25. *Deutschnationaler Kolonialverein.*
26. *Verein der Deutschen aus Ungarn.*
27. *Bund der Deutschösterreicher im deutschen Reich.*
28. *Antiultramontaner Reichsverband.*
29. *Deutscher Schatzmarkenverein.*

30. *Gobineau Vereinigung.*

31. *Evangelischer Hauptverein für deutsche Ansiedler und Auswanderer in Witzenhausen a. d. Werra.*

32. *Deutsche Kolonialschule in Witzenhausen a. d. Werra.*

33. *Evangelische Gesellschaft für die protestantischen Deutschen in Amerika zu Barmen.*

34. *St. Raphael-Verein um Schutze katolisch-deutscher Auswanderer.* (Limburg).

35. *Kolonialwirtschaftliches Komitee.*

36. *Deutscher Frauenbund.*

37. *Deutscher Verein für des nördliche Schleswig.*

38. *Kreditbank Scherrebek.*

39. *Deutscher Ansiedlungsverein in Rödding in Nordschleswig.*

40. *Evangelischer Verein für Waisenpflege in der Ostmark.*

41. *Deutsch-evangelisches Waisenhaus in Kobissau.*

42. *Evangelische Waisen- und Erziehungsanstalt Bethlehem zu Gross-Tillitz.*

43. *Deutsche Besiedelungsgesellschaft zu Berent* (West Prussia).

44. *Deutsche Hilfskasse* (Gilgenburg, East Prussia).

45. *Deutscher Verein zur Hebung und Pflege der Muttersprache in Belgien.*

46. *Deutscher Volksrat für Böhmen.*

47. *Deutscher Volksrat für Mähren.*

48. *Deutscher Volksrat für Ostschlesien.*

49. *Deutscher Volksrat für Wien und Niederösterreich.*

50. *Deutscher Volksrat für Salzburg.*

51. *Deutscher Volksrat für Untersteiermark.*

52. *Deutscher Volksrat für Krain.*

53. *Deutscher Schulverein.*

54. *Bund der Deutschen in Böhmen.*

55. *Deutscher Böhmerwaldbund.*

56. *Deutscher Verein Germania für Trebnitz.*

57. *Deutsche Volksbank für Böhmen.*

58. *Verein Nordmark.*

59. *Bund der Deutschen Nordmährens.*

60. *Bund der Deutschen Südmährens.*

61. *Verein Südmark.*

62. *Südmärkische Volksbank und Spargenossenschaft für die Alpenländer in Graz.*

63. *Ulrich Hutten Bund*—Innsbruck.

64. *Bund der Germanen in Wien.*

65. *Deutschnationaler Verein für Osterreich.*

66. *Selbsthilfe Genossenschaft " Ostmark ".*

67. *Bund der christlichen Deutschen in der Bukowina.*

68. *Bund der christlichen Deutschen in Galizien.*

69. *Deutscher Volksverein für Südtirol zu Bozen.*
70. *Tiroler Volksbund in Innsbruck und München.*
71. *Deutschnationaler Wählerverein in Innsbruck.*
72. *Bund der Deutschen Niederösterreichs.*
73. *Verein zur Erhaltung des Deutschtums in Ungarn.*
74. *Zentralbank der deutschen Sparkassen in Prag.*
75. *Deutsch-Alpenländische Volksbank in Innsbruck.*
76. *Salzburger Hochschulverein in Salzburg.*
77. *Deutscher Verein in Livland.*
78. *Verein der Deutschen in Kurland.*
79. *Deutscher Verein in Estland.*
80. *Deutscher Frauenbund,* Riga.
81. *Moskauer deutscher Verein.*
82. *Petersburger deutscher Bildungs und Hilfsverein.*
83. *Deutsch-amerikanischer Nationalbund* (Philadelphia, Pa.)
84. *Verband deutscher Vereine der Stadt Chicago*—(Chicago, Ill.)

APPENDIX III

GERMAN CHAUVINIST PUBLICATIONS OTHER THAN THOSE
ISSUED BY THE PAN-GERMAN LEAGUE

The following publications were neither sponsored nor issued by the Pan-German League and the latter was in no way responsible for them. The list is offered as a partial check-list of German chauvinist publications but makes no pretense to being in any way complete or definitive. The titles have been gathered from three sources:

(1) The collection belonging to the Mainz local branch of the Pan-German League, now to be found in the Mainz *Stadtbibliothek*.
(2) Some of the publications advocated and reviewed in the *Alldeutsche Blätter*.
(3) German chauvinist works published before the war, which were gathered together in a general collection of chauvinist German, French, Italian, British and American publications by a German professor interested in combating German jingoism and the Pan-German League. This collection is now in the Columbia University Library.

While the writer has not been able to investigate all the works mentioned, she has looked over a great mass of them in order to ascertain that they were not publications of the Pan-German League.

The titles have been alphabetically arranged under subject headings as far as possible and the large number that defied such classification have been grouped separately in alphabetical order.

AUSTRIA-HUNGARY

Berg, Rudolf, *Über böhmisches Staatsrecht.* Prague, 1897. 12 p. M.[1]

Deutschböhmen als Wirtschaftsgrossmacht. Reichenberg, 1903. 203 p. M.

Deutschbund (editors), *Verzeichniss Ortsnamen in Oesterreich.* Hanover, 1900. 24 p. M.

Deutsche evangelische Bund für den Ostmark, *Unser Verhältnis zu den nicht deutschen Evangelischen in Oesterreich.* Munich, 1907. 20 p. M.

Deutsch-Oesterreicher, *Die Zukunft der deutschen Oesterreichs.* Munich, 1899. 25 p. M.

Deutsch-ungarischer Katechismus. Reprint from *Export* No. 42, 1902. 11 p. M.

Flugschriften des alldeutschen Tagblatts.

Lischka, Victor, *Die Sonderstellung Galiziens,*

Schalk, Anton, *Der Hauptstreich gegen die Deutschen in Oesterreich,* Vienna, 1906. 63 p. M.

Gross-Oesterreich, *Zeitstudie eines Deutschoesterreichers.* Reichenberg, 1908. 80 p. M.

Gutberlet, Heinrich, *Böhmerland Deutschesland! Kampflieder aus der Ostmark.* Dresden, 1898.

Heimfelsen, J., *Die deutschen Kolonien in Bosnien.* Vienna, 1911. 119 p. M.

Hungaricus, *Das magyarische Ungarn und der Dreibund.* Munich, 1899. 61 p. C.

Jahresbericht des Vereins Angehöriger des deutschen Reiches in den siebenbürgischen Teilen des Königreiches Ungarn zu Hermannstadt über das Vereinsjahr. Hermannstadt, 1902. M.

Korn, Arthur, *Aufreizung! Gedichte aus dem Banat.* Munich, 1905. 72 p. M.

Korodi, Lutz, *Ungarische Rhapsodien, politische und minderpolitische.* Munich, 1905. 112 p. M.

Das Magyarentum und die pangermanische Gefahr. Berlin, 1902. 11 p. M.

Oesterreichs Zusammenbruch und Wiederaufbau. Munich, 1899. 14 p. C.

Politiker, *Vor dem Abschluss der Balkan Krisen. Politische Bilanz Oesterrichs-Ungarns.* Leipzig, 1913. 45 p. C.

Der Pressprozess gegen Edmund Steinacher vor dem Szegadiner Schwurgericht am Febr. 7, 1903 wegen Aufreizung der Deutschen gegen die magyarische Nationalität. Kronstadt, 1903. 40 p. M.

Pröll, Karl. *Halt! Wer da? Lieder aus dem deutsch-oesterreichischen Feldlager.* Munich, 1897. 50 p. M.

Pröll, Karl, *Die Totengräber Oesterreichs: Kampfesworte und Fehdelieder.* Munich, 1899. 31 p. M.

---

[1] The abbreviations used in the Bibliography (see *supra*, p. 219) have been used here as well.

Schalk, Anton, *Die Wahrheit über die ungarische Frage und die oester-reichische Regierungspolitik.* Vienna, 1903. 31 p. M.

Schalk, Anton, *Warum ich Herrn Karl Hermann Wolf für ehrlos erklärt habe.* Vienna, 1902. 14 p. M.

Schubart, Hans von, *Die deutsche Frage in Ungarns Ostmark: Ein Wort für die Siebenbürgen Sachsen.* Leipzig, 1900. 20 p. M.

Schubart, Ottokar, *Die deutsche Mark am Südmeer. Schilderung der nationalen Verhältnisse im Oesterreich, Kürstenlande und im Italien.* Bischofteinitz, 1902, 44 p. M.

Schwarzenberg, Karl, *Kann sich die oesterreichische-ungarische Armee den Einflüssen der Nationalitäten-Kämpfe entziehen?* Munich, 1898. 24 p. M.

Tiroler Volksbund, *Kalender für 1909.* Innsbruck, 1908. 160 p. M.

Titta, J. *Der nationale Kampf an der Trebnitzer Sprachgrenze im Jahre 1902.* Trebnitz, 1903. 89 p. M.

Trebnitz Verein, *Bericht über die Tätigkeit des Deutschen Schulerhalt-ungsvereines Trebnitz. Ein Schuljahr.* 1902-1903. Trebnitz, 1903. 51 p. M.

Wastian, Heinrich, *Ungarns Tausendjährung in deutschem Lichte.* Munich, 1896. 191 p. C.

DEUTSCHER WEHRVEREIN

Schriften 1-6; 8-10. Berlin, 1912-14. 9 v. in 1. C.

    1. *Warum muss Deutschland sein Heer verstärken?* 1912.

    2. Reim, *Die Notwendigkeit eines deutschen Wehrvereins.* 1912. Litzmann, *Über die Entwicklung der deutschen Heeresmacht.* 1912.

    3. Osten-Sacken and v. Rhein, *Heeresvorlage und allgemeine Wehrpflicht.* 1912.

    4. *Das Unzureichende in der Heeresvorlage.* 1912.

    5. *Die Heeresvorlage im Reichstag.* 1912.

    6. *Wer die Wehrvorlage verwirft ist ein Volksfeind.* 1913.

    8. Schultz-Oldendorf, W., *Briefe eines Rekruten an seine Mutter.* 1913. 2nd edition.

    9. *Wehrfragen und Sorgen.* 1913.

    10. *Die Friedensbewegung und ihre Gefahren für das deutsche Volk.* 1914.

" DRANG NACH OSTEN "

Dehn, Paul, *Deutschland nach Osten!* Munich, 1886-1890. 276 p. M.

Dehn, Paul, *Deutschland und Orient in ihren wirtschaftspolitischen Beziehungen.* Munich, Leipzig, 1884. 378 p. M.

Dehn, Paul, *Deutschland und die Orientbahn,* Munich, 1883. 51 p. M.

Engelbrechten, C. U. v., *Kaiser Wilhelm's Orientreise und deren Bed-eutung für den deutschen Handel.* Berlin, 1890. B.

Grothe, Dr. Hugo, *Die asiatische Türkei und die deutschen Interessen.* Halle, 1913. 62 p. C.

Grothe, Dr. Hugo, *Die Bagdadbahn und das schwäbische Bauernelement in Transkaukasien und Palästina.* Munich, 1902. 53 p. C.

Kaerger, Dr. Karl, *Klein Asien, ein deutsches Kolonisationsfeld.* Berlin, 1892. B.

Körte, Alfred, *Anatolische Skizzen.* Berlin, 1896. B.

Littmann, Leo, *Das europäische Friedensproblem und der Balkan.* Munich and Leipzig, 1913. 65 p. C.

Martin, Rudolf. *Berlin-Bagdad.* Stuttgart and Leipzig, 1907. 160 p. C.

Menz, Rheinhold, *Deutsche Arbeit in Kleinasien.* Berlin, 1893.

Oberhummer, R. and Zimmerer Prof., *Durch Syrien and Kleinasien.* 1898. B.

Rohrbach, Dr. Paul, *Die Bagdadbahn.* Berlin, 1902. B.

Südenhorst, Alois E. v., *Die Eisenbahnverbindungen Zentral Europas mit dem Orient und deren Bedeutung für den Welthandelsverkehr.* Vienna, 1878.

Winterstettin. K. v., *Berlin-Bagdad. Neue Ziele mitteleuropäischer Politik.* Munich, 1914. 79 p. M.

EDUCATION

Address-Handbuch und Lehrmittel Verzeichniss für die deutschen Auslandsschulen. Wolfenbüttel, 1914. M.

Amrhein, Hans, *Die deutsche Schule im Auslande.* Leipzig, 1905.

Arjuna, Harold, *Klassisch oder volkstümlich? Auch ein Beitrag zur Lösung der Schulfrage.* Brussels, 1896. 108 p. M.

Deutsche Nationalschule, Wertheim am Main, gegründet in Mai, 1902. Karlsruhe, 1902. 3 p. M.

Deutsche Schule zu Johannesburg (Transvaal). Bericht 1, 1899. Leipzig, 1899. 37 p. M.

Golmen, Otto J. *Brandenburg, Preussen, Deutschland. Drei dramatische Gemälde aus der vaterländischen Geschichte.* Leipzig, 1904. 358 p. M.

Jahresbericht der Realanstalt am Donnersberg bei Mannheim in der Pfalz für das Schuljahr. Kirchheimbolanden, 1902. 30 p. M.

Kaiser Friedrich der Rotbart. Kirchheimbolanden, 1902. 32 p. M.

Schäfer, Erdmann A., *Die Erziehung der deutsche Jugend im Auslande.* Leipzig, 1900. 219 p. M.

Schmitt, F. A., Schenckundorff, E. v., editors, *Jahrbuch für Volksspiele und Jugendspiele.* Leipzig, 1900. 276 p. M.

Streich, A., editor, *Beiträge zu einer Pädagogik für die deutschen Schulen des Auslandes.* Hanover. M.

ENGLAND

Der alte Gott lebt noch! Oder der Buren Sieg and Kampf. Chemnitz
1901. 16 p. M.

*Amtliche Berichte des Generals J. H. de la Rey, J. C. Smuts und P. J.
Liebenberg sowie andere Urkunden über den südafrikanischen
Krieg.* Munich, 1902. 32 p. M.

Beowulf, *Der deutsch-englische Krieg. Vision eines Seefahrers.*
Berlin, 1906. 123 p. M.

Bley, Fritz, *Der Burenkrieg in Bild und Wort.* Munich 1901. 32 p. B., M.

Bley, Fritz, and Grabein M., *Britische und deutsche Handelspolitik. Ein
Mahnwort in ernster Stunde.* Liepzig, 1899. B.

Böttger, Hugo, *Deutschland voran!* Berlin, 1900. 37 p. M.

Bürger, Alexander, *Unsere Englischen Vettern und Wir!* Leipzig,
1912. 34 p. C.

Der Burenfreund. Offizieles Organ des vereinigten Buren Comités.
Berlin, 1901. 44 p. M.

Von einem Deutschen aus Südafrika, *Südafrika englisch oder deutsch-
holländisch?* Berlin, 1899. 31 p. M.

Deutschland am Scheideweg. Leipzig, 1901. 63 p. M.

Doyle, Sir Arthur Conan, *Der Krieg in Südafrika, seine Ursache und
Führung* (translation). London, 1902. 188 p. M.

Dyckerhoff, Traugott Wilhelm, *Deutsche und Engländer.* Essen. B.

Eckenbrech, Helene etc., *Deutsch Südwestafrika Kriegs-und-Friedens-
bilder. Selbsterlebnisse.* Leipzig, 1907. 79 p. M.

Eisenhart, Karl, *Die Abrechnung mit England,* Munich, 1900. 75 p. M., C.

Elss, H., *Die Buren, der deutsche Brüderstamm in Südafrika.* Bielefeld.

Generalstabsoffizier (French) *Die englische Invasion in Deutschland.*
Transl. from the French. Berlin, 1912. 38 p. C.

Gildesmeister, Andreas, *Deutschland und England.* Berlin, 1905.

Hartmann, Dr. George, *Krieg oder Friede mit England?* Berlin, 1912, B.

Henkel, Fritz, *Aus dem Burenkriege.* Schalke, 1901. 112 p. M.

Herggelet, Marian, *Über die Wahrscheinlichkeit eines Krieges zwischen
Deutschland und England.* Leipzig, 1912, 110 p. C.

Jooste, J., *Aus der zweiten Heimat,* Berlin, 1904. 159 p. M.

Jürgensen, Eduard, *Söss plattdütsche Burenlieder.* Berlin, 1901. 8 p. M.

Der Lügner Chamberlain. Leipzig, 1901. 32 p. M.

Martin, Rudolf, *Deutschland und England.* Hanover, 1908. 94 p. C.

Martin, Rudolf, *Kaiser Wilhelm II und König Edward VII.* Berlin,
1907. 95 p. C.

Meyer, Ernst Teja, *Los von England!* Rostock, 1902. 29 p. C.

Moriturus, *Mit deutschen Waffen über Paris nach London.* Hanair,
1906. 84 p. M.

Du Moulin-Eckart, Richard, *Englands Politiik und die Mächte.* Munich,
1901. 80 p. M.

Pfister-Schwaighusen, H. v., *Alt-Englands Ansprüche, geschichtliche, staatsrechtliche, volkstümliche, völkische Abhandlungen.* Wiesbaden, 1902. 41 p. M.

Pfui Chamberlain. Berlin, 1902.

Plehn, Hans, *Weltpolitik.* Berlin, 1907.

Proosch, W., *Englands Verbrechen an Transvaal und Mr. Chamberlain's Verleumdung der deutschen Kriegsführung.* Offenbach a/M, 1902. 20 p. M.

Protest-Versammlung gegen den Angriff des englischen Kolonialministers Chamberlain auf die Waffenehre der deutschen Krieger am 14 Nov. 1901 zu Köln. Cologne, 1901. 24 p. M.

Rompel, Frederik, *Siegen oder Sterben. Die Helden des Burenkrieges.* Stuttgart, 1901. 192 p. M.

Salomon, Dr. Felix, *Britischer Imperialismus von 1871 bis zur Gegenwart.* Leipzig, 1916. 131 p. C.

Stead, Wm., *Die Hölle ist losgelassen!* (translation). Munich, 1900. 4 p. M.

Steffen, Gustav F., *Aus dem modernen England.* Leipzig, 1897. M., B.

Steffen, Gustav F., *England als Weltmacht und Kulturstaat.* Stuttgart, 1899. 432 p. M.

Stoll, Prof. Adolf, *Wir England Dank Schuldig?* Cassel, 1902. 24 p. C.

Suksdorf, Henry F., *Eine kritische Stunde in der Entwicklungsgeschichte unseres Volkes.* Berlin, 1900. 143 p. M.

Titus, *Die Bluthochzeit der Königin von England.* Berlin, 1900. 11 p. M.

Trampe, L., *Englands Lügenprophet.* Leipzig, 1914. 90 p. C.

Vallentin, Wilhelm, *Die Ursachen des Krieges zwischen England und den Buren-Republiken.* Berlin, 1900. 91 p. M.

Vigilans sed Aequus, (Wm. Thomas Arnold) *German Ambitions as they affect Britain and the United States.* London, 1903. 132 p. B.,N.

Weber, Edmund, *Krieg oder Friede mit England?* Stuttgart, 1913. 54 p. C.

Wesendong, Karl, *Musste es sein?* Munich, 1904. 184 p. M.

Wittenbauer, Ferdinand, *Trutz England! Lieder der Erbitterung.* Graz, 1901. 15 p. M.

FRANCE

Ehrlich, Ernst Traugott (Hans Spieser), *Deutschlands Unfähigkeit das Elsass zu entwelschen.* Zürich, 1909. 40 p. C.

Ghibellinus (Heinrich Fränkel), *Eine Frage an das französische Volk: Ist der Verrat der Kultur an die Barbarei eine Thatsache?* Weimar, 1892.

Koettschau, C., *Der nächste deutsch-französische Krieg.* 2 v. Strasburg 1886-87. 2 v. in 1. C.

Krieg mit Frankreich? Wohin muss die deutsche Marokko-politik führen? Berlin, 34 p. M.

Rommel, Otto, *Au pays de la revanche deutsch; Frankreich gerichtet
durch sich selbst.* Mannheim, 1886. 235 p. C.

Schmidt, K. E., *Deutschland und die Deutschen in der französischen
Karikatur seit 1848.* Stuttgart, 1907. 133 p. C.

Sommerfeld, Adolf, *Frankreichs Ende im Jahre 19??* Berlin, 1912.
80 p. C.

Strantz, Kurd v., *Ihr wollt Elsass und Lothringen? Wir nehmen ganz
Lothringen und mehr.* Berlin, 1912. 72 p. C.

GOBINEAU

Bericht über die Gobineau Vereinigung. 1903. 11 p. M.

Eulenberg—Hertefeld, Prince P. zu, *Eine Errinnerung an Graf Arthur
Gobineau.* Stuttgart, 1906. 47 p. M.

Schemann, Ludwig, *Die Gobineau-Sammlung der kaiserlichen Univer-
sitäts und Landesbibliothek zu Strassburg.* Strasburg, 1907. 32 p. M.

Schemann, Ludwig, *Graf Arthur Gobineau. Ein Errinnerungsbild aus
Wahnfried.* Stuttgart, 1907. 32 p. M.

COLONIAL POLICY

Hansch, Bruno Felix, *Die Aufteilung Afrikas und die Ziele der deutschen Afrikapolitik.* Leipzig, 1912. 27 p. M.

Hübbe-Schleiden, Wilhelm, *Warum Weltmacht? Der Sinn unserer
Kolonialpolitik.* Hamburg, 1906. 42 p. M.

Martin, Dr. Friedl., *Unsere Kolonien—deren Verwaltung und Wert.*
Munich, 1901.

Paul, Karl, *Die Mission in unseren Kolonien.* Dresden, 1905. 166 p. M.

Pfeil, Joachim Graf v., *Zur Erwerbung von Deutsch-Ostafrika. Ein
Beitrag zu seiner Geschichte.* Berlin, 1907. 231 p. M.

*Samoa—Freimütige Äusserungen über diplomatische und völkische
(nationale) Weltpolitik.* Berlin, 1899. 39 p. M.

Scharlach, William, *Zur Vertheidigung von Dr. Karl Peters. Rede vor
dem Diciplinarhofe zu Berlin.* Berlin, 1898. M.

Tiedemann, Adolf v., *Mit Karl Peters zu Emin Pascha.* Berlin, 1907. B.

Vollmer, Edm., *Was ist Lüderitzland wert?*

Die Wahrheit über die deutschen Kolonien. Berlin, 1905. M.

Wirth, Dr. A., *Marokko, Streiflichter auf die Weltpolitik.* Frankfurt
a. M. and Berlin, 1908. B.

LANGUAGE

*Betrachtungen über das geschichtliche Recht der deutschen Sprache in
bernischen Jura.* Berne, 1904. 46 p. M.

Brodbeck-Arbenz, J., *Die Fremdwörter im Geschäftsverkehr.* Zürich,
1902. 30 p. M.

Trautmann, Moritz, *Der Staat und die deutsche Sprache.* Leipzig, 1911.
76 p. M.

THE NAVY

Bitter Not ist uns eine starke deutsche Flotte. Berlin, 1899. 29 p. M.

Deutscher Flottenverein, *Deutschland Sei Wach!* Berlin, 1912. 216 p. C.

Deutscher Flottenverein. *Jahrbuch 1900-1902.* Berlin, 1900-1902. 3 v. C.

Deutscher Flottenverein, *Marine-austellung.* Berlin, 1900. 63 p. M.

Deutscher Flottenverein, *Verzeichniss des Präsidiums, des Vorstandes, des geschäftsführenden Organs.* Berlin, 1900. M.

Entwurf einer Novelle zum Gesetze betr. die deutsche Flotte, vom 19 April 1898. With a supplement. Berlin, 1899. 92 p. M.

Erdmann, Gustav Adolf. *Frei die See.* Leipzig, 1905. B.

Die Ergebnisse der von der Allgemeine Zeitung veranstalten Flotten-Umfrage. Special supplement to the *Münchner Allgemeine Zeitung,* 1898, numbers 1-23. 186 p. M.

Zur Flottenfrage—Darlegungen der Norddeutscher Allgemeinen Zeitung. 1899, 1900. 390 p. M.

Die Flotten Manöver von 1899. Berichte des Wolff'schen Telegr. Bureaus an die Deutsche Presse. 1889. 34 p. M.

Fokke, Arnold, *Volldampf voraus! Eine zeitgemässe Betrachtung zur Flottenfrage.* Düsseldorf, 1900. 35 p. M.

Freie Vereinigung für Flottenvorträge, *Handels und Machtpolitik. Reden und Aufsätze.* Stuttgart, 1900. 222 p. M.

Gersdorf, A. Graf von, *Ist die deutsche Flotte ein Luxus oder eine Notwendigkeit?* Berlin, 1912.

Grantoff, Ferdinand, *Seestern " 1906" Der Zusammenbruch der alten Zeit.* Leipzig, 1907. 203 p. M.

Hartmann, Hans, *Warum hat jederman im Volke ein Interesse an einer starken deutschen Flotte?* Berlin, 1899. 31 p. M.

Hoepner, *Hamburg und Bremen in Gefahr.* Altona, 1906. 108 p. M.

Hoepner, *Der Wert unserer deutschen Schlachtflotte.* 1906. 44 p. M.

Land und See Krieg. Leipzig, 1900. 7 p. M.

Nauticus, *Jahrbuch für Deutschlands Seeinteressen.* Berlin, 1899. 439 p. M.

Nauticus, *Neue Beiträge zur Flottenfrage,* Berlin, 1898. 218 p. M.

Rassow, H., *Deutschlands Seemacht.* Elberfeld, 1905. 40 p. M.

Reichs-Marine Amt (editors), *Die Seeinteressen des deutschen Reichs.* Berlin, 1898. 61 p. M.

Reventlow, Graf Ernst zu, *Die deutsche Flotte—Ihre Entwickelung und Organisation.* Zweibrücken, 1901. B.

Reventlow, Graf Ernst zu, *Deutschland in der Welt voran?* 1905. B.

Schäfer, Dietrich, *Was lehrt uns die Geschichte über die Bedeutung der Seemacht für Deutschlands Gegenwart?* Munich, 1900. 27 p. M.

Schubart, Hartwig, *Die deutsche Schlachtflotte.* Berlin, 1911. 23 p. C.

Vaterlandsfreund, *Eine starke Flotte eine Lebensbedingung für Deutschland.* Reprint from the *Norddeutsche Allgemeine Zeitung.* 1897. 43 p. M.

Wenckstern, Adolf von, *1%—die Schaffung und Erhaltung einer deutschen Schlachtflotte.* Leipzig, 1899. 65 p. M.

Weyer, Bruno, *Deutschlands Seegefahren.* Munich, 1898.

Weyer, Bruno (editor) *Taschenbücher der deutschen Kriegsflotte.* Munich, 1900, 210 p.; 1901, 273 p. M.

Die Zukunft des deutschen Seehandels. Berlin, 1897. 27 p. M.

POLISH QUESTION

Gruhn, Dr. Albert, *Das deutsche Kapital und der Polonismus.* Berlin, 1895. B.

Kritik und Reform der Germanisation in Posen. Berlin, 1897.

Polen und Deutsche in der Provinz Posen, Berlin.

PERIODICAL LITERATURE IN THE MAINZ COLLECTION

Beiheft zum Amtsblatte des Reichspostamts. Berlin, 1900. Nos. 23, 24; 1902, no. 3.

Der Burgwart, vol. 3, no. 6. Berlin, 1902.

Deutsche Erde, 1902. Gotha.

Deutsche Monatsschrift für das gesamte Leben der Gegenwart. Vol. 1, nos. 1, 4; Berlin, 1901-2.

Deutsche Monatsschrift für Kolonialpolitik und Kolonisation. Berlin, 1904, 1905.

Die deutsche Schule im Ausland. 1902-1914 (incomplete).

Deutsche Zeitschrift.

Geographische Zeitschrift. 1899.

Germania—Tijdschrift voor Vlaamische Bewegung, Brussels—1898-1905 (incomplete).

Grenzboten (Flugblatt). Leipzig, 1897.

Hammer—Blätter für deutschen Sinn. 1902-1909 (incomplete).

Hessische Blätter für Volkskunde. Leipzig, 1902-1908. And supplement—*Volkskundliche Zeitschriftenschau,* 1903-1907.

Der Kynast. 1898-1899; continued as *Deutsche Zeitschrift.*

Mitteilungen des Verbandes deutscher Vereine für Volkskunde. 1905-1908 (incomplete).

Nordafrika. Berlin, 1903-1904; continued as *Deutsche Monatsschrift für Kolonialpolitik und Kolonisation.*

Nord und Süd, Berlin, 1900.

Politisch-anthropologische Revue. 1903.

Werdandi, 1908-1912.

MISCELLANEOUS

Alexis, Wilibald (Wilhelm Häring) *Ruhe ist die erste Bürgerpflicht.* Leipzig, 1913. 53 p. M.

Amicus Patriae, *Armenien und Kreta.* Leipzig, 1896.

Amyntor, J., *Die neue Zeit, wie sie geworden ist.* Dresden, 1913. 38 p. M.

Becker, E., *Die grossherzoglich hessische (25) Division in der Schlacht bei Gravelotte—St. Privat.* Darmstadt, 1913. 196 p. M.

Bernhardi, F. v., *Deutschland und der nächste Krieg.* Stuttgart and Berlin, 1912. 333 p. C., M.

Bonhard, Philip, *Was lehren uns die Ergebnisse der Reichstagswahlen?* Heidelberg, 1902, 110 p. M.

Braun, Dr. Otto, *Deutsches Leben und deutsche Weltanschauung.* Berlin, 1912. B.

Brecht, Th. *Schwarz-weiss-roth. Eine Ethik des Patriotismus.* Halle, 1890. B.

Bruchausen, Karl v., *Der kommende Krieg.* Berlin, 1906. 55 p. M.

Büchi, Dr. Robert, *Die Geschichte der pan-Amerikanischen Bewegung.* Breslau, 1914. 189 p. C.

Bürger, F., *Soziale Thatsachen und sozialdemokratische Lehren.* Berlin, 1904. B.

Burger, Alexander, *Zum Streit um die Wehrfähigkeit des deutschen Volkes,* Berlin, 1912. 24 p. C.

Chamberlain, Houston Stewart, *Wehr und Gegenwehr.* Munich, 1912. 108 p. C.

Class, Heinrich, *Die Reichsfeststätte bei Mainz.* Mainz, 1897. 19 p. M.

Clausen, Ernst, *Stillgestanden!* Leipzig, 1903. 47 p. M.

F. D., *Der Wille zum Sieg.* Leipzig, 1914. 102 p. M.

Dehn, Paul, *Bismarck.* Berlin, Leipzig, 1908. 112 p. M.

Dehn, Paul, *Kommende Weltwirtschaftspolitik.* Berlin, 1898. 139 p. M.

Dehn, Paul, *Das neue Nürnberg und seine internationale Bedeutung.* Munich, 1883. 51 p. M.

Denner, Richard, *Bedeutung und Ziele deutscher Weltpolitik.* Minden in W. B.

Deutsche-Amerikanischer national Bund der Vereinigten Staaten von Nordamerika. *Protokoll der Konvention.* Indianapolis, Ind., 1905, 110 p.; *Grundsätze und Verfassung,* Philadelphia, Pa. 1905. 8 p. M.

Von einem Deutschen, *Deutschland bei Beginn des 20 Jahrhunderts,* Berlin, 1900. 215 p. C.

Von einem Deutschen, *1870/71—19..* Oldenburg i. Gr. 72 p. C.

Von einem Deutschen, *Die Partei der Zukunft.* Leipzig, 1914. 245 p. C.

Ein deutsches Weltreich. Berlin, 1892, 30 p. C.

Deutschland Erwache! Leipzig, 1913.

Diplomaten, von einem aktiven, *Deutsche Auslandspolitik und ihre Verleumder im Lichte historischer Tatsachen.* Leipzig, 1910. 66 p. C.

Divinator, *Ein Blick in die Zukunft.* Vienna, 1912. 64 p. C.

Dix, Arthur, *Deutscher Imperialismus.* Leipzig, 1914. 110 p. C.

Dyckerhoff. Traugott Wilhelm, *Gesammelte Schriften.* Essen, 1903. B.

Ebhardt, Bado, *Die Marksburg.* Berlin, 1900. 32 p. M.

Eisenhart, W., *Deutschland erwache!* Leipzig, 1913. 63 p. C.

Fick, A., *Die geistigen Getränke, ihr Nutzen und Schaden.* Gräfen-
hainischen, 1905. 32 p. M.

Flade, Erich, *Der Kampf gegen den Alkoholismus, ein Kampf für unser
deutsches Volkstum.* Berlin, 1905. B.

Folkwin, Freimund, *Friedenskarte Europas.* Zweibrücken, 1900. 54 p. M.

Fritsche, Theodore, *Die neue Gemeinde,* Leipzig, 1903. 21 p. M.

Froelich, J., *Deutschtum und Menschheit.* Dresden, 1900. 35 p. M., B.

Frymann, Daniel, *Wenn ich der Kaiser wär'.* Leipzig, 1912. B.

Geiser, A., *Die deutschen Balten.* Munich, 1906. 31 p. M.

Von einem Grösstdeutschen, *Germania Triumphans.* Berlin, 1895.
78 p. C.

Grumbach, S., *Das annexionistiche Deutschland.* Lausanne, 1917. 471 p. C.

Guhlen, Fritz, Freiherr v., *Die Sprengung des Dreibundes.* Leipzig,
1898. B.

Hentschel, Dr. Willibald, *Vom aufsteigenden Leben; Ziele der Rassen-
hygiene.* Leipzig, 1913. 127 p. C.

Hentschel, Dr. Willibald, *Varuna.* Leipzig, 1907. 626 p. C.

Hermann, A., *Das Sedanfest in Braunschweig 1899.* Leipzig, 1899.
32 p. M.

Hettner, Alfred, *Das Deutschtum in Südbrasilien und Südchile.* Leipzig,
1903. 24 p. M.

Hönig, Fritz, *Die Scharnhorstische Heeresreform und die Sozialdemokratie.* Berlin, 1894. B.

Hötzsch, Otto, *Die Vereinigten Staaten von Nordamerika.* Leipzig,
1904. 180 p. M.

Holanbek, Georg, *Paul Pacher. Eine Gedenkschrift.* Salzburg, 1908.
222 p. M.

Holanbek, Georg, *Zwischen zwei Kaisern.* Salzburg, 1907. 12 p. M.

Horning, Fr., *Das Schlachtfeld bei Wörth im Elsass in Bildern.*
Fröschweiler, 1895. 56 p. M.

Hron, Karl, *Russland oder England.* Vienna, 1900. B.

Jacobsen, J. *Nordseebad "Lakolk" auf Röm.* Tondern, 1901, 57 p. M.

Jähns, Max, *Was ist des Deutschen Vaterland?* Berlin, 1900. 46 p. M.

Kaemmerer, Th., *Der "bevorstehende" Weltkrieg als Vorläufer des
Weltfriedens, zugleich ein Kampf ums Deutschtum.* Leipzig, 1909.
47 p. C.

Klingemann, Karl, *Buddhismus, Pessimismus und moderne Weltanschauung.* Essen, 1901. 58 p. C.

Knortz, Karl, *Deutsch in Amerika.* Leipzig, 1906. B.

Koch, Max, *Geschichte der deutschen Literatur.* Stuttgart. B.

Köhler, Hermann, *Die Sozialdemokratie die lachende Erbin des südafrikanischen Krieges.* Leipzig, 1901. B.

Krafft, Rudolf, *Glänzendes Elend.* Stuttgart, 1895. 88 p. M.

Kretzschmar, Fr., *Die kommende Krisis des Nationalismus und die
politische Konstellation Europas.* Auma, 1894.

Kuhn, Karl, "*Walhalla*". Charlottenburg, 1913. 295 p. C.

Lange, Friedrich, *Deutsche Politik.* Berlin, 1894. B.

Langemann, Ludwig, *Der deutsche Wille zum Leben.* Berlin, 1917. 80 p. C.

Langhans, Paul, *Der alte und der neue Reichstag.* Gotha, 1899.

Lehmann, J. F., *Verlags Prospeckt,* Munich, 15 p. M.

Liebert, E. v., *Fürst Bismarck und die Armee.* Berlin, 1912. 15 p. C.

Liedl, Dr. O., *Über Alldeutschtum.* 1910.

Liman, Paul, *Bismarck.* Berlin, 1899. 568 p. M.

Liman, Paul, *Der Kronprinz,* Minden in W., 1914. 295 p. C.

List, Guido, *Deutsch-mythologische Landschaftsbilder.* Berlin. B.

Lügen des Herrn Erzberger zur Aufklärung der deutschen Wähler. 1906.

Lüstenöder, Hans, *Die vlämische Bewegung.* Berlin, 1897.

Martin, Rudolf, *Stehen wir vor einem Weltkrieg?* Leipzig, 1908. 145 p. C.

Martin, Rudolf. *Die Zukunft Deutschlands—eine Warnung.* Leipzig, 1908. 153 p. C.

Mehrmann, Karl, *Die Aristokratie in der Weltpolitik.* Berlin, 1905. 127 p. M.

Meinhold, Eberhard, *Deutsche Rassepolitik und die Erziehung zu nationalem Ehregefühl.* Munich, 1908. 28 p. C.

Oberwinder, Heinrich, *Die Weltkrise und die Aufgaben des deutschen Reichs.* Dresden, 1905. 192 p. C.

Oppel, Alwin, *Kanada und die Deutschen.* Dresden, 1916. 160 p. C.

Peters, Emil, *Das Hohelied der Kraft.* Berlin, 1915. 154 p. C.

Peters, Dr. Karl, *Zur Weltpolitik.* Berlin, 1912. B.

Plehn, Hans, *Weltpolitik,* 1907. 213 p. M.

Die Preussen und die preussische Politik. Leipzig, 1910. 104 p. C.

Pröll, Karl, *Deutschnationale Märchen für die politische Kinderstube.* Leipzig, 1893. B.

Pröll, Karl, *Weltnational.* Berlin, 1894.

Pudor, Dr. Heinrich, *Deutschland für die Deutschen!* Munich and Leipzig, 1912. B.

Ratzel, Friedrich, *Das Meer als Quelle der Völkengrösse.* Munich and Leipzig, 1900. 85 p. M.

Ranter, Dr. D., *Gemeinsames Programm der Deutschen.* Berlin, 1892, B.

Reder, A. V., *Im alldeutschen Reich!* Berlin, 1901. B.

Reimer, Josef L., *Grundzüge deutscher Wiedergeburt.* Leipzig, 1906. 119 p. M.

Reimer, Josef L., *Ein Pangermanisches Deutschland.* Berlin and Leipzig, 1905. 403 p. C.

Reventlow, Graf Ernst zu, *Holder Friede, süsse Eintracht.* Leipzig, 1906. 87 p. C.

Reventlow, Graf Ernst zu, *Was würde Bismarck sagen?* Berlin, 1909. 19 p. C.

Reventlow, Graf Ernst zu, *Weltfriede oder Weltkrieg!* Berlin, 1907. 152 p. M., C.

Rhenanus, *"Vernunft-Europa".* Leipzig, 1911. 44 p. C.

Richter, J. W. Otto, *Deutschland in der Kulturwelt,* Leipzig.

Schäffle, Dr. Albert, *Deutsche Kern-und-Zeitfragen.* Berlin, 1894. B.

Schmidt, *Der Krieg als Kulturfaktor, als Schöpfer und Erhalter der Staaten.* Gibichenfels, 1912.

Schölermann, Wilhelm, *Massregeln oder Männer?* Berlin 1900. 12 p. M.

Schulte vom Brühl, Walter, *Sei Deutsch!* Weisbaden, 1891. B.

Schultheiss, Franz, *Deutscher Volksschlag in Vergangenheit und Gegenwart.* Munich, 1899. 39 p. M.

Schultz, W., *Deutschtum und Alkohol.* Basel, 13 p. M.

Schwarzseher von einem, *Unser Kaiser und sein Volk! Deutsche Sorgen.* Freiburg, Leipzig, 1906. 177 p. M.

Sembratowycz, Roman, *Das Zarentum im Kampfe mit der Zivilisation.* Frankfurt am Main, 1905. 35 p. M.

Sepp, Prof. Dr. J., *Deutschland einst und jetzt.* Munich, 1896. 24 p. C.

Severus, Claudius, *Flanderns Not.* Berlin and Brussels, 1916. 79 p. C.

Sommerfeld, Adolf, *Der italienisch-türkische Krieg und seine Folgen.* Berlin, 1912. 79 p. C.

Spieser, Hans, *Elsass-Lothringen als Bundesstaat.* Berlin, 1908. 131 p. M.

Stein, Adolf, *Wer wird siegen?* Berlin, 1893. B.

Suksdorf, H. F., *Der Weg zur Grösse unseres Volkes.* Berlin, 1903. 48 p. M.

Tannenberg, O. R., *Gross Deutschland—die Arbeit des 20ten Jahrhunderts.* Leipzig-Gohlis, 1911. 280 p. C.

Teja, Graf, *Der Abgrund.* Leipzig, 1914. 203 p. C.

Unold, J., *Grundlegung für eine nationale und ideale Sittenlehre.* Leipzig, 1896. B.

Unold, J. *Die höchsten Kulturaufgaben des modernen Staates.* Munich, 1902. 171 p. M.

Wagner, Klaus. *Krieg.* Jena, 1906. 259 p. C.

Waldersee, G., *Was Deutschland braucht.* Berlin, 1895. 15 p. C.

Wirth, Dr. Albrecht, *Männer, Völker und Zeiten.* Hamburg and Berlin, 1911. B.

Wirth, Dr. Albrecht, *Weltgeschichte der Gegenwart.* Hamburg, 1913. 549 p. M.

Wreschen und die Interpellation Fürst Radziwill im Reichstag. 1902. 31 p. M.

INDEX